"It's the perfect antidote for the restlessness and boredom that kids tend to suffer over the long summer break."
- Craig Shafer, Santa Maria Sun

"If you're looking for things to do for the summertime, this is the way to go. ...I didn't realize there was this much stuff to do. ...It's not just for kids."
- Jay, Morning Show, KSNI Sunny Country 102.5

"Divided into clear, concise sections using maps and directions to hundreds of vacation venues, Best Family Adventures brings California's landscape of San Luis Obispo County to reality, infused with passion for curiosity, taking a fresh look at Central Coast history, trails, parks, art galleries, beaches, libraries, theaters and more. A guide to many of California's popular destinations, find the reasons why visitors enjoy California Coast vacations; with an endless wealth of exciting possibilities."
– California Tour & Travel

Best Family Adventures:
San Luis Obispo County
(Second Edition)

IMPORTANT LEGAL NOTICE AND DISCLAIMER

Many activities listed, described or otherwise implied in this book are potentially dangerous. Users of this book should take necessary precautions to protect themselves and their families if they choose to participate in any of the activities listed, suggested or implied by this publication.

All information in this book is subject to change including, but not limited to, locations, contact information, prices and hours of operation. Call ahead for most current information including closures, price changes, new location and rules that may affect the use of any given facility.

The author, editors, contributors, publishers and distributors accept no liability for any errors or omissions in this book or for any injuries or losses incurred while using it as a resource.

Pen & Pad Publishing
P.O. Box 2995
Orcutt, CA 93457
(805) 345-9066
www.bestfamilyadventures.com
JBest@BestFamilyAdventures.com

Best Family Adventures: SanLuis Obispo County
(Second Edition)
Text and Photos Copyright © 2011 Jennifer Best
All rights reserved.

Printed in the United States of America
ISBN 10: 0-9769050-3-5
ISBN 13: 978-0-9769050-3-5
Library of Congress Control Number: 2011930143

Maps: Richard Cole
Researchers: Jennifer Best, Erica Best, Valerie Best,
    Stephen Best, Julia Cabreros
Editors: Lynn Peterson, Julia Cabreros
Design & Photography: Jennifer Best

ACKNOWLEDGEMENTS

Thanks to a wonderfully supportive, adventurous community that is my native county, the first edition of *Best Family Adventures: San Luis Obispo County* sold out in 2011. Since its release in 2006, readers have stopped me to give thanks on trails, on streets, in stores, even on the road. (Our van's not hard to identify, thanks to the shameless self promotion emblazoned on nearly every window.) They've told me tales of highlighting, dog-earing, and otherwise defacing their copies of that initial book throughout their own adventures both with and without children in tow. In addition to helping support our family through their purchases of these books, they've given me the gifts of heartfelt thanks, tremendously brilliant smiles and energetic hugs. Then they've asked, repeatedly, for a second edition.

Dear Readers: Your wish is my command. I'm honored to present to you *Best Family Adventures: San Luis Obispo County, Second Edition*. May it lead down the path to a lifetime of adventure for you and your families: the family by blood; the family through marriage; and the family that can only be formed through true friendship.

For my dad,
Randy Peterson,
who taught me you can never be lost
when every path leads to another adventure.

Contents

Introduction

As a San Luis Obispo native, I learned early the value of great days spent outside. I pedaled my bicycles along the city's streets, hiked the trails, climbed some of its best rocks, and relaxed with great books in the dappled shade of its beautiful trees. Like so many teens, however, I chose to leave home for college, then to see a bit of the world. My travels were fantastic, but there there really is no place like home, particularly for those of us spoiled by the natural beauty, idyllic weather and special places of the Central Coast.

Still, why *Best Family Adventures*? I've written my fair share of travel articles, as well as sponsored travel guides. The guides are fun and informative, but their first purpose is to serve the association members, not to provide a comprehensive guide for readers. And while there are wonderful books (p. 226) dedicated to the area's hiking or mountain biking, wining or dining, none presented the myriad family-friendly venues and activities available throughout the county.

This book was born out of my obsessive need to write, a genetic predisposition to explore, one editor's refusal to let me retire, and readers who kept asking for more. The week before our first child was born in 2000, I resigned from my job as education reporter at *Santa Maria Times* in favor of full-time parenthood. My editor, Wayne Agner, had other plans for me. Within months of leaving my desk, Wayne and I settled on an assignment that fit the paper's needs and those of my family – I'd write weekly features on family-friendly activities anywhere within 150 miles of Santa Maria. We would work around the baby's schedule. Here was an opportunity to hit the trail with my child while continuing my career and adding a little something to the college fund. How could I refuse? The stories ran almost weekly for more than two years.

Readers wanted more. Was there some guide to which they could turn for reference? Turns out, there wasn't. I'd learned about many of these places as a Central Coast native, or by talking to friends and strangers. Regular readers told me they were putting the articles together in binders, compiling their own reference books. So *Best Family Adventures* was born.

Many potential readers misunderstand the title. "I don't have kids, so this book's not for me," they say. But families come in a variety of configurations from the nuclear to the good ol' college gang. This is a guide to all things family-friendly – it's not a guide to nightlife or the club scene, fine dining establishments or local watering holes. You can enjoy these venues with your children or your pastor, your conservative grandmother or your future in-laws.

HOW TO USE THIS BOOK

This adventure guide is meant to be tossed in your backpack, left on the coffee table, spilled on, marked up, dog-eared and otherwise abused. My dream for this book is that you'll explore its pages in which you'll discover new places and perhaps be reminded of old favorites. My hope is that you'll explore with your children or spouse, best friends or new friends, go it alone or get a group together. The point of it all is to get out and explore all that

San Luis Obispo County has to offer.

Best Family Adventures: San Luis Obispo County is divided into chapters by community, with Outlying Areas and Points East each earning its own dedicated chapter. For quick reference, turn to the community you're most interested in researching. If you have more time, grab a highlight marker, a drink and a snack, curl up in your favorite reading chair and have at it. The index should help you find, quickly, any activity in which you may be interested throughout the county. And the clubs and organizations list is designed to help you find support for just about any special interest that can be explored in a group.

Each chapter is divided into five subject areas: Letters for libraries and the like; Arts for galleries and other artistic venues; History for venues of particular historical interest; Nature for venues and activities with a bent toward science and nature; and Other Adventures for those things that were tough to pigeonhole. Golf may be a good walk spoiled, but does it really belong in the Nature category? And if a farm is organic, it's natural, right? Still, it offers more than a walk in the trees.

Each entry includes its address, phone number and Web site address where available, driving directions and a description. You'll also find symbols representing the cost of admission. All of this information is subject to change, but was accurate at press time, including price ranges:

FREE! = Free of charge

$ = $10 or less per person

$$ = $11 to $20 per person

$$$ = $21 or more per person

☞ = Best Bets (when time's too short to hit them all)

TERMINOLOGY & TECHNICAL DETAILS

You'll find some repeated phrases here that had my editors in fits. Rather than repeat their explanation at each listing, let's cover the basics here.

Adventure Pass is a day-use pass required for motorists using high-impact recreation areas in the Los Padres National Forest, including Hi Mountain Road, the Pozo area and routes inland of Highway 1 on the San Simeon and Big Sur coast. To be on the safe side, carry a day pass in your vehicle every time you venture into the forest, or pick up the annual pass to cover your bases. The passes only are required for visitors traveling by motorized vehicle. Hikers and cyclists are exempt. Depending on the site, there may be additional fees required for camping. Check the forest service Web site (www.fs.fed.us/r5/lospadres) for detailed information about the program, including sales locations.

The **Black Gold library system** (blackgold.org) connects libraries throughout the Central Coast for resource sharing. Anyone with a library card (free) has access to books, recorded books, movies and other resources loaned by libraries from Piru in eastern Ventura County to Templeton in northern San Luis Obispo County. Titles can be ordered online and delivered to your local library, which may charge a nominal fee for the delivery service.

Cal Poly Lands are expansive and largely open for public use. Camping is allowed on Poly land, but no fires, stoves or tents are allowed and there are no restroom facilities. Plan accordingly.

Disc golf, also known as Frisbee golf, is an outdoor activity related somewhat to traditional golf. Take a good old flying disc, fling it toward a target basket, then repeat and you have yourself a short game of disc golf. Avid disc golfers carry their own bags of specialized discs, but a backpack-friendly flying disc works just as well.

"Skinned infield" refers to baseball or softball diamonds where grass has been removed from the infield, making them safer for competitive play.

The Central Coast's wild places are home to potentially dangerous wild animals, including **bears, mountain lions, coyotes** and **rattlesnakes**. Chances are you'll come across the occasional rattlesnake, but you're unlikely to see the larger animals of concern. They typically avoid people but can be surprised by quiet explorers. Before heading out, acquaint yourself with the proper procedures for avoiding these dangers, and steps to take in the unlikely event you meet one of the creatures. Educate any children who may be exploring with you, and keep them close at hand. The California Department of Fish and Game (www.dfg.ca.gov/news/issues/lion) is a great resource for detailed information. Essentially, make noise while you explore, and don't stick your hands into holes or other potential dens.

Ticks love the Central Coast's natural areas. They most often hitch rides with passersby who rub against brush or tall grass where ticks lay in wait for any warm body. To protect yourself, wear long-sleeved shirts, long trousers, long socks, close-toed shoes and a brimmed hat. Periodically check yourself and your hiking buddies throughout your adventures. No need to panic if you see one. Just flick it off with your finger or a safe object like a leaf.

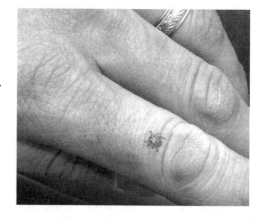

Poison oak is the common name for the bush scientists like to call toxicodendron diversilobum — poisonous branching plant with opposing leaves. That about sums it up. The plant flourishes along the Central Coast and is a serious issue for many people. Like its relatives, poison sumac and poison ivy, this coastal shrub emits oil that serves as an irritant when it comes in contact with skin. Within a week to 10 days, the oil causes a rash that bubbles, itches and oozes. Did the leaves, or even dormant branches, rub on your boots? Then the oil is there and will continue to cause issues until you clean them. Did you get it on your clothes? Backpack? The dog? Ditto.

Though this rule doesn't hold true for its cousins, poison ivy and poison sumac, it does seem to ring true most of the time: leaves of three, let it be. Poison oak presents leaves in sets of three. They are a vibrant green in early spring and turn to a rich, dark, glossy green before turning sunset red and finally dropping from the plant completely for winter. The bushes can grow to

25 feet, though tend to top out at 6-8 feet in these parts. It's most difficult to identify in winter when the leafless branches look much like those of any number of other deciduous plants.

The best way to prevent irritation from poison oak is to avoid contact with any part of the plant. Even the sticks of overwintering bushes carry the oil. Just stay out of areas where it is known to exist. Then again, that doesn't sound like fun, so here are some other options:

— Wear long-sleeved shirts, long pants, long socks and boots to cover as much skin as possible

— Prior to exposure, use products like EnviroDerm's Ivy Block, or Tecnu's Poison Oak-n-Ivy Armor

— Wash every stitch of clothing used to remove any residual oils, which can affect anyone who comes in contact with them for weeks to come.

— Immediately upon return to civilization, use cool water and a grease-cutting soap, such as TecNu, though Dawn and other grease-cutting dishwashing soaps have been known to do the trick. Be sure to scrub under your nails, as the oil can hide here and cause problems later. The FDA suggests beginning the entire cleaning process with a complete rubdown in rubbing alcohol. Others add that suds (and rinse) should be done with cold water. The idea is that the oil won't be able to spread deeper into the pores

— Wash the dog. Man's best friend can be poison oak's best carrier. Unless you wash the dog thoroughly, it doesn't matter how much you wash your own belongings and exposed skin. One good scratch of an oily Fido means lots of scratching for you in the near future.

I did all that and got it anyway. Now what?

It probably took up to a week for the rash to show, but now it's there in all its itching, oozing glory. You can try to tough it out, or resort to a variety of anti-itch treatments including over-the-counter hydrocortisone, calamine lotion or poison oak itch treatments available at your local pharmacy. It'll take about a week for the thing to begin to subside and up to three weeks for the damage to disappear completely.

If images of scratching off your own arm (or leg or whatever's affected) are invading your dreams, or the rash appears anywhere near your eyes, it's time to see your doctor. She can provide prescription treatment ranging from prednisone to a fantastic topical called fluocinonide.

The web is full of useful resources about Poison Oak, including the National Institutes of Health, U.S. Food and Drug Administration and poisonivy.aesir.com.

All these warnings aside, we live in a pretty great place full of family-friendly activities. Do your teens doubt it? Toss this book their way, let them pick a few places to explore, and then help them find their way.

Happy Trails!

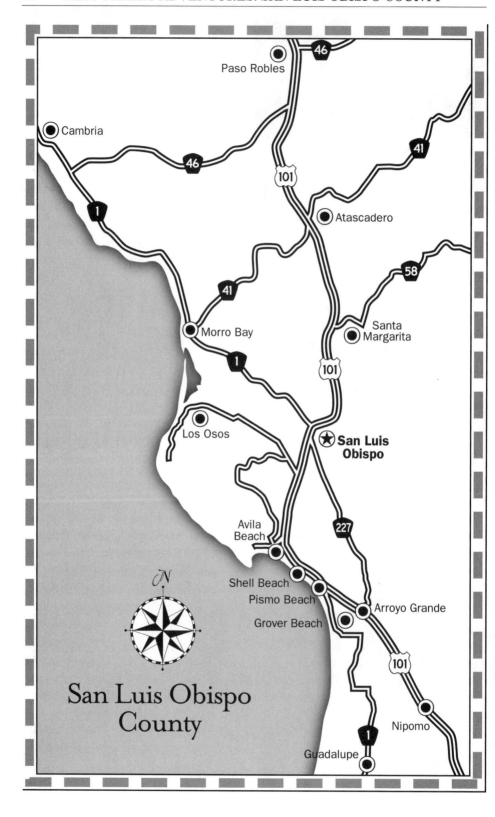

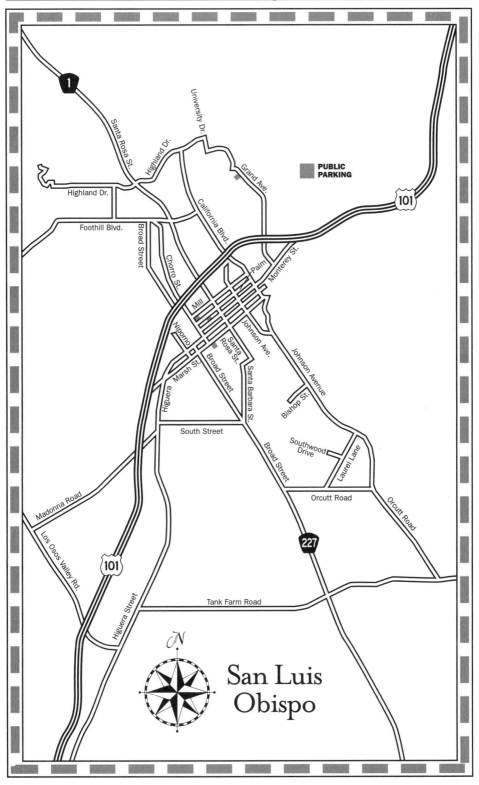

Chapter 1
San Luis Obispo

San Luis Obispo is a haven for families with children of any age. The county seat and namesake boasts a chain of 65-million-year-old volcanic peaks, rolling hills, meandering creeks, arts opportunities and parks as well as a variety of activities designed specifically with children in mind and eateries to please any palate.

It is little wonder so many people have made this temperate valley home. The centrally located city within a few minutes' drive of beaches, lakes and mountains was home to the Chumash people for centuries before Mission San Luis Obispo de Tolosa was established here in 1772. The fifth of the state's original 21 missions remains the focal point downtown. Services are still held in the chapel, festivals are celebrated in the plaza, children continue throwing rocks across the creek while the smells of good food and sounds of live music float through the fresh air.

San Luis Obispo is home to more than 30 parks including pocket parks locals may hardly notice and sports complexes that play home to tournaments throughout the year. Many of the larger parks have group areas available by reservation.

The arts also flourish here. Galleries abound and many studios offer hands-on lessons for artists of all ages and abilities. Check the community calendar on any given week for special events, classes, performances and workshops.

On-street parking in downtown San Luis Obispo is metered and often hard to find, but the city provides ample parking in a number of centrally located parking garages where the first hour is free: on Marsh Street at Chorro Street; on Palm Street between Chorro and Morro streets; or off Palm Street at Morro Street.

California Polytechnic State University (Cal Poly) is just outside city limits.

ARTS
Anam-Cré Pottery Studio
570 Higuera St. #140
(805) 544-1850
anamcre.com
$$

From Highway 101, take the Marsh Street exit, turn left onto NipomoStreet, then left onto Higuera Street. The studio is in The Creamery.

Eight pottery wheels, a slab roller, three kilns, a variety of texture molds and a group of dedicated instructors keep this pottery studio centered. Activities include classes for adults and children alike, from beginning

San Luis Obispo offers an abundance of outdoor adventures for explorers of all ages, from frog-catching preschoolers to monster mountain bikers. Terrace Hill, shown here, is popular for its short walk to open space and primte kite flying conditions.

sculptors to advanced potters. Open studio hours are also available by subscription. The studio also takes part in Art After Dark, a community wide art event held the first Friday of each month until 9 p.m. at participating galleries.

Art Central

1329 Monterey St.

(805) 788-0887

artcentralslo.wordpress.com

FREE!

From Highway 101, take the Marsh Street exit and continue straight into town. Turn left onto Osos Street then left onto Monterey Street.

What began as an art store quickly became home to a sizable gallery. The store's owner, an artist in her own right, features works by local artists. Open Mondays through Saturdays. This gallery takes part in Art After Dark, a community wide art event held the first Friday of each month until 9 p.m. at participating venues.

ARTS Space Obispo

570 Higuera St., Suite 165

(805) 544-9251

artsobispo.org

FREE!

From Highway 101, take the Marsh Street exit and continue straight into town. Turn left onto Nipomo Street, then left onto Higuera Srteet. The gallery is in The Creamery.

The home gallery of the San Luis Obispo County Arts Council is used to host a variety of cultural events including poetry readings, art exhibits, workshops and art-related meetings. It's an intimate space for musical performances and the epicenter of Art After Dark, a community wide art event held the first Friday of each month until 9 p.m. at participating venues. The space's regular exhibit hours are Mondays through Fridays from 10 a.m. to 4 p.m. and Saturdays 10 a.m. to 2 p.m. Closed holidays.

ASI Craft Center Gallery

First Floor of Julian McPhee University Union, Cal Poly

(805) 756-1266

www.asi.calpoly.edu/craftcenter

FREE!-$$$

From Highway 101, take the Grand Avenue exit north onto the Cal Poly campus. For the mandatory parking pass, stop at the information booth on the right side of the road immediately upon entering campus. The gallery is inside the student union at the intersection of Perimeter Road and Grand Avenue.

This art center and gallery features student works and public workshops, special sales and an annual Throwfest, a 24-hour clay throwing event held each February. The gallery, available to students and community members 18 or older, is generally open Sunday through Wednesday from noon to 6 p.m., though hours vary. Call ahead.

The gallery often shows works of ceramic, clay, stained glass, blown glass and photography. The center offers public arts and craft classes and workshops. Other activities include surfboard shaping, candle dipping, tie dye, hemp projects, soap making, clay work and stained glass. Workshops vary to fit participants' ages. Call for schedule and reservations.

☞ Boo Boo Records Kids Music
978 Monterey St.
(805) 541-0657
www.booboorecords.com
FREE!
From Highway 101, take the Marsh Street exit and continue straight into town. Turn left onto Osos Street then left onto Monterey Street.

Every Wednesday at 10 a.m. babies and toddlers crowd into the record store's back room to dance, wiggle and drum to their little hearts' content. Music changes weekly and occasionally there are special guests.

Cal Poly Performing Arts Center
1 Grand Ave.
(805) 756-7222
www.pacslo.org
$$$
From Highway 101 take the Grand Avenue exit and head north onto the Cal Poly Campus. Parking information and passes are available at the booth to the right immediately on entering campus.

The center includes the Christopher Cohan Center, featuring a world-class, 1,282-seat concert hall. It also houses the 497-seat Cal Poly Theatre, a 170-seat recital hall and a pavilion. Local organizations and professional troupes from around the world take the stage here throughout the year. Check the center's calendar for current offerings.

Rules regarding children are strictly enforced, so beware when purchasing tickets. Babies and children are only allowed when expressly stated in an event's advertising. All children must have a ticket, even if they are small enough to fit on an adult's lap. Any child disrupting a performance will be ushered from the theater along with one guardian and will not be allowed to return to the seating area until intermission.

Compact Gallery
1166 Higuera St.
(805) 235-3256
compactgallery.net
FREE!

From Highway 101, take the Monterey Street exit, turn left onto Toro Street, then right onto Higuera Street.

No doubt the city's smallest art space may also be the most eclectic. Founded by a relocated New Yorker, the gallery strives to provide alternative works from artists abroad. Open Wednesdays through Saturdays from noon until 5 p.m. The gallery remains open until 9 p.m. for new exhibit receptions which are held on the first Friday of each month to coincide with Art After Dark, a community wide art event held at participating venues.

Cuesta College Cultural & Performing Arts Center
Highway 1

(805) 546-3198

academic.cuesta.edu/performingarts/

FREE!-$$

From Highway 101, take the Santa Rosa Street/Highway 1 exit and turn north. Continue out of town about 5 miles. Turn left onto Hollister Road, right onto Romauldo Road, then left on the access road just past the track to get into parking lot 2. Parking fee.

Cuesta Community College is alive with performing arts ensembles including Jazz band, wind ensembles, choirs, theatre troupes and more, many of which perform at the campus's own Cultural & Performing Arts Center.

The campus is also home to its own art gallery (academic.cuesta.edu/finearts/) which features student and faculty works as well as shows by other influential artists. The gallery is located in room 7170 in the art building near the performing arts center.

Downtown Centre Cinemas
888 Marsh St.

(805) 546-8600

www.themovieexperience.com

$

From Highway 101 take the Marsh Street exit and continue straight into downtown.

While it focuses on playing blockbusters, this theater's unique location underground may give it added interest value. Drop down the big steps to seven screens of escapism.

☞ Fremont Theater
1025 Monterey St.

(805) 541-2141

www.themovieexperience.com

$

From Highway 101, take the Marsh Street exit and continue straight into town. Turn left onto Osos Street, then right onto Monterey Street.

To give children a true movie experience, bring them to this Art Deco cinema. The Fremont was built in 1942 and has served generations of movie goers in style with a truly big screen and plenty of comfortable seats for a crowd. Murals of sea nymphs on horseback adorn the interior walls. Other touches include the neon-illuminated swoops on the ceiling, floor-to-ceiling velvet drapes and inlaid walkways.

The theater generally screens blockbusters, but it also features special showings including the ongoing Screening Room Classics series. It is also the featured theater during the San Luis Obispo International Film Festival (slofilmfest.org) held annually in March.

The neighboring Mission Cinemas adds three modern screens to the mix.

Gallery at The Network
778 Higuera St., Suite B

(805) 788-0886

galleryatthenetwork.com

FREE!

From Highway 101, take the Marsh Street exit, turn left onto Garden Street.

This eclectic commercial gallery includes works by local artists as well as pieces from further afield. On any given day, customers may view jewelry, oil paintings and pottery, or book art, water colors and fiber arts. Open daily with extended hours first Friday evenings ('til 9 p.m.) for Art After Dark, a community wide art event held at participating venues.

Hands Gallery
777 Higuera St.

(805) 543-1921

handsgallery.com

FREE!

From Highway 101 take the Marsh Street exit and continue straight into town. Turn left onto Chorro Street, and then left onto Higuera Street. The gallery is on the left.

Local artists and more show their works at this commercial gallery. Kids who can keep their hands to themselves are appreciated in this store full of breakable but intriguing works of art including utilitarian pieces for all ages. This gallery takes part in Art After Dark, a community wide art event held the first Friday of each month until 9 p.m. at participating galleries.

Just Looking Gallery
746 Higuera St., Suite 1

(805) 541-6663

justlookinggallery.com

FREE!

From Highway 101 take the Marsh Street exit and continue straight into town. Turn left onto Chorro Street, and then left onto Higuera Street. The gallery is in the Mission Mall on the right.

For nearly 30 years this locally owned gallery has offered limited editions, original works and pieces that offer humor, beauty and "serious" art.

Linnaea's Café
1110 Garden St.
(805) 541-5888
linnaeas.com
FREE!
From Highway 101 take the Marsh Street exit, then turn left onto Garden St.
Works of art rotate regularly on the walls and in the garden of this popular coffee house which also serves as a venue for poetry readings, musical performances and other cultural events. The café takes part in Art After Dark, a community wide art event held the first Friday of each month until 9 p.m. at participating venues.

☞ Palm Theatre
817 Palm St.
(805) 541-5161
thepalmtheatre.com
$$
From southbound Highway 101 take the Chorro Street exit, take the first two rights to get onto Chorro Street, then turn left onto Palm Street. From northbound Highway 101 take the Broad Street exit and continue straight, then turn left onto Palm Street.
The nation's first solar-powered movie theater offers three screens of everything no other theater in San Luis Obispo County does: the best of cinema. Come here for foreign films, low-budget festival award winners, documentaries and occasional exceptional blockbusters. You'll also find a reasonably priced snackbar and friendly staff at this locally owned gem.

The Photo Shop
1027 Marsh St., Suite B
(805) 543-4025
photoshopslo.com
FREE!
From Highway 101 take the Marsh Street exit.
While primarily a commercial enterprise specializing in digital and print photo equipment, supplies and services, the store also features ongoing exhibits by photographers. The shop takes part in Art After Dark, a community wide art event held the first Friday of each month until 9 p.m. at participating venues.

Public Art
FREE!
Whether you walk the creek, meander downtown streets and alleys or

pedal the bike paths, you're bound to discover art in public places throughout San Luis Obispo. For current maps of public art check the SLO Arts Council website (sloartscouncil.org), SLO Parks & Rec website (www.slocity.org/parksandrecreation/publicart.asp) or stop by the San Luis Obispo Museum of Art (1010 Broad St., 805-543-8562) or San Luis Obispo Chamber of Commerce Visitors Center (1039 Chorro St., 805-781-2777.

☞ San Luis Obispo Museum of Art

1010 Broad St.

(805) 543-8562

sloma.org

FREE!

From Highway 101 take the Marsh Street exit and follow Marsh into town. Turn left onto Broad Street. The center is two blocks up and on the right.

The museum located on the western edge of Mission Plaza features three galleries of fine art and craft exhibits that change regularly. The museum specializes in sharing works of local professional artists. It also offers classes, workshops and its annual Plein Air Festival. Works of member artists are on sale throughout the year. Take a tour led by a friendly docent, or let your children take the lead. Admission is free, but donations are welcomed.

This museum also takes part in Art After Dark, a community wide art event held the first Friday of each month until 9 p.m. at participating galleries.

San Luis Obispo Little Theatre

888 Morro St.

(805) 786-2440

slolittletheatre.org

$$

From Highway 101 take the Marsh Street exit and follow Marsh into town. Turn left onto Morro Street. The theater is three blocks up and on the right.

For more than 60 years, this non-profit community theater company has continued to promote non-professional theater through a variety of offerings including: plays, musicals, readers' theater, and classes and workshops for adults and children.

SLO ART Gallery

339 Marsh St.

(805) 542-9000

tinyurl.com/4xeapvu

FREE!

From Highway 101 take the Marsh Street exit and continue straight into town. The gallery is in the Frame Works building on the right.

This gallery features framed works by local artists and special guest artists. Shows rotate every three months or so. Check the gallery's website or swing in to find details on current and future exhibits, hours and special events. The gallery also takes part in Art After Dark, a community wide art event held the first Friday of each month until 9 p.m. at participating venues.

Steynberg Gallery
1531 Monterey St.
(805) 54-0278
steynberggallery.virb.com
FREE!

From Highway 101 take the Monterey Street exit and proceed straight.

This gallery and coffee house features regularly rotating collection of works by local and international artists. Live music, poetry readings, open mic nights an other cultural events are often offered here as well. Steynberg Gallery also takes takes part in Art After Dark, a community wide art event held the first Friday of each month until 9 p.m. at participating venues.

☞ Sunset Drive-in Theater
255 Elks Lane
(805) 544-4475
www.fairoakstheatre.net
$

From northbound Highway 101 take the Prado Road exit and turn left onto Prado Road at the end of the offramp. From southbound Highway 101, take the Madonna Road exit, turn left onto Madonna Road, right onto Higuera Street, then left onto Prado Road at the old cemetery.

For a fun, affordable, all-American family night gather pillows, beanbags, sleeping bags, beach chairs, mattresses (whatever makes you comfortable) and head to one of only two drive-in theaters on the Central Coast. (The other is the Hi-Way Drive-in in Santa Maria.) The price is right for affordable family fun. If the movie is appropriate for youngsters, this might be just the place to introduce them to moving pictures on a big screen; children 5 and under get in free.

In the 1950s, these outdoor theaters were all the rage. Through the decades they dwindled, thousands closed, but San Luis Obispo never went without, and generations of families have enjoyed the experience together.

The best way to enjoy the drive-in is NOT in your own designated seats, but snuggled together in some fashion: a mattress in the bed of a pickup truck; comfy bean bags on the ground (or in aforementioned pickup); crammed in the back of the minivan, seats removed, hatch up; side by side in beach chairs; all while bundled under blankets as needed.

LETTERS

☞ San Luis Obispo County Library
995 Palm Street
(805) 781-5775 (children's desk)
slolibrary.org

FREE!

From Highway 101 take the Marsh Street exit and continue straight into town. Turn left onto Morro Street. The library is at the corner of Morro and Palm streets.

This relatively large library, open Tuesdays through Saturdays, has a long history of excellent story times catering to preschoolers and toddlers as well as a long list of services and events for the community. Storytimes are held Tuesdays and Thursdays at 10:10 a.m. with another session held in Spanish at 4:15 p.m. on the first Tuesday of the month. A hypo-allergenic canine reading buddy visits at 5:15 p.m. the second Tuesday of each month.

The library offers an entire room dedicated to local history and hosts the genealogical society which offers free family research assistance. Ongoing events include reading programs for children and adults, Book Club in a Box and more. Special events are also presented here throughout the year and have included Teddy Bear Tea, science programs, lectures, readings, film presentations and musical performances.

HISTORY

Ah Louis Store
800 Palm Street
visitslo.com
FREE!

From Highway 101 take the Broad Street exit. Turn north one block to Chorro Street, then east on Chorro to Palm Street.

The two-story brick structure was the first Chinese store in San Luis Obispo County when it opened in 1874. It served as the hub of San Luis Obispo's Chinatown. Ah Louis sold general merchandise, herbs and Chinese goods. His store also served as a bank, counting house and post office for the Chinese immigrants who dug the eight tunnels through the Santa Lucia Mountain Range from 1884 to 1894.

The store remains in the hands of the Louis family, which operated it as a retail shop for decorative items from China until 2006. It has since housed retail establishments with no evident ties to Chinese culture.

Camp San Luis Obispo Historical Museum
5 miles north of San Luis Obispo on Highway 1
(805) 594-6517
www.militarymuseum.org/campsanluisobispo.html
FREE!

*From Highway 101, take the Santa Rosa Street/Highway 1 exit and turn north. Continue out of town. Camp San Luis Obispo is on the left. **To enter the camp, driver must show proof of insurance, registration and driver's license.***

Since the 1920s, Camp San Luis Obispo has been home to the California National Guard. The 223rd Infantry Regiment, among other training and logistic operations and programs, calls the facility home. The grounds also serve as a living memorial and museum. Static displays include an Army aviation display area with fixed and rotary wing aircraft from the 1950s and '60s. The central mall includes various vehicles, examples of sculpture by Italian prisoners of war interned at the camp during World War II, and a Bataan Memorial. There is a small indoor museum to the right shortly after entering the camp. In addition, the camp houses the California Conservation Corps State Museum which documents the history of the *Civilian Conservation Corps* and the present *California Conservation Corps*.

Central Coast Veterans Memorial Museum

Veterans Memorial Hall
801 Grand Ave.
(805) 543-1763
vetmuseum.org
FREE!
From Highway 101 take the Grand Avenue exit. Turn south onto Grand Ave.
Young history buffs in the making may enjoy this museum of war memorabilia including cannons, helmets, uniforms, maps, flags and military patches, among other items. Hours are Wednesdays through Saturdays from 10 a.m. to 3 p.m.

Civilian Conservation Corps State Museum

1536 Modoc, Camp San Luis Obispo
www.militarymuseu.org/cccmuseum.html
FREE!
From Highway 101, take the Santa Rosa Street/Highway 1 exit and turn north. Continue out of town and pass Camp San Luis Obispo. Turn left onto Hollister Avenue/Cuesta College, turn left onto O'Conner Road, turn right onto Madera, and then turn left onto Modoc.
The museum is located in four barracks at Camp San Luis Obispo and is open by appointment only. The buildings feature the past, present and future of the corps that was established in 1933 by President Franklin Delano Roosevelt. Roosevelt hoped the corps forestry work would prevent soil erosion, provide flood control and complete other projects as the needs arose, but said the chief focus would be "the moral and spiritual value of such work." A library and research center includes more than 100 binders of letters home, information about works completed, and more.

Dallidet Adobe & Gardens

1185 Pacific St.
(805) 543-0638
historycenterslo.org/?page_id=33
$
From Highway 101, take the Marsh Street exit and continue straight into town. Turn right onto Santa Rosa Street then left onto Pacific Street.

This historic adobe home, owned since 1953 by the San Luis Obispo County Historical Society, provides a field trip experience back to the 1830s. The furnished home was once home to Pierre Hypolite Dallidet and Ascención Salazar, developers of the first commercial winery on the Central Coast. It has also been designated California State Historical Landmark No. 720. The garden is open to the public Thursdays from 2:30 p.m. to 5:30 p.m. Docent-led tours of the adobe are held from 1 p.m. to 4 p.m. Sundays from Memorial Day to Labor Day weekends.

Jack House & Gardens
536 Marsh Street
(805) 781-7308
www.slocity.org/parksandrecreation/jackhouse.asp
$
From Highway 101 take the Marsh Street exit. The house is on the left about two blocks down.
This historic Victorian house built in 1880 and related garden are home to a variety of special events, some of which cater to children. It's a good stop for children learning about the Victorian era. The garden includes a group barbecue area and there are restrooms on the site. Tours are held from 1 p.m. to 4 p.m. Sundays. (Groups of 10 or more should call ahead for reservations, 781-7300.) Children accompanied by adults are admitted free of charge.

☞ Mission San Luis Obispo de Tolosa
Monterey Street between Chorro and Broad streets
(805) 543-6850
www.missionsanluisobispo.org
FREE!

From Highway 101 take the Marsh Street exit. Turn right onto Chorro Street. The mission is on the right midway through the second block.
This historic Catholic mission, the fifth of the 21 missions established in California, was founded in 1772. More than 200 years later it remains the focal point of downtown San Luis Obispo and serves as a great tool for bringing history lessons to life. It is California State Historical Landmark No. 325. The main chapel, which houses a particularly unique vestibule/bell tower, still houses Catholic church services regularly in addition to special services, concerts and other public events

throughout the year. The chapel, mission and gardens are open for public tours daily from 9 a.m. to 4 p.m. (5 p.m. in summer), and guided tours are held most Sundays at 2 p.m. Additional tours for groups are available by reservation. Donation requested.

Octagonal Barn
About 4400 South Higuera Street
(805) 544-9096
FREE!
From Highway 101 take Los Osos Valley Road east, turn right onto South Higuera Street.
Though this barn is on private property, it is an interesting and rare structure clearly visible from the public roadway. Local groups have raised tens of thousands of dollars to restore the barn, which is one of only three of its kind remaining in California. Call ahead to arrange a tour.

☞ History Center of San Luis Obispo County
Carnegie Library
696 Monterey St.
(805) 543-0638
historycenterslo.org
FREE!
From Highway 101 take the Marsh Street exit and head straight into town. Turn left onto Broad Street, then right onto Monterey Street. The museum is on the left inside the Carnegie Library.
Just a skip across the street from Mission San Luis Obispo is the county's most extensive collection of publicly available historical documents. The building, a Carnegie Library completed in 1905, served as the city's central library until 1955. The following year the San Luis Obispo County Historical Society entered into a lengthy lease agreement with the city. A retrofit and remodel in 2001 gave rise to an expanded exhibit area and public research room. Today, rotating exhibits feature local history and culture. The museum is open Wednesdays through Sundays from 10 a.m. to 4 p.m.

San Luis Obispo Historic Railway District
Railroad Ave.
(805) 544-6531
www.slorrm.com
From Highway 101 take the Marsh Street exit. Turn right onto Osos Street and continue straight. Follow the jog to the left at the triangular park, and continue straight into the parking lot.
In 1876, San Luis Obispo was linked by the narrow-gauge Pacific Coast Railway to Harford's Wharf at Port San Luis. The railway, which connected to cities as far south as Los Alamos in Santa Barbara County, transported goods and passengers traveling by steamship up and down the coast until the

standard-gauge Southern Pacific finally made it to town in 1894.

Today, the railroad and the people who built it are featured in a variety of projects in the district. The restored **Ramona Railroad Depot** (1100 Railroad Ave.) remains in use today by Amtrak passengers. Bring the kids by to watch the big diesels pass, take a trip, or check out old photos in the depot.

Just down the tracks, the **San Luis Obispo Railway Museum** strives to spotlight the history of the Central Coast's rail systems, including the full-gauge rails still in operation and the narrow gauge rails that made many Central Coast communities what they are today. The museum collects, restores and displays railroad artifacts including locomotives, boxcars, cabooses and other rolling stock, even a velocipede. The museum website (slorrm.com) offers a fabulous (and free) walking-tour guide to the district.

Stenner Creek Trestle
Stenner Creek Road
FREE!
From Highway 101 take the Santa Rosa Street/Highway 1 exit. Head north and continue straight out of town. Turn right onto Stenner Creek Road.

This 953-foot-long, 90-foot-tall trestle was built on the East Coast, then shipped around Cape Horn for installation here in 1894. More than 100 years later it remains a signature portion of California's coastal rail route, and a nifty place to catch a different perspective of passing trains.

NATURE
San Luis Obispo City Park Rangers lead monthly hikes through various open spaces. Call (805) 781-7300 for current schedule.

Anholm Park
870 Mission St.
(805) 781-7300
www.slocity.org/parksandrecreation
FREE!
From Highway 101 take the Marsh Street exit and continue straight into town. Turn left onto Chorro Street, then right onto Mission Street.

This small (less than a quarter acre) pocket park has a play structure, picnic table and benches. No restroom.

☞ Bishop Peak Natural Reserve
(805) 781-7300
www.slocity.org/parksandrecreation/bishop_peak.asp
FREE!
From Highway 101 take Santa Rosa Street north, turn left onto Foothill Boulevard, then right onto Patricia Drive. Turn left onto Highland Drive and follow the cul-de-sac to its end. Parking is limited to space available on the street. If all parking is taken, return to Patricia, turn left, park near Anacapa Court and begin your adventure on the Patricia Street Access which dovetails

into the Ferrini trail.

The picturesque 1,559-foot Bishop Peak that dominates the horizon west of San Luis Obispo is one in a chain of nine prominent lava plugs left by volcanoes formed more than 20 million years ago. "The Nine Sisters" or "the morros" stretch from Morro Bay to Edna Valley southeast of San Luis Obispo. They include, from west to east, Morro Rock, Black Hill, Cerro Cabrillo, Hollister Peak, Cerro Romauldo, Chumash Peak, Bishop Peak, Cerro San Luis and Little Islay Hill. Morro Rock, Hollister Peak, Cerro Romauldo and Chumash Peak are closed to the public.

Giant volcanic stones balance precariously atop Bishop Peak which is covered with soil, grasses, wildflowers, oaks and bay trees. The morro is home to the original Cal Poly "P," a giant, whitewashed letter emblazoned on the rocky mountainside by enthusiastic students of yesteryear. The mountain also was home to a granite quarry that supplied

Bishop Peak is a challenging trail for youngsters but still accessible for active adults.

the stones for the historic Presbyterian Church at the corner of Marsh and Morro streets in downtown San Luis Obispo. The quarry has long been defunct and decades of winter storms and summer sunshine have faded the old "P," but the peak remains a popular destination for local hikers and rock climbers.

A fairly fit adult carrying a toddler in a pack can make the 2-mile trip to the peak in 1½ hours, which includes stops to watch deer, butterflies and plentiful lizards. The walk down takes about 45 minutes with no stops. The hike is strenuous, rocky and the trails do not provide access for people in wheelchairs or of limited physical capacity. There are no services. Bring plenty of water and snacks, and carry out whatever you carry in.

There are other, more youngster-friendly options in the reserve including Felsman's Loop. This 2.7-mile hike meanders along the morro's northwestern foothill.

No fires, overnight camping, or bicycles are allowed. Dogs must be on leash. Hikers are asked to stay on trails.

Bowden Ranch Open Space
East end of Lizzie Street
(805) 781-7300
www.slocity.org/parksandrecreation/bowden_ranch.asp
FREE!

From Highway 101 take the California Avenue exit, turn south onto California, right onto San Luis Drive, left onto Johnson Avenue then left onto Lizzie Street.

One of the city's newest open space acquisitions makes legal a long-time local favorite hike over the ridge into Reservoir Canyon (p. 47). There is nothing easy about this strenuous, uphill climb which rises 1,120 feet in less than one mile. The route is not stroller or wheelchair friendly, nor are mountain bikes allowed.

Still, the views from the ridge are superb and surprises await intrepid adventurers. For an extended excursion, continue southeast along the ridge about half a mile to find the top of the Reservoir Canyon trail, then descend into its cool depths. But remember, what goes down, must come up.

Broad Street Community garden
500 block South Broad Street
(805) 781-7069
www.slocity.org/parksandrecreation
$$

From southbound Highway 101 take the Broad Street exit. From northbound 101, take Broad Street exit, turn left onto Peach Street, left onto Chorro Street, left onto Lincoln and then left onto Broad Street.

Eighteen garden plots are available for rent to city residents on a first-come, first served basis.

Buena Vista Park

Buena Vista Avenue between Hope and McCollum streets

(805) 781-7300

www.slocity.org/parksandrecreation

FREE!

From Highway 101 take the Grand Avenue exit. Head north, turn right onto Loomis Street then left onto Buena Vista Avenue.

This nearly-half-acre pocket park is something akin to a roundabout with no services, but offers the neighborhood a bit of open space to stretch out or play catch.

☞ Cal Poly animal units

(805) 756-2419

www.calpoly.edu

FREE!

From Highway 101, take the Grand Avenue exit north onto the Cal Poly campus, stopping for a parking pass at the information booth immediately on your right upon entering campus.

Cal Poly's learn-by-doing spirit extends to visitors at its various animal units which are open for public tours during daylight hours. Children who ask questions of students at work are likely to find the answers for themselves through hands-on experience. Call ahead for tours.

Swine Unit

From the information booth at Grand Avenue, take Grand Avenue north, turn right onto Perimeter Road, turn right onto Via Carta then left onto Sports Complex Road.

Breeder hogs kept outside are friendly and welcome pats and scratches from visitors. While children may be aware of the oinks and snorts hogs are known for making, give these beasts a good scratch between the shoulder blades for a new sound experience. The area also includes a farrowing barn (where litters are born) that is sometimes available for tours and a shoat barn, home to the weanlings.

Dairy Unit

From the information booth at Grand Avenue, take Grand Avenue north, turn right onto Perimeter Road, right onto Via Carta, left onto Highland Drive, then right onto Mt. Bishop Road.

Check out the milking barn and hundreds of dairy cows at this facility. Calves are sometimes available for petting here, too.

Horse Unit

From the information booth at Grand Avenue, take Grand Avenue north, turn right onto Perimeter

Road, turn right onto Via Carta and follow it to its end at the horse unit.

The breeding and training facility managed by students is home to plenty of friendly mares itching for a scratch. Watch little ones' fingers which horses could easily mistake for scrumptious carrots or other favorite treats. (But please don't feed the animals.)

Poultry Unit

From US 101, take Highway 1 toward Morro Bay, then turn right onto Stenner Creek Road.

This student-led commercial endeavor was built in 1995 to accommodate up to 14,000 egg-producing chickens, 7,000 replacement pullets, 7,000 broilers and 2,500 chickens for other projects. Today, the unit partners with outlets throughout the Central Coast to sell campus produced eggs and a major corporation for meat production.

Sheep Unit

From US 101, take Highway 1 toward Morro Bay, then take the first right after Stenner Creek Road.

Ever since Cal Poly opened its doors in 1903, sheep production has been a course of study. Today, more than 100 white-face, production-grade sheep are regularly housed on Cheda Ranch. Here, students focus on animal care and husbandry as well as range management techniques. At any one time, 24 of the 26 paddocks may be empty

Tours are not normally provided, but the unit is open for public enjoyment throughout the year. Keep in mind that this is a working farm and the facilities were developed with sheep, not children or careless adults, in mind. Steer clear of the high-tensile, electric fences designed to keep out predators. Treat all such fences as if they were live. Do not climb on panels, leave gates as you find them, and stay out of the ram pens.

If you're into watching little lambs romp and play, your best bet is to visit between March 15 and May 1. For the lambs' safety, please do not cuddle them.

Cal Poly Conservatory

www. plantconservatory.calpoly.edu

FREE!

From Highway 101, take the Grand Avenue exit north onto the Cal Poly campus, stopping for a parking pass at the information booth immediately on your right upon entering campus. Parking information and maps to the conservatory are available here.

The glasshouse in the center of campus plays home to a variety of rare and endangered plants as well as native species and other plants used in biology and plant science courses. Tours are available on a limited basis by reservation only (756-2775).

Cal Poly Farm Hike

polyland.calpoly.edu

FREE!

From Highway 101 turn north onto Highway 1, right onto Highland Drive, left onto Mount Bishop Road and park in the Crop Unit parking lot.

Cal Poly encourages hiking throughout its lands. Just remember to leave gates as you found them.

This easy hike meanders past several agricultural units including the beef unit, experimental farm, dairy and poultry units. From the parking lot walk west to Stenner Creek then follow the dirt road north along the creek past the orchards, lagoon and Parker Ranch. Turn left onto the paved road (Mount Bishop Road) and continue past the beef unit. After the beef unit turn right onto Stenner Creek Road, then circle the poultry unit. Just north of the poultry unit is an intersection with an unnamed dirt road. Take the trail at the south east corner and continue through the open grassland and onto a dirt road that leads past the organic experimental farm, south to the dairy unit then back to Mount Bishop Road and, eventually, the car.

Cal Poly Plant Shop

(805) 756-1106

polyplantshop.com

FREE!

From Highway 101, take Grand Avenue exit north onto campus. Stop for a parking pass at the kiosk at campus gate. Turn right onto Perimeter Road, right onto Via Carta. The plant shop and greenhouse are on the right directly across from the horse stables.

Student-grown plants of many varieties are on display and for sale here. Bring a picnic and enjoy the tree-shaded lawn and deck that separates the greenhouse from the equine unit. Bring some cash to pick up seasonal flowers and other plants started here. Open Mondays through Saturdays from 10 a.m. to 5 p.m. Closed all academic holidays.

Cal Poly U-pick

(805) 756-2296 (hotline)

www.calpolyfruitenterprises.calpoly.edu

$-$$$

From Highway 101, take the Grand Avenue exit north onto campus. Stop for a parking pass at the kiosk at campus gate. Crop locations vary. Call ahead for specific directions.

Cal Poly students lead this enterprising effort to share the crops they grow. The public is welcome to take part picking whatever crop is in season including stonefruits, citrus and pumpkins. School and other group tours of the pumpkin patch have also been available in the fall when a corn maze has been created. Pumpkin picking is available late in season.

☞ Cerro San Luis Natural Reserve

(805) 781-7300

www.slocity.org/parksandrecreation

FREE!

From San Luis Obispo, take Marsh Street west toward southbound Highway 101. After crossing under the freeway, take an immediate right onto

Fernandez Road (the last right before entering the highway).

This 118-acre reserve has long been the primary public access to Cerro San Luis, one of the city's signature peaks complete with its historic "M" commemorating Mission Preparatory High School in San Luis Obispo. Trails in the reserve vary, but all involve a climb. Sites include outcroppings of cactus that protect a variety of plant species seldom seen elsewhere in the city, an old lemon grove, and access to the "M."

The hike to the peak is fairly strenuous in that it involves a continuous uphill walk, but, due to the relatively clear path and graded incline, it is regularly traveled by people of all ages and physical abilities. This is also an excellent mountain bike ride with wide paths that accommodate both bikers and hikers.

There is also public access to the peak is via Laguna Lake (p. 41).

Cheda Ranch
Stenner Creek Road
polyland.calpoly.edu/places (click on "Cheda Ranch")
FREE!

From Highway 101 take the Santa Rosa Street/Highway 1 exit. Head north and continue straight out of town. Turn right onto Stenner Creek Road.

Park just before you get to the trestle, then walk back to the last paved road before the trestle and proceed to the ranch.

This relatively flat trail along Stenner Creek meanders past Middlecamp Reservoir, Nelson Reservoir and straight on to the parabolic Cheda Ranch milking barn. The barn has been converted to serve as home to more than 100 head of black-face sheep. If the hike to the barn and back isn't enough, on the return trip to the car take the trail north around the east side of Nelson Reservoir. The trail climbs gently as it loops past Frog Pond to a viewpoint overlooking the ranch, sheep unit (p. 31), trestle vineyard and Chorro Valley.

Chorro Creek
Cal Poly Chorro Creek Road
polyland.calpoly.edu/topics/recreation/x330/chorrocanyon.htm

FREE!
From Highway 1, turn south onto Education Drive, then immediately right onto Cal Poly Chorro Creek Road
Although adjacent to the Cuesta College campus, this 582-acre ranchland is owned and maintained by Cal Poly. Take this generally flat, pleasant walk through vineyards, past a lagoon and down Chorro Creek. The path also leads past an "educational flying range" maintained by the university's College of Engineering and used regularly by local model aircraft enthusiasts.

C.L. Smith Joint Use Park
1375 Balboa Street adjacent to C.L. Smith Elementary School
(805) 781-7300
www.slocity.org/parksandrecreation
FREE!
From Highway 101 take Los Osos Valley Road west, turn right onto Oceanaire, then right onto Balboa Street.
This 4.8-acre park includes ball diamonds, athletic fields, play structures and basketball courts.

☞ Cuesta Canyon County Park
East end of Loomis Street
(805) 781-5930
www.slocountyparks.org
FREE!
From Highway 101 take the Grand Avenue exit. Take Grand Avenue north, and then turn right onto Loomis Street which feeds directly into the parking lot.
Although it appears to be in San Luis Obispo, Cuesta Park is a county park. San Luis Creek bubbles through the center of the park which also houses play structures, horseshoe pits, playing fields, picnic areas, large pit barbecues, a hiking trail and restrooms.

Dairy Creek Golf Course
El Chorro Regional Park, across Hwy. 1 from Cuesta College
(805) 782-8051
Centralcoastgolf.com
$$-$$$
From Highway 101 take the Santa Rosa Street/Highway 1 exit and proceed north out of San Luis Obispo. About 5 miles past Highland Drive, turn right into El Chorro Regional Park and follow the signs to the course.
Reservations are accepted up to one week in advance for one of the newest public golf courses in San Luis Obispo County. The 18-hole, 6,548-yard, par 71 course designed by John Harbottle serves up some local challenges, not the least of which is the erratic coastal breeze that can whip across the fairways at a moment's notice. Fees are reduced for golfers under age 17, students and seniors. Cart rentals are available.

Dairy Creek is also home to the Central Coast Golf Academy. The training program offers short game seminars, equipment analysis, driving range, video analysis and stay-and-play golf for on-course strategy sessions.

Damon-Garcia Sports Fields
South Broad Street
(805) 781-7300
www.slocity.org/parksandrecreation
FREE!

From Highway 101 take the Los Osos Valley Road exit. Turn right onto Los Osos Valley Road, left onto South Higuera Street, right onto Tank Farm Road, then left onto Broad Street/Highway 227. The complex is on the left.

This 20-acre sports complex features a specialized grass designed to withstand the tests of turf sports. The park can accommodate 4 to 9 playing fields, depending upon configuration. There is also a concession stand and restrooms. While there are no play structures at this new park as of press time, it remains a fine expanse of grass ideal for letting kids run out some of their bottled up energy.

☞ East Cuesta Ridge
FREE!

Take Highway 101 north out of San Luis Obispo and up Cuesta Grade (the big hill just north of town). Mt. Lowe Road is just past the summit on the right side of the road. The unmarked road is little more than an extended pullout with room to park before the locked gate.

(Note: The safest access is from northbound U.S. 101; access from southbound side absolutely not advised.)

Public access to this graded dirt road is limited to pedestrian and bicycle use. Unless you're feeling particularly strong and bring another such adult along to help heft strollers over the locked gate, you're better off leaving it at home and opting for the kid carrier.

Once over the gate obstacle, visitors are rewarded with a long, winding ascent to and along the ridge high above the highway and canyons, through native oak groves, and past two radio facilities and several peaks including Mt. Lowe, Black Butte, Lopez Mountain and Gay Mountain. The 7½-mile unrelenting climb can be grueling for small children and adults unaccustomed to such ascents, but the road provides clear and relatively smooth travel. The views from the top are among the best in the area, and the ride down is invigorating.

☞ El Chorro Regional Park

Off Highway 1 about 5 miles north of Highland Drive
(805) 781-5930
slocountyparks.com
FREE!

From Highway 101, take the Santa Rosa Street/Highway 1 exit and turn north and continue about 5 miles past the city limits.

This 490-acre county park has unique play structures, artificial rocks for bouldering, 62 campsites, three trails, a fenced dog park (805-528-1537), barbecue facilities, volleyball courts, horseshoe pits, softball fields, an 18-hole golf course and a busy calendar of events. The park is also home to the 150-acre San Luis Obispo Botanical garden (805-546-3501) and Education Center which provides exhibits about the garden and sustainable design such as straw bale construction and passive solar heating.

Hikes in the park include Dairy Creek (a 1.2-mile, stroller-friendly, relatively smooth, flat trail), Eagle Rock (a strenuous ¾-mile climb culminating in expansive views of the Chorro Valley) and the moderately strenuous, 1½-mile Oak Woodland Trail. Watch for poison oak, Chumash mortar holes, oak woodlands, wood rat nests, and plentiful native wildflowers including shooting stars, sticky monkey flower, popcorn flower, soap plant, wild rose and meadow lupine.

Ellsford Park

San Luis Drive between California Blvd. and Cazadero St.
(805) 781-7300
www.slocity.org/parksandrecreation
FREE!

From Highway 101, take the California Boulevard exit. Go south on California Boulevard, turn left onto San Luis Drive.

Two grassy areas compose this pocket park that totals 1 acre. The park features benches and an extremely steep drop off to San Luis Creek.

Emerson Park

Bounded by Nipomo, Pacific, Pismo and Beach streets
(805) 781-7300
www.slocity.org/parksandrecreation
FREE!

From Highway 101 take the Marsh Street exit and continue straight into town. Turn right onto Nipomo Street.

This city-block park was once the home of Emerson School. Today the park includes a playing field installed by the parents of Emerson School students decades ago. More recent additions include play structures, adult fitness zone, basketball courts, picnic tables and the city's parks and recreation department headquarters. There are no restrooms.

The park also includes Emerson Community garden, a mix of 38-plots of varying sizes, some in raised beds. The plots are available for rent to city residents on a first-come, first-served basis (805-781-7069).

French Park
Poinsettia Street
(805) 781-7300
www.slocity.org/parksandrecreation
FREE!

From Highway 101 take the Los Osos Valley Road exit. Turn right onto Los Osos Valley Road, left onto South Higuera Street, right onto Tank Farm Road, and then right onto Poinsettia Street.

This 10-acre park includes a multi-use court, youth baseball/softball field, sand volleyball court, tennis court, horseshoe pits, barbecue areas, picnic tables, play structures and a restroom.

Garden of the Seven Sisters
2156 Sierra Way
(805) 781-5939
tinyurl.com/648cwfp
FREE!

From Highway 101 take the Santa Rosa Street exit, turn south onto Santa Rosa Street, left onto Marsh Street, right onto Johnson Avenue, right onto Ella Street, then left onto Sierra Way.

The University of California Cooperative Extension Master Gardener Program maintains this living classroom where master gardeners provide workshops on sustainable, science-based gardening practices for the home gardener. Topics may include water conservation, soil preservation, composting, habitat for beneficials and healthy harvests.

The garden is open when events are scheduled, but is otherwise closed to public access.

☞ Irish Hills Natural Reserve
access from Prefumo Canyon Road
(805) 781-5939
www.slocity.org/parksandrecreation
FREE!

Take Highway 101 to Los Osos Valley Road exit. Turn west onto Los Osos Valley Road, then turn left onto Prefumo Canyon Road. At 2 miles, watch for a locked gate on the left side of the road after the bridge. Park alongside the roadway.

To access the Madonna Road Trailhead, from Highway 101 take Los Osos Valley Road toward Los Osos, turn left on Madonna Road and park at the end of the street. A short walk up a dirt road leads to this trailhead.

Eventually city officials hope to create a trail system linking San Luis Obispo to Montana de Oro State Park to the west. When they do, the Irish

Hills will be the jumping off point. Until then, the 1,090-acre reserve provides opportunities for pleasant family adventures on foot, mountain bike or horseback. In 2009, the addition of neighboring Froom Ranch made way for 5 additional miles of trails for a total of 13 miles of potential adventure. Quick and relatively easy access may be had at the Madonna Road trailhead, but the Prefumo Canyon access may be preferable for visitors seeking more solitude. Within a 30-minute hike from either trailhead, sweeping views from the ridge encompass the entire chain of morros, or mountains.

The Prefumo Canyon trailhead offers the most-challenging entry into this network of trails. Loose gravel and a continuous incline along this rutted section increase the difficulty level along this route, which is most enjoyed by rugged outdoorsfolks training for climbs beyond SLO County. Side trails lead to caves and views. Throughout much of the area, shade is in short supply. There are no watering holes or facilities along the way, so plan accordingly.

For more family-friendly ascents, begin at Madonna Road. Here, follow Mariposa Trail straight up the hill for a direct but rewarding ascent through dappled shade and hillside meadows, or take the fairly flat, single-track trail to the left for an easy walk to Froom Creek. The Froom Creek trail asends gently up the watershed for more than half a mile to the first potential loop turnoff. Here, take either the short, steeper Canyon View cutoff over to the midpoint of Mariposa Trail, or continue another half mile up the watershed to Poppy Trail which loops back to Mariposa Trail.

Trailside flora includes plenty of poison oak, monkey flower, white globe lily or white fairy lantern, Scotch broom, larkspur, and Indian paintbrush. Wildlife is often spotted here including deer, foxes, and a variety of reptiles

and birds.

All trails except the step Bog Thistle route off Prefumo are open to mountain bike use and dogs on leash are welcome throughout the system.

Islay Hill Open space
Tank Farm Road east of Broad Street
(805) 781-7300
www.slocity.org/parksandrecreation
FREE!

From Highway 101 take the Los Osos Valley Road exit. Turn right onto Los Osos Valley Road, left onto South Higuera Street, right onto Tank Farm Road, right onto Spanish Oaks, left onto Sweet Bay Lane. Parking is on this neighborhood street, so be mindful of local residents.

This local hike has grown more popular with the development of neighborhoods nearby including the addition of Islay Hill Park just a few blocks away. The climb is moderately strenuous at points, but most active children can make the trek which is the shortest among the area's peaks, and affords a great view. Beware of the poison oak along the trail and at the top. No mountain bikes are allowed on this trail, and there are no facilities along this 2-mile round-trip route.

Islay Hill Park
Tank Farm and Orcutt roads
(805) 781-7300
www.slocity.org/parksandrecreation
FREE!

From Highway 101 take the Los Osos Valley Road exit. Turn right onto Los Osos Valley Road, left onto South Higuera Street, and right onto Tank Farm Road.

This popular 5-acre neighborhood park features play structures, youth baseball/softball field, basketball court, tennis court, sand volleyball court, picnic areas and restrooms.

Islay/French Parks Bike Path
(805) 781-7300
www.slocity.org/parksandrecreation
FREE!

From Highway 101 take the Los Osos Valley Road exit. Turn right onto Los Osos Valley Road, left onto South Higuera Street, and right onto Tank Farm Road.

This winding bike/pedestrian path invites trikes, strollers and scooters, too, on its course connecting two neighborhood parks. A set of stairs midway along the path adds a bit of a challenge.

Johnson Park

1020 Southwood Drive

(805) 781-7300

www.slocity.org/parksandrecreation

FREE!

From Highway 101 take the Los Osos Valley Road exit. Turn right onto Los Osos Valley Road, left onto South Higuera Street, and right onto Tank Farm Road. Turn left onto Broad Street/Highway 227, left onto Orcutt Road, then left onto Laurel Lane. Turn left onto Southwood Drive.

This oft-shaded 4 1/2-acre park includes play structures, barbecue area, multi-use court, picnic tables, restrooms, outdoor basketball courts, group barbecue area and a bike path along the creek.

Johnson Open space

5182 Ontario Road

(805) 781-7300

www.slocity.org/parksandrecreation/johnson_ranch.asp

FREE!

From northbound Highway 101 take the South Higuera Street exit, turn left under the freeway, then right across Ontario Road and into the unpaved parking lot. From southbound 101, take the South Higuera Street exit loop and turn left across Ontario Road to enter the parking area.

This public open space just a stone's throw from city limits provides 3.9-miles of relatively easy trails on 242 acres. From the trailhead, follow the seasonal runoff up the canyon to the left, then follow the swtichbacks and otherwise gentle climb up and across the watershed's incline. At mile 1.6, a short cutoff leads to the final .6-miles of trail leading to the parking lot. Or skip the cutoff and continue along the 1.3-mile route through a pleasant oak grove and fantastic picnic rock before meeting up with the final, gentle descent.

This trail does offer some shade, but the exposed areas, particularly south-facing hillsides, can be brutally warm for coastal folks. As always, wear sturdy shoes and carry plenty of water.

Laguna Lake Golf Course

11175 Los Osos Valley Road

(805) 781-7309

Lagunalakegolfcourse.org

$-$$

From Highway 101 take the Los Osos Valley Road exit and proceed north.

The city's parks department prides itself on offering affordable golf for the whole family on this 10-hole, 1,344-yard, par-32 executive course. The course, driving range, club, cart rentals and lessons are available from 7 a.m. to dusk daily. The facility offers student and senior rates (no charge for players over age 90) and First Tee, a golf education program for youth ages 4 to 17. In

2011, the facility added a short-order restaurant with beer and wine license.

Laguna Hills Park

Bounded by Valecito and San Adriano courts and Mirada Drive
(805) 781-7300
www.slocity.org/parksandrecreation
FREE!
From Highway 101 take Los Osos Valley Road west. Turn left onto Diablo
Drive, and then left onto Mirada Drive.
This neighborhood park on 3½ acres includes a play area and picnic tables,
but no restrooms.

Laguna Lake Open space

500 Madonna Road
(805) 781-7300
www.slocity.org/parksandrecreation
FREE!
From Highway 101 take the Madonna Road exit and turn west.
This 360-acre reserve features a system of hiking trails for varying
abilities. Take a gentle walk along the flats or climb up to the 540-foot ridge
overlooking downtown SLO and Los Osos Valley. This park is immediately
adjacent to Laguna Lake Park.

Laguna Lake Park

500 Madonna Road
(805) 781-7300
www.slocity.org/
parksandrecreation
FREE!
From Highway 101 take the
Madonna Road exit and turn west.
This 375-acre park has everything
a city park needs and then some: play
structures, dog park, hiking trails,
barbecue areas, sand volleyball court,
fitness trail, picnic tables, restrooms
and a 180-acre lake that can be used
for fishing, sail boarding, row boating,
and power boating under 1 horsepower.
The lakeside is a popular duck-feeding
area, but beware of the geese, some
of which are downright aggressive.
The park is adjacent to the city's 360-
acre Laguna Lake Open space which
features a system of hiking trails.

Las Praderas Park

Mariposa Drive

(805) 781-7300

www.slocity.org/parksandrecreation

FREE!

From Highway 101 turn east onto Los Osos Valley Road. Turn left onto South Higuera Street and left onto Praderas Drive. The park is at the T intersection of Praderas and Mariposa drives.

A pocket park of grass on nearly a quarter acre.

Laurel Lane Community garden

1200 block Laurel Lane

(805) 781-7069

www.slocity.org/parksandrecreation

$$

From Highway 101 take the Marsh Street exit and continue straight into town. Turn right onto Broad Street, left onto Orcutt Road, then left onto Laurel Lane.

Immediately adjacent to the fire station are 16 garden plots ready for planting. The plots, some of which are in raised beds, are available to city residents on a first-come, first-served basis.

Leaning Pine Arboretum

Via Carta, Cal Poly

(805) 756-2888

www.leaningpinearboretum.calpoly.edu

FREE!

From Highway 101, take the Grand Avenue exit north onto the Cal Poly campus, stopping for a parking pass at the information booth immediately upon entering campus. Continue along Grand Avenue, turn right onto Perimeter Road, and turn right onto Via Carta. The plant shop and greenhouse are on the right directly across from the horse stables.

Families with well-supervised children are welcome to picnic or simply wander the 5-acre grounds of the arboretum from 10 a.m. to 5 p.m. Monday through Saturday when school is in session. The grounds include gardens dedicated to specific geographical areas which are comparable to the climate offered on the Central Coast. Featured regions include New Zealand, Australia, California, Chile, South Africa and Mediterranean. Other gardens are devoted to specific groupings including a primitive garden, formal garden and an area full of unusual conifers.

Pick up a garden walk guide at the kiosk near the entrance or in the neighboring Cal Poly Plant Shop. Interpretive signs also offer a bit of education, or make a reservation for an interactive group tour. The arboretum is also home to a variety of special events throughout the year.

Visitors are asked to stay on designated paths. Gardeners use reclaimed water throughout the garden, so children should be strongly discouraged from playing in any water, puddles, hoses, taps or other water sources within the garden.

Meadow Park
Meadow Avenue at South Street
(805) 781-7300
www.slocity.org/parksandrecreation
FREE!

From Highway 101, take the Madonna Road exit and head east. Turn left onto South Higuera Street, then immediately right onto South Street. Turn right onto Meadow Avenue.

This 14-acre park is the only park in town with an area designated specifically for slacklining, a skill akin to tightrope walking with a slackened length of webbing stretched between two trees or other above-ground anchors. Slackliners must use designated trees, are required to bring and use tree protection and are not allowed to position their lines more than 5 feet off the ground or across walkways. Slacklining is only allowed during daylight hours.

The park is also home to Rotary Garden, a community garden with 40 plots available for rent on a first-come, first-served basis (805-781-7069). For $24/year, city residents can adopt one of these plots and make garden to their hearts' delight.

There is also plenty of room for more traditional park play and has long been a local favorite for kite flying. Facilities include barbecue areas, horseshoe pits, picnic tables, sand volleyball courts, basketball court, fitness course, walking trails, playground, softball field and restrooms.

☞ Mission Plaza
Monterey Street between Chorro and Broad streets
www.slocity.org/missionplaza.asp
FREE!

From Highway 101 take the Marsh Street exit. Turn right onto Chorro Street. The mission is on the right midway through the second block.

This open-air walkway between Mission San Luis Obispo de Tolosa and San Luis Creek is a fun place to let the kids run, give parents a rest and take in any of a number of public events held throughout the year such as the I Madonnari Italian Street Painting Festival, Plein Air Festival and Concerts in the Plaza, a live music series held every Friday evening throughout summer months. Children delight in feeding ducks or tossing rocks in San Luis Creek below the bridge. A shallow fountain in front of the mission features Paula Zima's "Qiqsmu" sculpture depicting a Chumash girl, a bear and two cubs. There are benches and grassy mounds nearby for the weary. The plaza also includes public restrooms, an amphitheater, an arbor patio area, the historic Murray Adobe and access to San Luis Creek.

Mitchell Park

Bounded by Santa Rosa, Pismo, Buchon and Osos streets

(805) 781-7300

www.slocity.org/parksandrecreation

FREE!

From Highway 101 take Marsh Street and drive straight into downtown.
Turn right onto Osos Street.

This city center park encompasses an entire city block. Amenities include play structures, a bandstand, picnic tables, a barbecue area and restrooms.

Osos/Triangle Park

Osos Street and Railroad Avenue

(805) 781-7300

www.slocity.org/parksandrecreation

FREE!

From Highway 101 take the Marsh Street exit and continue straight into
town. Turn right onto Osos Street. The park is on the left at the Y intersection
of Osos Street and Santa Barbara Street.

A one-third-acre grassy triangle of a pocket park with one picnic table.

Pennington Creek/Escuela Ranch

polyland.calpoly.edu/places/WestRanch

FREE!

From Highway 1 north of San Luis Obispo, turn right onto Education Way,
turn right at the Y onto Pennington Creek Road, continue past the ranch, and
over a bridge. The trailhead is past the first gate on the left after the bridge.

This relatively little-known 1,819-acre Cal Poly property 5 miles north of the main campus is open to hikers and mountain bikers. The property is maintained primarily as an agricultural education facility with emphases on grazing and grape, hay and alfalfa production. A biological preserve has also been set aside. With few visitors, wildlife abounds on the old ranch property. Watch for deer, coyotes and bring binoculars for birding.

The easiest portion of the trail follows a graded, dirt road along Pennington Creek to a grove of olive trees at the confluence of four creeks. Families with small children not used to hiking or inclines may want to turn back here.

For a more lengthy (and more challenging) hike, continue along the unmaintained loop trail past the stone corral, around the north side through an oak grove and eventually the top of the hill, then follow a four-wheel-drive road along the ridge and back to the dirt road.

☞ Poly Canyon

Poly Canyon Road, Cal Poly campus

www.polyland.calpoly.edu/places/PolCan

FREE!

From Highway 101, take the Grand Avenue exit north onto the Cal Poly campus, stopping for a parking pass at the information booth immediately upon entering campus. Turn right onto Perimeter Road, then right onto Poly Canyon Road. An often-locked gate keeps out motorists, but bicycles, pedestrians and equestrians are welcome.

A graded dirt road along Brizzolara Creek gives way to a variety of hiking, biking and equestrian trails that meander to the Design Village, scenic ridges and eventually to Stenner Creek. All trails discussed in this section can be walked in either direction.

The most difficult thing about Poly Canyon is finding parking. For a quick and easy answer to legal parking, stop at the information booth at the Grand Avenue entrance to campus. Parking permits (required) are also sold there.

Once at the Poly Canyon gate (which is often locked since vehicular access beyond the gate is supposed to be limited to residents and campus authorities), enjoy an easy stroll on the well-maintained, graded dirt road.

There are several trail options.

About three-quarters of a mile from the gate are a trail and bridge on the right side of the road. Follow this sometimes steep climb through a swale and finally to the ridge above the Poly "P" east of the dorms. Once on the ridge, the walk is easy and often breezy. This loop can be completed by following the path down the western slope of the hill with a quick stop for an alphabet lesson atop the "P."

The most unusual stop in the canyon is Design Village, a 9-acre experimental architectural design and construction area in a park-like setting. To find the village, take the easy walk up Poly Canyon Road past the "P" fork. Take the trail that passes under the stone archway to the left of the road and follow the clearly marked pathway to the village. A handful of architecture students live in the canyon which is also home to the annual international Design Village competition started here in 1974. Existing structures particularly attractive to many children include the shell house, tensile structure, stick house, underground house, geodesic dome and the canyon's first student-built landmark: the 1963 concrete blade structure which was rebuilt in 2004.

For a longer, more challenging loop, continue along the main road about 25 yards past the stone archway to the gate on your left. Hop the gate and continue along this road as it turns into a single track. The trail loops around the backside of the knoll before heading back downhill through Horse Canyon and to the main campus via the equine unit.

The Great Loop is a 6.5-mile trail that also can begin in Poly Canyon. Rather than turn left and climb the gate, continue straight on through the gates at Pennington Ranch (p.44), a Poly-owned property, being sure to leave all gates as you found them. This loop trail continues up the hill toward the train tracks, along the hillside, then back down Stenner Creek Canyon past working ranches, an impressive train trestle, the campus farms and back to the main campus.

Trails are numerous in the canyon. For detailed information, check the Cal Poly website or the biking and hiking books listed in the resources section (p. 226).

Camping is allowed on Poly land, but no fires, stoves or tents are allowed and there are no restroom facilities. Plan accordingly.

Poly Canyon serves as a fantastic hands-on classroom for a variety of scientific studies.

Prefumo Canyon Road
FREE!

Take Highway 101 to Los Osos Valley Road exit. Turn west onto Los Osos Valley Road, then turn left onto Prefumo Canyon Road.

This is a beautiful drive, walk or bike along a winding canyon road that meanders through oak groves and over San Luis Obispo's legendary rolling hills. Views from the 1,360-foot summit are spectacular during the day, but the area is equally popular at night for stargazers seeking dark skies away from any viewing obstacles.

Double back and return to San Luis Obispo or continue on to See Canyon and Avila Valley.

Priolo-Martin Park
Vista del Collados at Vista del Arroyo
(805) 781-7300
www.slocity.org/parksandrecreation

FREE!

From Highway 101 turn west onto Los Osos Valley Road. Turn right onto Descanso Street, then left onto Vista del Arroyo.

A quarter-acre pocket park with trail and benches featuring views across Laguna Lake to Cerro San Luis and Bishop Peak.

Railroad Recreational Trail

(805) 781-7300

www.slocity.org/parksandrecreation

FREE!

From Highway 101 take the Marsh Street exit and follow Marsh into town. Turn right onto Osos Street and continue straight. Follow the jog to the left at the triangular park, then park in the lot near the rail station.

This 1.2-mile paved trail from Jennifer Street Bridge to Orcutt Road offers a peaceful alternative for cross-town bicycle commuters. The relatively flat, family-friendly route follows the southwest perimeter of Sinsheimer Park (p. 49), a good place to stop for restrooms, a picnic or a jaunt through the play structure.

☞ Reservoir Canyon Open space

Reservoir Road about 1 mile north of SLO off Highway 101

(805) 781-7300

www.slocity.org/parksandrecreation

FREE!

Take Highway 101 north through San Luis Obispo. After the last SLO exit (Monterey Street), watch closely for side roads. The second right is Reservoir Canyon Road. Turn right here. Follow the road to the dirt parking area near the locked gate.

Ask locals about Reservoir Canyon and they're likely to shrug or stare blankly, but the city has owned acreage in the canyon for more than a century. The long-abandoned reservoir and the old road leading to it returned to nature decades ago, but they left behind a clear path that offers a pleasant creekside hike through cool, dense shade of sycamore and oak minutes away from the city center.

The 3.2-mile trail through the

city's 487-acre open space meanders along Reservoir Creek, which can run briskly in winter storms then slow to a trickle by early autumn. The route is not stroller friendly and bicycles are not allowed. Smaller children who are relatively sure of foot will have no problem following the gurgling creek. After 1.2 miles, parents may have to take hold of little ones' hands or put them in the carrier to clime 1,100 feet in just 1 miles. The payoff for the effort includes fantastic canyon views.

At this point, hikers may continue onto Bowden Ranch (p. 29) for a one-way hike, or double back, then continue downstream to find two small cascades, one of which hides a 70-foot-deep cave. At any rate, watch for poison oak which is prevalent along many segments of this hike.

San Luis Blues
Sinsheimer Stadium
900 Southwood Drive
www.bluesbaseball.com
(805) 512-9996
$-$$$
From Highway 101 take the Los Osos Valley Road exit. Turn right onto Los Osos Valley Road, left onto South Higuera Street, and right onto Tank Farm Road. Turn left onto Broad Street/Highway 227, left onto Orcutt Road, then left onto Laurel Lane. Turn left onto Southwood Drive.

This summer collegiate baseball program provides a professional atmosphere and top amateur play Memorial Day weekend through early August.

San Luis Creek
Various points throughout San Luis Obispo
FREE!
San Luis Creek was the mission's first source of water. Today its route through the city is largely channeled under streets and buildings, but emerges at various parks for public enjoyment.

The easternmost public access to San Luis Creek is at Reservoir Canyon (p. 47). Upon entering the city, water sometimes rushes but most often bubbles peacefully through Cuesta County Park before heading into a residential neighborhood and, finally, into the tunnels. The creek sees daylight again at Mission Plaza (p. 43) where it is a popular spot for ducks, families and downtown business people. Here it includes three blocks of walkways, parks, benches, viewing areas, bridges and boulder crossings within view of creekside shops and restaurants. Artwork along the creek includes the iconic Johns Ausburger's Tank Head Fish (1977) and Sandra Johson's Web of Life Sphere (1999).

Santa Rosa Park
Santa Rosa and Oak streets
(805) 781-7300
www.slocity.org/parksandrecreation

FREE!

From Highway 101, take Santa Rosa Street/Highway 1 north.
The 11-acre park is home to, among other things, San Luis Obispo Skate park. The unsupervised skate facility offers wood ramps and quarter pipes, but extensive plans for an elaborate concrete park have been approved and fundraising efforts continue. City parks rangers stop by frequently to enforce the helmet-and-pads rule.

The popular park also offers access to San Luis Creek (pp. 43 & 48), play structures, barbecue areas, horseshoe pits, softball field, baseball field, basketball/roller hockey court and restrooms.

Sinsheimer Park
North end of Southwood Drive
(805) 781-7300
www.slocity.org/parksandrecreation
FREE!

From Highway 101 take the Los Osos Valley Road exit. Turn right onto Los Osos Valley Road, left onto South Higuera Street, and right onto Tank Farm Road. Turn left onto Broad Street/Highway 227, left onto Orcutt Road, then left onto Laurel Lane. Turn left onto Southwood Drive. The park is at the end of the drive.

This 23½-acre sports complex, also accessible via the Railroad Recreational Trail (p. 47), is home to San Luis Obispo Baseball Stadium, Stockton Softball field and the SLO Swim Center which features an Olympic-sized outdoor heated pool, therapy pool, locker rooms and restrooms. The park also includes batting cages, tennis courts, play structure, sand volleyball court, running and bike trails, horseshoe pit, a nine-hole disc golf course and barbecue areas. The pool is open daily for lap swimming and has regularly scheduled recreational swim hours and lessons. It is also home to the San Luis Obispo Swim Club and serves as the home pool for San Luis Obispo High School swimming, diving and water polo.

South Hills Open space
(805) 781-7300
www.slocity.org/parksandrecreation
FREE!

There are two main access points: For the northwestern access, from Highway 101 take the Madonna Road exit from Highway 101. Turn right onto Madonna Road, left onto South Higuera then immediately right onto South Street. Turn right onto Exposition. For the southeastern access, continue along South Street, turn right onto Broad Street, right onto Stoneridge Drive and left onto Bluerock Drive. The trailhead is at the back of Stoneridge Park on the right.

This 131-acre preserve includes a prominent ridge

that divides the southern portion of the city. Trails are open to pedestrian traffic only. From the pocket park off Bluerock Drive, the trail offers an easy walk up an abandoned road to the ridge where views of the city and nearby peaks are superb. The top of the ridge is a great place to teach kids about the state rock, serpentinite, which abounds here.

Stagecoach Road
Somewhat parallel to U.S. 101 north of San Luis Obispo to Cuesta Ridge
FREE!
To begin at the top, take Highway 101 north out of San Luis Obispo and up Cuesta Grade (the big hill just north of town). A left-hand-turn lane at Cuesta Summit leads the way to the old road. Once off the freeway, take a left onto Stagecoach Road. The graded dirt road meanders down the canyon wall and back to Highway 101. To begin at the bottom, take Highway 101 north to Stagecoach Road, (the first handy left past Monterey Street).

The old dirt road that once served as the main route for the stage line remains open as a public thoroughfare. The unrelenting incline winds through oak groves to the summit goal. It is a fun ride for fit cyclists interested in out-and-back rides as well as skilled riders interested in a somewhat technical and potentially speedy descent that drops down the Cal Poly side of the mountain.

Stenner Springs Natural Reserve
End of Stenner Canyon Road
(805) 781-7300
www.slocity.org/parksandrecreation
FREE!
From Highway 101 take the Santa Rosa Street / Highway 1 exit. Head north and continue straight out of town. Turn right onto Stenner Creek Road which ends in about 2.5 miles at the open space.

This 49-acre public space offers limited hiking trails that are minimally maintained, but they provide access to Stenner Spring Natural Reserve, Los Padres National Forest and Cal Poly lands. The area is particularly favored by experienced mountain bikers heading for routes including Shooters, Morning Glory, Botanical, Eucalyptus and Elevator. Inexperienced cyclists should steer clear of the area, but hard-core mountain bikers may want to try the grueling Botanical route. From Stenner Creek, the route climbs 800 technical feet up switchbacks to the Bontanical Garden on the ridge, then dives down the fast, fun, potentially hazardous Shooter route. No restrooms.

Stoneridge Park
Bluerock Drive
(805) 781-7300
www.slocity.org/parksandrecreation
FREE!

From Highway 101 take the Madonna Road exit from Highway 101. Turn right onto Madonna Road, left onto South Higuera then immediately right onto South Street, right onto Broad Street, right onto Stoneridge Drive and left onto Bluerock Drive.

A half-acre grassy pocket park with picnic tables and trailhead for the South Hills Open space hiking trails. No restroom.

Terrace Hill Open space

(805) 781-7300

www.slocity.org/parksandrecreation

FREE!

From Highway 101 take California Boulevard south, turn right onto San Luis Drive, left onto Johnson Avenue, and then right onto Bishop Street.

While the volcanic peaks tend to dominate San Luis Obispo's skyline, Terrace Hill is but a large mound begging to be hiked, run and explored. A very short walk up a wide, graded-dirt access road leads to the flat-top park at 501 feet above sea level. This is a good place to let the kids take a run up (and down, and up, and down) the hill, a longtime favorite with local athletic teams and keen individuals. Shade is limited on the hill, but there are a couple of picnic benches and plenty of space to arrange picnic blankets. The open sky here and the winds rising up the sides of the hill make this a splendid spot for kite flying. No restrooms.

Throop Park

510 Cerro Romauldo Ave

(805) 781-7300

www.slocity.org/parksandrecreation

FREE!

From Highway 101 turn north onto Highway 1, left onto Foothill Boulevard, right onto Ferrini Road and left onto Cerro Romauldo Avenue.

This neighborhood park includes a play structure, softball field, picnic tables and restroom.

Vista Lago Park

Vista del Lago at Laguna Lane

(805) 781-7300

www.slocity.org/parksandrecreation

FREE!

From Highway 101 take Los Osos Valley Road west, turn right onto Laguna Lane, then right onto Vista del Lago.

A ½-acre pocket park with picnic and play areas, but no restroom.

West Cuesta Ridge

FREE!

Take Highway 101 north out of San Luis Obispo and up Cuesta Grade (the big hill just north of town). A left-hand-turn lane at Cuesta Summit leads the way to TV Tower Road that generally follows the ridge. Once off the freeway, take a right and continue up the poorly maintained road (and watch for nasty potholes among other obstacles).

The highlight of this ridge is the view west along the morros to the Pacific Ocean. A 1,334-acre botanical area featuring Sargent cypress trees is also worth a stop on this national forest land. The trees occur naturally only in California. The dirt road that extends from Highway 101 is popular among mountain bikers and motorists seeking scenic views. The ridge and associated trails are great places to see spring wildflowers and to sneak above the marine layer for sunrise or sunset. The ridge trail from the botanical area to Cerro Alto is a popular route among fit area hikers and mountain bikers.

The dirt road can be terribly rough for passenger cars, particularly those with low clearance. This road is not recommended for vehicles with trailers or RVs due to tight turns, potholes and other obstacles along the route.

OTHER ADVENTURES

Apple Farm Inn Millhouse

2015 Monterey St.

(805) 544-2040

applefarm.com/millhouse

FREE!

From northbound Highway 101 take the Monterey Street exit. Continue straight onto Monterey Street for about half a block. From southbound Highway 101, take the Monterey Street exit, turn left at the top of the ramp, then left onto Monterey Street.

The replica of a 19th Century millhouse at this inn and restaurant is probably the most interesting part of the property to children (and many adults). Bring the kids to watch the miller make ice cream, press cider or perform other feats with machinery that utilizes the 14-foot working waterwheel. The mill generally operates from 10 a.m. to 4 p.m. Monday through Thursday, but call in advance to check current schedule.

The property also includes a hotel and a restaurant featuring desserts large enough for a small family to share (not that you'll want to).

Automobilia Museum at McCarthy's Wholesale

11 Higuera St.

(805) 544-1900

www.mccarthywholesale.com

FREE!

From Highway 101 take the Madonna Road exit and head east, then turn right onto Higuera Street.

Although this property is primarily a used-car lot, the showroom includes a collection of antique and specialty cars, glass cases full of toy cars and other automotive and air travel goodies. Open most days from 10 a.m. to 5 p.m.

☞ Bubblegum Alley
700 block of Higuera Street
FREE!

From Highway 101 take the Marsh Street exit. Follow Marsh into town, turn left onto Garden Street then left onto Higuera Street. The pedestrian-only alley is on the left side of the street midway between Garden and Broad streets.

In a town surrounded by beautiful mountains, filled with parks and packed with activities ideal for families, it may seem odd to point out a spot where people have been spitting out their gum for nearly half a century. Some call the alley lined with discarded chewed gum absolutely disgusting; others call it a hoot. Kids usually just ask for a piece of gum to chew so they can make their marks on the wall.

No one knows exactly when the gum collection began, but local lore has it that some time in the 1950s kids started slapping their gum on the wall. It may have been a team tradition, or merely a place to put their gum. Some gum artists have opted to make more extravagant marks. Some have chewed stick upon stick of gum in a concerted effort to spell complete words, leave their Greek letters or sculpt more detailed contributions.

Love it or hate it, Bubblegum Alley serves as a point of interest in which children delight.

Cal Poly Associated Students Inc. Epicenter
Second floor, Julian McPhee University Union
(805) 756-1281

www.asi.calpoly.edu

FREE!

From Highway 101, take the Grand Avenue exit north onto the Cal Poly campus, stopping for a parking pass at the information booth immediately upon entering campus. Continue north on Grand Avenue to Perimeter Road.

One-stop shopping for student-sponsored activities, many of which are open to the general public.

Cal Poly Athletics

(866) 756-7267

gopoly.com

FREE!-$$$

This university offers all sorts of athletic programs for its students, which means plenty of opportunities for fans. Catch a ball game, swim meet, tennis match or other sporting event with the family.

Cal Poly Associated Students Inc. Children's Center

Building 133 on Campus Way

(805) 756-1267

www.asi.calpoly.edu/children_s_center

$$$

From Highway 101, take the California Boulevard exit and head north. Turn right onto Campus Way.

The center provides daycare for children ages 4 months to 6 years. It also runs Poly Trekkers, a summer program for school-age children.

Cuesta Community College

Highway 1

(805) 546-3100

www.cuesta.edu

FREE!-$$

From Highway 101, take the Santa Rosa Street/Highway 1 exit and turn north. Continue out of town about 5 miles to the college.

In addition to its growing performing arts presence (p. 18), Cuesta College hosts athletic contests and provides additional facilities which, while designed first for student use, are often made available to the general public. There is also a North County campus in Paso Robles, currently dedicated to student academic needs, and the college uses Lucia Mar Unified School District facilities in the South County to provide classes there.

Among the main campus's most fantastic facilities is a beautiful outdoor swimming pool complex open for student and public programs (www.communityprograms.net). The complex includes an Olympic-sized pool with a rare 3-meter diving board. Seasonal aquatic offerings for youth have included water polo camp, swimming lessons and diving classes. For pool information, call (805) 546-3207.

For current athletics schedules, check academic.cuesta.edu/athletics. For class schedules open to the community at large, including youth, go to the college's main website.

Downtown Trolley

Serving downtown – hours vary

(805) 541-2877

www.slocity.org/publicworks/transit.asp

$

Pickup points along Monterey Street: in front of the Apple Farm Restaurant, Grand Avenue, California Boulevard, Toro Street, across the street from Fremont Theater, and ½ block east of Mission Plaza. Other pickup points include Higuera Street between Chorro and Garden Streets, Nipomo Street just outside Foster's Freeze, Marsh Street at Chorro Street and Osos Street ½-block south of Monterey Street.

Small children delight in every form of transportation. For an inexpensive thrill, hop on the trolley that connects downtown with the hotels on the north end of Higuera Street. Ride a block or take the whole loop.

The Downtown Trolley runs year-round on Thursdays 3 p.m. to 10 p.m. (on a modified route due to Thursday Night Farmers' Market – p. 57). It also operates from 1 p.m. to 10 p.m. Fridays and Saturdays from April through October.

Kennedy Club Fitness Multiplex

188 Tank Farm Rd.

(805) 781-3488

kennedyclubs.com/san-luis-obispo

$$

From Highway 101 take Los Osos Valley Road east, turn left onto South Higuera Street, then right onto Tank Farm Road.

Non-members can access this 50,000-square-foot club with purchase of a day pass. Facilities include the gym, outdoor sand volleyball courts and a six-lane, 50-meter swimming pool. The aquatics program includes Masters swim team, private and semi-private swim lessons, water polo, family swim, youth stroke school and adult swim clinics.

Madonna Inn

100 Madonna Road

(805) 543-3000

madonnainn.com

FREE!-$$$

From Highway 101 take the Madonna Road exit and turn west. Madonna Inn is on the right.

For half a century the family of Alex and Phyllis Madonna has owned and operated its original inn featuring 110 uniquely decorated rooms, many of which include features such as rock or waterfall showers. A favorite historical feature of the property is the lion house just across the parking lot from the main entrance. (No lion has been housed here in decades.)

Enjoy a tea and pastry party in the Copper Café, or check out the swinging lady and other features decorating the inn's various dining areas. Young men may be particularly interested in using the restrooms (and the girls can peek in once the coast is clear). No white porcelain for this family of creative minds. Instead, Alex Madonna installed a motion-activated waterfall urinal in the facility near the wine cellar.

The property is also home to the 20,000-square-foot Alex Madonna Expo Center which hosts public and private events throughout the year. And hotel guests as well as day spa guests are welcome to enjoy two Jacuzzis, a fitness center and a European-style, beachfront-entry pool with an infinity edge overlooking San Luis Obispo.

☞ San Luis Obispo Children's Museum
1010 Nipomo Street
(805) 545-5874
slocm.org
FREE!-$
From Highway 101 take the Marsh Street exit and follow Marsh into town. Turn left onto Nipomo. The museum is two blocks up and on the right.

This three-story-tall children's museum has a history of providing great educational entertainment to children in a safe, friendly environment that is comfortable for kids and parents alike. Children are invited to dress up and hit the big stage, cook up something special in the play kitchen, explore stop-action film-making, discover geology and more during regular operating hours Tuesdays through Sundays (call for current schedule and special extended schedules).

Interactive staff regularly schedules activities, and the museum maintains a calendar of special events. Admission is free to children under three. There are discounts for seniors and members of the military, and groups that call in advance may receive discounts as well.

San Luis Obispo County Regional Airport
903 Airport Drive
(805) 781-5205
sloairport.com
FREE!
From Highway 101 take the Marsh Street exit and proceed straight into downtown, then turn left onto Broad Street. Continue out of town and then turn right on Airport Drive.

Still a relatively small town airport, this strip provides plenty of viewing area for young aeronautics enthusiasts.

SLO-OP Climbing Gym

289 Prado Road

(805) 720-1245

www.slo-opclimbing.org

$

From northbound Highway 101, take Prado Road exit and continue straight to the gym. From southbound 101, take Madonna Road exit, turn right onto Madonna Road, right onto South Higuera Street, and then left onto Prado Road.

The nation's first non-profit, co-op gym has dedicated its entire 3,500-square-foot facility to bouldering and community building. While the gym is open 24 hours a day to members, visitors and prospective members are generally welcome from 6 p.m. to 10 p.m. Monday through Thursday. Members may bring no more than one guest at a time, and children under age 14 must be supervised by an adult.

SLO Sportsmen's Association

3270 Gilardi Road

(805) 541-5755

slosa.org

$

From northbound Highway 101, take Santa Rosa Road/Highway 1 toward Morro Bay for 7.5 miles, then turn right onto Gilardi Road.

This expansive venue provides year-round firearms and archery range facilities in an organized setting. It is regularly home to competitions, special events and educational programs including 4H and Boy Scout projects and hunter safety courses.

Facilities include several ranges designed for specific uses: pistol, rifle, trap and skeet, as well as archery. Hours and events are highly organized and include blackpowder muzzleloaders competitions monthly, a high-power rifle program, cowboy action shooting as well as action pistol events. Call or check the website for current schedule.

☞ Thursday Night Farmers' Market

Higuera Street from Nipomo Street to Osos Street

(805) 541-0286

downtownslo.com (click on "farmers' market")

FREE!

From Highway 101 take the Marsh Street exit and follow Marsh into town. Head straight for the Chorro Street parking structure on the right immediately past the intersection of Chorro and Marsh streets.

There are farmers' markets, then there's Thursday Night Farmers' Market in downtown San Luis Obispo. It's as much a street carnival as it is a market of fresh fruits, vegetables and flowers. Every week the street is closed to motorists for four hours to make room for thousands of pedestrians who spill

from sidewalks to street to sample farmers' offerings, eat at various barbecues and enjoy live entertainment that ranges from bands to jugglers to belly dancers. There's always something of particular interest to children.

Setup begins at 5:30 p.m. every Thursday (only significant rainfall cancels), but vendors are strictly forbidden from selling before the 6 p.m. bell rings. Booth and performers pack up at 9 p.m. By city ordinance, no dogs are allowed.

YMCA
1020 Southwood Drive
(805) 543-8235
sloymca.org
FREE!-$$$

From Highway 101 take the Los Osos Valley Road exit. Turn right onto Los Osos Valley Road, left onto South Higuera Street, and right onto Tank Farm Road. At Broad Street/Highway 227 turn left, turn right onto Orcutt Road, turn left onto Laurel Lane, and then turn left onto Southwood Drive.

This American standby offers after school programs, family fun nights, racquetball courts, more than 40 class offerings, fun runs, special events, specialty camps, and fitness memberships that include access to Sinsheimer Pool. Kids Gym, a preschool program held in two-hour sessions from 8:30 a.m. to 2:30 p.m., includes activities for $5 per child per session. Children must be potty trained. Healthy Kids Club is a drop-in program for older children held daily from 2:30 p.m. to 7 p.m. There are also occasional free events including Halloween at the YMCA and Happy Holidays at the YMCA. Call for current offerings.

Poly Canyon offers several options for hands-on outdoors experiences for the young, the young at heart, and the hard-core outdoorsman. For nearly half a century, the Design Village has been the university's hands-on training area for architects of the future. The fairly easy walk to the scenic village is one of SLO's best kept outdoor secrets.

Chapter 2

Avila Beach & Port San Luis

The best sunbathing and swimming beach in San Luis Obispo County shares sheltered San Luis Bay with Port San Luis, Fishermen's Beach, Pirate's Cove and Olde Port Beach, also known among locals as Cal Poly

Beach. Gentle waves lap the shore along this compact section of California coastline, providing fantastic opportunities for kayakers, paddlers, sailors, skim boarders, beginning surfers and body boarders.

Even when fog blankets the coast along the 160-mile stretch from Point Piños to Point Concepción, the sun pokes through at Avila Beach. While Pismo Beach, Oceano Dunes and the Guadalupe-Nipomo Dunes Complex bear the brunt of on-shore winds, Avila Beach enjoys protection from a jut of land that curves around the western edge of the bay.

Avila Valley, which stretches from Highway 101 to the beach, also serves up some interesting weather and family fun.

The presence of humans in the Avila area dates back some 5,000 years, according to the Port San Luis Harbor District, which serves these neighboring beaches. The area's modern history dates back to 1869 with the construction of People's Wharf. The town of Avila was founded five years later.

HISTORY

San Luis Obispo Light Station (aka Port Harford Lighthouse)
Pecho Coast Trail
(805) 541-8735
www.sanluislighthouse.org

FREE!-$$

From Highway 101 take Avila Beach Drive west through Avila Beach and
park either in the Olde Port lot or in the pullout across the road from the
power plant entrance.

Access to this 30-acre historic landmark located inside the Diablo Canyon
Nuclear Power Plant security buffer zone is limited to docent-led hikes,
guided tours and special events. The Point San Lighthouse Keepers provide
trolley service by reservation (540-5771) on the first and third Saturday of
each month and for groups of 20-50 on some Sundays.

Hikers who register at least two weeks in advance for one of the semi-
weekly hikes are rewarded with a beautiful adventure culminating in a tour
around the light station property. The 7.5-miles out-and-back route to the
lighthouse is open to hikers ages 9 and older and the age limit is strictly
enforced. It's a moderately strenuous trek over uneven terrain along the
edge of the Pacific.

The bluff top parcel includes the foghorn building and a duplex that once housed
lighthouse keepers and their families. The light station, which operated from 1890-
1933, is listed on the National Register of Historic Places.

NATURE

☞ **Avila Beach**
(805) 595-5400
portsanluis.com
FREE!

From Highway 101 take Avila Beach Drive west.

The best local beach for small children is Avila Beach with its gently sloping sand that encourages waders and young body boarders to venture into the sea. While lifeguards are on duty during summer months, parents should keep an eye on their little ones and weak swimmers should steer clear of waves, though they're typically small here during summer months.

Fishing is a popular activity from atop the pier where no fishing license is required. Other popular attractions include the old-fashioned, high-flying playground on the sand just west of the pier and the pirate-themed **Avila Beach Community Park** just inland from the western end of the beach. The beach area also includes barbecues, picnic tables, restrooms, outdoor showers and the tile spiral of history inlaid in the pedestrian plaza east of the pier.

Avila Beach Sea Life Center
50 San Juan Street
(805) 595-7280
www.sealifecenter.org
$$$

From Highway 101 take Avila Beach Drive west, turn left onto 1ˢᵗ Street and immediately right onto San Juan Street.

This nonprofit facility located on the edge of Avila Beach Community Park (aka Pirate Park) offers group tours, visitors' hours, camps and workshops focused on hands-on marine science education programs. Open to the public 10 a.m. to 4 p.m. Saturdays and Sundays from September through May, and 10 a.m. to 5 p.m. Wednesdays through Sundays from June through August.

☞ Bob Jones Trail
Ontario Road to Avila Beach Drive
FREE!

From Highway 101 take San Luis Bay Drive west, then turn immediately left onto Ontario Road. The parking/staging area is on the left.

This 2½-mile paved pathway dedicated for walkers, bikers and skaters offers an easy, peaceful, scenic route through Avila Valley. Because it is largely flat and away from traffic, it is popular for families with young cyclists as well as strollers.

The path's inland terminus is off Ontario Road about one-third of a mile from San Luis Bay Drive. From there it winds along the route determined largely by San Luis Creek which it parallels. The path sneaks behind the orchards of Avila Valley Barn, the backside of the Sycamore Springs Resort Labyrinth and Mediation Garden before crossing San Luis Bay Drive. It later merges with the course pathways at Avila Beach Golf Resort before crossing heavily traveled Avila Beach Drive.

To lengthen your ride or walk, turn right onto Avila Beach Drive and continue to the road's end at Port San Luis. Due to potentially heavy traffic, this portion is not recommended for young children or inexperienced riders/skaters. An off-street connector is in the plans for this stretch, but erosion in the area and lack of funding both threaten the project.

Fishermen's Beach offers great tidepooling when the tide is right.

Fishermen's Beach

(805) 595-5400

www.portsanluis.com

FREE!

From Highway 101 take Avila Beach Drive west through Avila Beach, over the high bridge along the coast at San Luis Creek and past Olde Port Beach.

If Olde Port Beach wasn't small enough for you, try out Fishermen's Beach, as the westernmost stretch of sand is called. This little-advertised nook on the harbor is particularly nice for families more interested in digging in the sand and watching sailboats than surfing or playing on playgrounds.

It is only accessible at low tide.

Fishermen's Memorial

Eastern end of Port San Luis parking lot

(805) 595-5400

www.portsanluis.com

FREE!

From Highway 101 take Avila Beach Drive west through Avila Beach. The memorial is on the right side of the road shortly before the Olde Port parking lot at the end of Avila Beach Road.

A scenic spot for a picnic a short hop away from the sand. The dolphin fountain holds the interest of some kids long enough for them to enjoy their lunches at nearby picnic tables before returning to the sand or the car.

Olde Port Beach (aka Cal Poly Beach)

(805) 595-5400

www.portsanluis.com

FREE!

From Highway 101 take Avila Beach Drive west through Avila Beach and over the high bridge along the coast at San Luis Creek. Olde Port Beach is around the bend.

This lesser-known little stretch of sand nearly disappears at very high tides, but it is a great swimming beach with little or no wave action. Don't expect to catch the Last Great Wave here, but do bring along some hotdogs and firewood for an evening blaze. Fires are permitted in the heavy steel fire rings provided. (No pallet fires are allowed.) A vehicle ramp provides drive-on short-term access to the beach for dropping off/picking up supplies and loading/unloading watercraft. Dogs also run without leash on this rare stretch of canine-friendly sand.

Pirate's Cove

Cave Landing Road

FREE!

From Highway 101 take Avila Beach Drive west. Turn left up the hill at Cave Landing Road which leads directly to a large, dirt parking area.

Whether or not a nude beach should be included in a family-oriented book may be a bone of contention, but the beauty of this cove is beyond reproach. If

you're not afraid to take off your skivvies in public, or prefer to do so, venture half a mile up Cave Landing Road to Pirate's Cove. The picturesque cove is well protected from the wind by steep cliffs on three sides. The waves are ideal for frolicking but generally too small and shallow for good surfing.

Nudists strip down on the sand, but there are other aspects of this area that can be explored even by the most reserved, including a tunnel along the bluff from which fishing is quite popular.

Beach access is difficult due to a steep, unimproved trail down to the beach.

☞ Port San Luis Pier
(805) 595-5400
www.portsanluis.com
FREE!
From Highway 101 take Avila Beach Drive west to its end.

The Port San Luis pier draws fishermen venturing out for the hunt as well as landlubbers seeking to simply purchase fresh fish and crab. It remains a popular spot for pier fishing, commercial sport fishing, you-pick-'em live crab, a live seafood market and on-pier dining featuring fresh local fare. Patriot Sportfishing (805-595-7200) has long provided charter sportfishing cruises and offers whale watching tours generally from December to April.

See Canyon
See Canyon Road between San Luis Bay Drive and Prefumo Canyon Road
FREE!
From Highway 101, take San Luis Bay Drive exit and head west. Turn right onto See Canyon Road and follow the road to its peak where it becomes Prefumo Canyon Road then returns to San Luis Obispo at Los Osos Valley Road.

This winding coastal canyon is home to apple orchards that thrive in the cooler conditions found here. Nights come earlier in this deep canyon and temperatures drop below that of other areas in the region creating ideal conditions for crisp apples. Longtime orchard standouts include:

Gopher Glen, 2899 See Canyon Road, (805) 595-2646, www.gopherglen. com – More than 60 varieties of popular and heirloom apples, kitchen shop, cookbooks, apple pears, fresh homemade cider, baskets and fruit; open late July through December.

See Canyon Fruit Ranch, 2345 See Canyon Road, (805) 595-2376 - focuses on old-time apple varieties; open September through October.

☞ Sycamore Mineral Springs Labyrinth & Meditation Garden

1218 Avila Beach Drive
(805) 595-7302
www.smsr.com/play/labyrinth-meditation-gardens.php
FREE!

From Highway 101 take Avila Beach Drive west.

It's fun to watch the kids' faces twist in confusion as they wind their way first toward, then away from the center of the labyrinth before reaching their goal. Unlike a maze, there is only one path through the labyrinth, so there's no way to get lost.

While adults may prefer a soothing massage at Sycamore Mineral Springs Resort across the road, children seem more elated by some time in the tire swings and garden sunshine. The labyrinth and garden are owned by the resort which provides them both free to the public.

The property is also home to Sycamore Crest Trail, a 1-mile trek to the ridge overlooking San Luis Bay. The trail begins as a dirt road just beyond the restaurant.

Initially, it meanders through oak woodland, but it narrows further uphill as it approaches open grassland. Follow your steps to return to the resort, explore the ridge, or continue southeast on the ridge until the trail descends and doubles back to the Bluffs Coastal Trail (p. 70).

OTHER ADVENTURES

Avila Beach Golf Resort
6464 Ana Bay Drive
(805) 595-4000 ext. 1
avilabeachresort.com
$$-$$$
From Highway 101 take Avila Beach Drive west through Avila Beach, over the high bridge, and then take the first right.

This scenic golf resort welcomes young and experienced golfers alike. The par-71, 6,500-yard championship course runs from the oak-lined Avila Valley to the estuary just off Avila Beach. The resort offers clinics, lessons, a pro shop and restaurant.

☞ Avila Valley Barn
560 Avila Beach Drive
(805) 595-2810
avilavalleybarn.com
FREE!
From Highway 101 take Avila Beach Drive west. The barn is on the right just past Ontario Road.

What started as a simple roadside produce stand selling out of fruit crates quickly turned into one of the county's premier harvest season family attractions. Throughout summer and fall, the barn comes to life with a variety of produce from local growers and special events. Families are encouraged to pack their own lunches and enjoy picnics on the lawn under dancing trees, enjoy a day on the farm, feed and pet farm animals (just stop by the barn and ask for feed – staff gives away bags of scraps like corn husks and apple pieces), and pick produce from peaches to pumpkins.

The addition of a sweets shop featuring homemade ice cream complements the barn's collection of fresh-baked goods that have traditionally included breads, cakes, pies, turnovers and tarts.

Picking opportunities vary by season but generally follow this schedule: Olallieberries in May-June; peaches in July-August; apples in September-October; pumpkin picking and hay bale mazes each October; Christmas trees for sale (though not grown on site) in November. The barn generally closes in December and typically reopens in March.

Avila Valley Hot Springs
250 Avila Beach Drive
(805) 595-2359

avilahotsprings.com

$

From Highway 101 take Avila Beach Drive west.

Generations of families have enjoyed the naturally warm water of Avila Hot Springs. Visitors now enjoy a 50-foot-by-100-foot pool featuring 86-degree water, water slides and a 20-foot-by-20-foot mineral pool maintained at 104 degrees all year round.

Other facilities include a restaurant, arcade, barbecue and picnic areas, Laundromat, cabins and campgrounds boasting hot showers and RV hookups. The staff provides swimming lessons and summer swim camps, bike rentals and massage services. Generally open seven days a week from 8 a.m. to 8 p.m.

PG&E Energy Education Center

6588 Ontario Road

(805) 546-5280

www.pge.com/education_training/about_energy/diablo_canyon/plant_tours/

FREE!

From Highway 101, take the San Luis Bay Drive exit and head west. Turn immediately left onto Ontario Road.

Open from 9 a.m. to 1 p.m. Monday through Friday for self-guided exhibits designed to provide public education about Diablo Canyon Nuclear Power Plant. The plant, operated near this center, generates up to 2,200 megawatts of electricity. Docents may be available to lead tours of the center by reservation.

Chapter 3
Shell Beach

North of the ever-popular Pismo Beach and south of Avila Beach stretches a coastline full of cozy coves, bluff-top parks and public walkways. They're not exactly secret, but when Pismo Beach is crawling with visitors, Shell Beach coves remain relatively serene.

Technically part of the city of Pismo Beach, Shell Beach has long maintained its own identity. The relatively quiet neighborhood is bounded on one side by the Pacific Ocean and the other by Highway 101 and features spectacular ocean views.

Throughout its early years of construction, developers repeatedly found signs of Chumash history here: bones, household items, beads. Though the Chumash people and earliest investors saw the value of this spot, investors were slow to catch on. While the city near the pier was growing, Shell Beach remained a quiet farming area literally a stone's throw from the ocean.

After World War II the entire Central Coast saw a boom in real estate. Scenic Shell Beach was no exception.

Unlike its sandy southern portion, the attraction in this half of the city is its coves where tidepooling, kayaking, beachcombing and sunbathing are

Shell Beach

popular activities. Although quiet coves beckon visitors at low tide, high tide often inundates the coves and, in some cases, brings waves crashing directly against the bluffs.

Swimming is permitted in all areas, and surfing is popular in many of them. Currents can be dangerous at all tides. There are no lifeguards on duty in any of the coves.

Kayaking offers visitors opportunities to get up close and personal with wildlife that forages in the kelp beds immediately offshore. Seals are plentiful, and dolphins are often spotted in the area. Local kayak rental and guide companies typically do not rent boats if conditions are too rough for boaters' safety, but parents should make their own assessment before taking children out.

The community is home to a plethora of parks from bluff perches to inland historical venues. All parks in Shell Beach are free and open during daylight hours. Many include picnic/barbecue areas and some have large group areas available by reservation.

LETTERS

Shell Beach Library
230 Leward Ave.
(805) 773-2263
FREE!
From Highway 101 take the Spyglass Drive exit and turn west. Turn left onto Shell Beach Road, then right onto Leward Avenue.

This compact branch of San Luis Obispo County Library provides access to a small collection of works during open hours Tuesday, Wednesday and Friday. There are also occasional special events as well as summer reading programs and access to the interlibrary loan program.

NATURE

Bluffs Coastal Trail
Parking off Bluff Drive past the end of Indio Drive
(805) 773-7039
FREE!
From Highway 101 take Avila Beach Drive exit. Turn north onto Palisades Road, turn left onto El Portal Street, and then curve right onto Indio Drive, also known as Cave Landing Road. Drive around the median divider at the gated end of the road, and then turn right into a clearly marked parking lot built specifically for bluff trail traffic.

The easiest, most stroller-friendly walk in Shell Beach is also among the most scenic – a public walkway that winds along the bluff top at the far northern edge of Shell Beach in front of multi-million-dollar homes. The walk along paved trails is extremely easy and wheelchair accessible.

The 1-mile out-and-back paved pathway offers spectacular views south beyond the sandy expanse of Pismo Beach, over the Oceano State Vehicular

Recreation Area and Guadalupe-Nipomo Dunes Complex and on toward
Point Sal some 19 miles directly south. The view north includes Mallagh
Landing (aka Pirate's Cove) and Point San Luis.

This trail is a great spot for introducing children to nature's scent
garden, particularly in the spring when native plants are at their
blooming peak. Hummingbirds swoop past visitors as they follow the trail
to the Y that takes visitors down to the cove overlook. Though Pirate's

Cove is a nude beach,
the overlook was placed
strategically to protect
the privacy of sunbathers
while providing a view of
the beautiful cove. The
viewpoint is ideal for
spotting otters and seals.

A post fence keeps walkers
on the paved trail most of
the way, but at the overlook,
a wide gap has been left
in the fence, presumably
so hikers may continue, at
their own risk, closer toward
the edge. The portion of trail
beyond the asphalt path is
very rough, not maintained
and dangerous. The area
beyond the fence is **not** safe.

Though the pathway is
intended for pedestrians, a
fun paved, loop bike ride for
experienced cyclists begins
and ends at the pathway
parking lot. Follow Cave

Landing Road north past the big homes, up and down the bluff-top hills, past the cove parking lot and down the backside to Avila Beach Drive. Turn right onto Avila Beach Drive and pedal to Palisades Road. Turn right onto Palisades Road, right onto El Portal Drive, and right onto Indio Drive back to the parking lot.

For a more challenging hike (and absolutely without stroller), walk away from the bluff parking lot and cross Indio Drive. Follow the fire access road that runs somewhat parallel to El Portal Drive and watch for the trail to the left just before the fire road turns to dirt. Follow this gentle climb along the foothill toward the freeway, then as it curves more steeply toward the ridge. At the ridge, turn left toward the ocean and continue along the ridge for spectacular views and wonderful displays of native wildflowers in season. This route meets with Sycamore Crest Trail.

Dinosaur Caves Park
Off Price Street at Cliff Ave.

(805) 773-7039

pismobeach.org

FREE!

From Highway 101 take the Spyglass Drive exit and turn west. Turn left onto Shell Beach Road, then right onto Cliff Avenue.

The first thing many wonder about Dinosaur Caves is: Where's the dinosaur?

The 11-acre open space on Shell Beach Road known as Dinosaur Caves Park is easy enough to spot, dinosaur or no dinosaur. It is the first large vacant lot south of Shell Beach and it is usually dotted with locals walking their dogs along the bluffs. Kayakers like cruising the kelp beds and paddling in and out of the caves below.

Local history has it that an amusement park once called this property home. H. Douglas Brown began building a concrete dinosaur here in 1948, but never finished due to public outcry. The headless behemoth was removed in the 1950s.

The 11-acre lot with the million-dollar views from above and sea caves below is the city's newest seaside park. Topside, Dinosaur Caves offers wonderful views and wildlife too. Regular sightings include squirrels, rabbits, ducks and myriad birds, sea lions, dolphins, otters, and pelicans. The park includes public restrooms, a playground, trails and lawn, and an amphitheatre with its own natural seating area. The park is also home to Art in the Park, a public display of local artisans, on the first Sunday of the months of May through October.

The bluff beyond the fence is unstable, so hikers are strongly advised to heed posted warnings and remain on firm footing.

Ebb Tide Park
Off Ebb Tide Court

(805) 773-7039

pismobeach.org

FREE!

From Highway 101 take the Spyglass Drive exit and turn west. Turn right onto Shell Beach Road, then left onto Ebb Tide Way which ends at the park.

Like most of the parks in Pismo Beach and Shell Beach, Ebb Tide Park

offers stupendous views of the Pacific coast. The bluff-top park is limited to a grassy area and short, paved pathway, but you can access the beach below from the neighboring hotel property where a public easement leads visitors down the stairs to the surf. There are no public restrooms at the park or on the beach.

Eldwayen Ocean Park

Ocean Boulevard between Palomar and Vista del Mar
(805) 773-7039
pismobeach.org
FREE!

From Highway 101 take the Spyglass Drive exit and turn west. Turn left onto Shell Beach Road, then right onto Vista del Mar which leads directly to the park.

This is the cove about which locals don't want to tell you. Benches, picnic tables and barbecues sit atop the 1½-mile bluff. Two sets of stairs lead down to a lovely cove often visited by seals and otters. This is a popular dog-walking beach for residents and includes both sandy stretches and tide pools. No restrooms.

Margo Dodd Park/Thousand Stairsteps

Western end of Cliff Avenue at Ocean Boulevard
(805) 773-7039
pismobeach.org
FREE!

From Highway 101 take the Spyglass Drive exit and turn west. Turn left onto Shell Beach Road, then right onto Cliff Avenue.

This tiny bluff-top park next door to Dinosaur Caves Park (p. 72) is most famous for its gazebo and views. Kids enjoy dancing in the gazebo, running on the grass, and checking out the hundreds of pelicans that often roost on the neighboring bluff isolated from the mainland by some 20 yards of ocean.

Just north of the park is a long, steep set of stairs from a rugged outcropping at the end of Palisade Avenue to the beach below. This is a popular spot for tidepooling, but be aware that the pools and most of the beach quickly diminish with the rising tide.

Memory Park
Seacliff Drive & Baker Avenue
(805) 773-7039
pismobeach.org
FREE!

From Highway 101 take the Spyglass Drive exit and turn west. Turn left onto Shell Beach Road, then right onto Seacliff Drive which leads directly to the park.

Another bluff-top park with a well-maintained lawn, benches, picnic tables and extremely treacherous access to a small cove. Sea walls protect cliff-top homes from erosion and detract from the beauty of this cove.

A narrow public pathway from nearby Naomi Street leads to Naomi View Platform, a public viewing area.

Palisades Park
Shell Beach Road at Encanto Ave.
(805) 773-7039
pismobeach.org
FREE!

From Highway 101 take the Avila Beach Drive exit west. From the south, cross under the freeway, and then turn left onto Shell Beach Road. From the north, continue straight off the end of the exit ramp and onto Shell Beach Road.

This 6-acre neighborhood park includes basketball courts, tennis courts (across Shell Beach Road), play structures, plenty of room to run on the grass, and picnic areas complete with barbecues. A portable restroom is sometimes located in the tennis court parking lot.

South Palisades Park
Indio Drive/Beachcomber Drive/Silver Shoals Drive
(805) 773-7039
pismobeach.org
FREE!

From Highway 101 take the Avila Beach Drive exit west. From the south, cross under the freeway, and then turn left onto Shell Beach Road. From the north, continue straight off the end of the exit ramp and onto Shell Beach Road. Turn right onto Beachcomber drive or Silver Shoals Drive.

The bluff-top park includes benches, picnic tables, barbecues, paved pathways and access to the coves below via often sketchy trails. From the end of Beachcomber Drive, follow the cliff trail down to the tide pools.

At low tide, this stretch of sand passes below Ebb Tide Park and connects with the Silver Shoals public access stairway at The Cliffs Resort. Silver

Shoals is a popular local surfing spot known for its glassy conditions, though it also offers plenty of rock hazards and kelp.

Shell Beach Playground

At Shell Beach Elementary School, 2100 Shell Beach Road

(805) 773-7039

pismobeach.org

FREE!

From Highway 101 take the Spyglass Drive exit and turn west. Turn left onto Shell Beach Road and right onto Terrace Avenue.

The playground and playing fields at this 4-acre park are available to the general public after school, on weekends and holidays.

Silver Shoals

Access from 2757 Shell Beach Road

(805) 773-7039

pismobeach.org

FREE!

From Highway 101 take the Spyglass Drive exit and turn west. Turn right onto Shell Beach Road.

This long, sandy cove runs from a public access stairway at The Cliffs Resort all the way north toward Beachcomber Cove below South Palisades Park (p. 74). This area is very popular among local surfers and is often referred to as "St. An's" or "St. Andrews."

Park in the public access spots at The Cliffs, and then follow the dirt pathway along the north side of the hotel and down the stairs to the beach.

Spyglass Park

Spyglass Drive & Solano Road

(805) 773-7039

pismobeach.org

FREE!

From Highway 101 take the Spyglass Drive exit and turn west to the park.

This 4½-acre park with a view of the ocean includes plenty of grass for a stretch, as well as play structures, picnic tables, benches and free-standing barbecues. There is beach access via a hazardous bluff trail down a ravine to what can, at times, be a tiny rocky cove. At low tide, the beach offers nearly a mile of sand and tide pooling opportunities. It is also popular among local surfers for winter surf.

Chapter 4

Pismo Beach

The greatest draw at Pismo Beach is its namesake stretch of gently sloping sand and its curvaceous waves. Where the sand stops, beautiful bluffs shelter contemplative coves, secret dynamic tide pools and provide scenic trails.

Perhaps more than anything else, Pismo Beach is about getting outside and making the most of all that the ocean and temperate climate provide. Popular activities here include kayaking, cycling, clamming, fishing, surfing, body boarding, kite surfing and paragliding. Check local phone books for current businesses that provide the necessary equipment and instruction. There is also a plethora of parks from bluff perches to inland historical venues. All parks in Pismo Beach are free and open during daylight hours. Many include picnic/barbecue areas and some have large group areas available by reservation.

Parking in Pismo Beach is free except in the popular and perennially packed pier district. Many of the beachfront hotels also provide limited spaces for visitors crossing the property for coastal access. Watch for signs or otherwise designated parking spots to avoid tickets or towaway hassles.

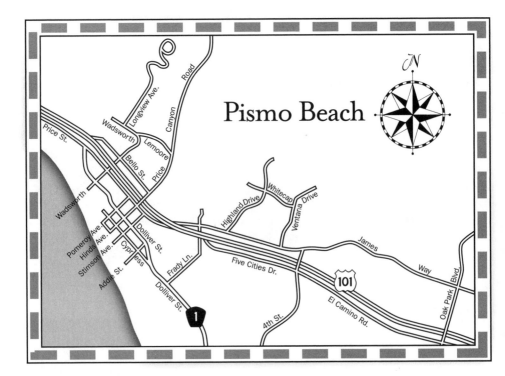

Pismo Beach's sandy stretch is a big draw on holiday weekends and throughout summer months, but the best weather is in the fall when coastal fog and valley tourists disappear for the season.

NATURE

Boosinger Park

Wadsworth Avenue at Lemoore Avenue

(805) 773-7039

pismobeach.org

FREE!

From southbound Highway 101 take the Price Street exit. Turn left onto Price Street, left onto Bello Street and right onto Wadsworth Avenue. From northbound Highway 101 take the Wadsworth exit and turn right onto Wadsworth Avenue.

This small neighborhood park offers sweeping 180-degree views of the coast. Amenities include play structures, drinking fountain, picnic tables, barbecues and benches. Come for the park; stay for the view, but remember there are no restrooms, so plan accordingly.

☞ Chumash Park

Off Ventana Drive near James Way

(805) 773-7039

pismobeach.org

FREE!

From Highway 101 turn east onto Fourth Street, left onto James Way, then right onto Ventana Drive.

Just across the frontage road from the husttle of Highway 101 is this 38-acre park that emphasizes its natural setting. Though there are fun play structures here, the park also includes a trail system along wetlands, through oaks and up a beautiful little valley. This is a nice, easy, fairly stroller-friendly walk for spring wildflower viewing. The park is also great for frog catch and release and general meandering. Restrooms also are available.

Some of Pismo's parks are great spots for catching frogs.

Cottage Inn Public Access

Access trails and beach via Cottage Inn By The Sea
2351 Price Street
(805) 773-7039
pismobeach.org
FREE!
From Highway 101 take Mattie Road west to Price Street/Highway 1 south.
Public bluff-top trails give way to miles upon miles of sand and surf. This public throughway on hotel property provides the northernmost access to the long stretch of sand that extends south into Santa Barbara County.

Elmer Ross Beach

Access via trail and stairs behind Shelter Cove Lodge, 2651 Price Street
(805) 773-7039
pismobeach.org
FREE!
From Highway 101 take Mattie Road west to Price Street/Highway 1 north.
A bluff-top walkway and stairs lead to this lesser-known beach, unlike many of its local counterparts, faces west. A large cliff at the southern end of the cove blocks sun from a significant portion of the cove at times. The peaceful little beach here is a treasure. It is also referred to as Shelter Cove.

Highland Park

Highland Drive at Whitecap Street
(805) 773-7039
pismobeach.org
FREE!
From Highway 101 turn east onto Fourth Street, left onto James Way, then right onto Highland Drive.
This lesser-known 7-acre gem includes play structures and picnic areas in a quiet neighborhood.

Ira Lease Park

East of Highway 1 at Addie Street
(805) 773-7039
pismobeach.org
FREE!
From northbound Highway 101 take the Price Street exit. Turn left onto Stimson Avenue, and then left onto South Dolliver/Highway 1.
This 1-acre park includes a creek-side trail, picnic areas, an expanse of grass and a very large barbecue pit.

Mary Herrington Park
West of Highway 1 at Addie Street
(805) 773-7039
pismobeach.org
FREE!
From northbound Highway 101 take the Price Street exit. Turn left onto Stimson Avenue, and then left onto South Dolliver / Highway 1.

A 1-acre grassy stretch along Pismo Creek includes picnic tables, barbecue facilities and restrooms.

☞ Monarch Butterfly Grove & Boardwalk
Pismo State Beach
Highway 1 north of Le Sage Drive
www.monarchbutterfly.org/grove.htm
FREE!
From Highway 101 take the Price Street exit. From the north, continue straight from the off ramp onto Dolliver Street / Highway 1. From the south, follow Price Street straight from the off ramp. Turn left onto Ocean View or Stimson avenues, and then left onto Dolliver Street / Highway 1. The grove is on the right south of North Beach Campground.

Every winter some 100,000 Monarch butterflies make this eucalyptus grove home. They float through the air, often landing on or near visitors. Docents who staff the area from 10 a.m. to 4 p.m. daily during butterfly season ask that no one touch the butterflies as doing so can permanently damage their wings. Instead, take binoculars (or use some on site provided by friends of the park), a camera, a jacket and a picnic. This is an ideal spot for a field trip lesson about lifecycles, metamorphosis and migration.

From the back of the grove, follow the dirt trail to the beach boardwalk which runs south through the dunes to Grand Avenue in Grover Beach.

☞ Pismo State Beach Pier, Promenade and Park
West end of Pomeroy Avenue
pismobeach.org
FREE!
From Highway 101 take the Price Street exit. From the north, continue straight from the off ramp onto Dolliver Street / Highway 1, turn right onto Pomeroy Avenue. From the south, follow Price Street straight from the off ramp. Turn left onto Pomeroy Avenue.

This 60-acre public beach is highlighted by its photogenic pier, classic swings, sand volleyball courts and the new addition of the Pismo Beach Promenade.

For more than 125 years a public pier has offered Pismo Beach visitors and locals alike a place to fish, walk, dance, dine, and peer down on shapely waves. Though storms have wreaked havoc on the pier, local authorities have rebuilt it bigger and better than before. Today the 1,370-foot icon remains a popular spot for fishing since it provides great access beyond the surf line (check out the fishing decks down the stairs near the west end of the pier) and fishing permits are not required. Top catches include perch, skates, halibut, jack smelt and flounder.

During the winter holiday season, the city erects a tree of lights at the end of the pier. On July Fourth the pier serves as the launching pad for the city's fireworks extravaganza. A variety of festivals are centered on the pier as are private fetes like weddings and reunions. The pier is lighted every night throughout the year, providing just enough light for night surfers and shark fishing.

Not a day goes by that surfers can't be found in the water below the pier. Most seem to enjoy the combination of a high tide and gentle breeze so if your key interest here is observing surfers or taking to the waves yourself, watch for these conditions.

According to the city, a million and a half people visit the pier every year. In recent years the city has expanded the base facilities to include a 550-foot first phase boardwalk that will eventually stretch from the pier to Grand Avenue in Grover Beach.The Pismo Beach Promenade is designed to match the Pismo Beach Municipal Fishing Pier which stretches into the Pacific Ocean about 40 yards further north. Benches are strategically placed off the 15-foot-wide pathway to provide rest and views. Half-round lights reminiscent of ship deck lights are mounted midway up the promenade banisters to continue the ocean theme. The promenade continues four blocks south to Addie Street.

Other facilities at the base of the pier include a public restroom with cold showers, free parking, fish-cleaning stations, benches and picnic tables.

Local businesses provide a variety of dining and shopping opportunities nearby. Public volleyball nets stretch across the sand for pickup games and occasional organized events. To reserve courts, call 481-8334. Nearby old-style swings offer rides to children and children at heart.

Pismo Beach Sports Complex
East end of Frady Lane
(805) 773-7039
pismobeach.org
FREE!
From southbound Highway 101 take the Hinds Avenue exit. Turn right onto Hinds Avenue, left onto Price Street, right onto Stimson, then left onto South Dolliver/Highway 1 before finally turning left onto Frady Lane. From northbound Highway 101 take the 4th Street exit and head south into Grover Beach. Turn right onto Grand Avenue, then right onto Highway 1, and then right onto Frady Lane.

Used largely for organized athletic events for all ages, this 5½-acre park includes three baseball fields, picnic areas and public restrooms.

Pismo Lake Ecological Preserve
Off Fourth Street west of Highway 101
www.coastalrcd.org
FREE!
From Highway 101 take the Fourth Street exit. Turn south onto Fourth St.

The 69-acre preserve consists of 30-acres of lakes that host myriad plant and animal life surrounded by a sea of humanity. At publication time, access to the area had been closed, but State Parks, Water Resources Board and city and county officials were developing a new plan that may again provide pedestrian access. Proposed developments include an observation platform, an interpretive center, trails and a docent guide program.

Pismo State Beach North Beach Campground
555 Pier Ave.
(805) 489-1869
www.parks.ca.gov
$$
From Highway 101 take the Price Street exit. From the north, continue straight from the off ramp onto Dolliver Street/Highway 1. From the south, follow Price Street straight from the off ramp. Turn left onto Ocean View or Stimson avenues, and then left onto Dolliver Street/Highway 1. The campground is on the right.

This 31-acre campground is separated from the Pacific Ocean only by a band of beach and foredunes. The 103 sites are developed. Reservations highly suggested.

Price Regional Park
580 Frady Lane
(805) 773-7039
pismobeach.org
FREE!-$

From Highway 101 take the Price Street exit. From the north, continue straight from the off ramp onto Dolliver Street/Highway 1, turn left onto Price Canyon Road, right onto Bello Street and right onto Frady Lane. From the south, follow Price Street straight from the off ramp. Turn right onto Price Canyon Road, right onto Bello Street and right onto Frady Lane.

This 38-acre historical museum park has been in the works for three decades. Once completed, it is slated to include historic residences emphasizing the life and times of Rancho Pismo,the John Michael Price family, and the Chumash who lived here before them. Plans also call for rock corral replicas, restoration of the Price Anniversary House built here in 1893, restoration of adobe structures on the site, a theater in an orchard, and a barn.

The lands are open for passive public use (walking, picnicking, seeing the sights). Call for docent-led tours of the property.

Shore Cliff Lodge Beach Access
Access via staircase behind Shore Cliff Lodge, 2555 Price St.
(805) 773-7039
pismobeach.org
FREE!

From Highway 101 take the Mattie Road exit. Turn west onto Mattie Road, then left onto Price Street.

Follow the spiral staircase for public access to this little known cove.

Wilmar Stairs
Oceanic end of Wilmar Avenue
(805) 773-7039
pismobeach.org
FREE!

From Highway 101 take the Mattie Road exit. Turn west onto Mattie Road, then left onto Price Street, then right onto Wilmar Avenue.

A long, steep set of stairs provides neighbors and visitors access to the lesser-visited northwestern end of Pismo Beach. Only a hop and skip from the Cottage Inn Public Access and bluff-top trails.

OTHER ADVENTURES
☞ **Pismo Bowl**
277 Pomeroy Ave.
(805) 773-2482

www.pismobeachbowl.com

$

From Highway 101 take the Price Street exit. From the north, continue straight from the off ramp onto Dolliver Street/Highway 1, turn right onto Pomeroy Avenue. From the south, follow Price Street straight from the off ramp. Turn left onto Pomeroy Avenue.

Not every bowling alley serves as a destination, but this family-owned and operated eight-lane throwback is nostalgic and fun for people of any age. Real wooden lanes may not be plum, but with the help of gutter bumpers, the kids are unlikely to notice.

While bowling alleys across the nation have suffered from decreased interest, Pismo Bowl continues to hop not only with league play for all ages and abilities, but also theme nights. Cosmic Bowling is one of those unusual events designed to attract an energetic crowd. The weekly Friday night event involves loud music, fog, blacklights, and strobes from 8 p.m. to midnight. The alley also offers a junior bowling league every Saturday for bowlers ages 6 to 21. Junior league play includes instruction and competition. Evening leagues offer those over 21 some alley time and senior leagues are held weekdays.

Bowling amenities also include automatic scoring, shoe rentals and ball rentals. Other activities here include billiards, video games, a pro shop, and a grill.

Chapter 5

Grover Beach

City namesake Dwight William Grover dreamed this coastal town would become a tourist center and transit hub. More than 110 years later, the 2¼-square-mile city has become instead a haven for families seeking relatively affordable homes in a safe, friendly coastal community. Its lack of major attractions and major events attest to the small-town mentality that contributes to this city's charm.

Grover Beach is rife with thrift shops, junk shops, and treasure shops. It also hosts a diverse range of restaurants featuring seafood to Mexican food, pizza to sushi.

The largest influx of visitors these days is headed for California's only

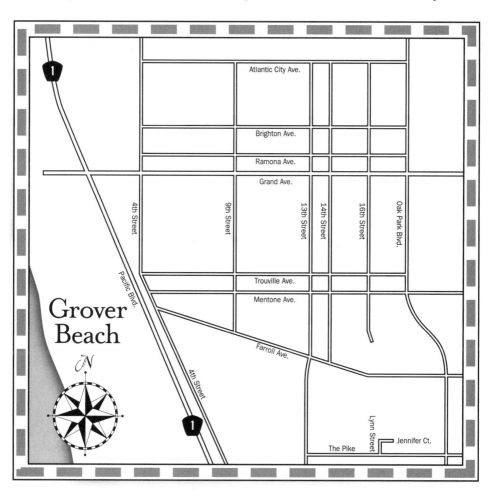

remaining drive-on beach: Oceano Dunes State Vehicular Recreation Area. According to California State Parks, 1.5 million visitors pass the kiosks to play in the sand with a variety of off-highway vehicles, family vehicles, RVs and campers. Most of those enter at Grover Beach's Grand Avenue ramp.

For those who want a quieter visit with nature, Grover Beach offers a pedestrian boardwalk through the dunes. The wooden walkway leads visitors away from the roar of engines toward the whisper of wings half a mile north at the Monarch butterfly grove in neighboring Pismo Beach.

LETTERS

Grover Beach Community Library

240 North 9th St.

(805) 481-4131

FREE!

From Highway 101 take 4th Street south, turn left onto Atlantic City Avenue, right onto 9th Street and right onto Ramona Avenue.

This very small, non-profit library operates outside the county library system. It focuses on the needs of community youth and seniors. Programs include regularly scheduled storytime as well as periodic special events.

NATURE

16th Street Park

On 16th Street between Nice and Mentone avenues

(805) 473-4580

www.grover.org

FREE!

From Highway 101 take Oak Park Boulevard south. Turn right onto Mentone Avenue.

The park includes a play structure, running room, covered group barbecue area, horseshoe pits, softball field and a grass volleyball court. No restroom.

Costa Bella Park

Corner of Oak Park Blvd. and Farroll Ave.

(805) 473-4580

www.grover.org

FREE!

From Highway 101 take Oak Park Boulevard south to Farroll Avenue.

This grassy park on the corner has become a popular spot for locals to walk their dogs. Do not bring children here if they are uncomfortable with dogs. Be aware that some dogs can be unpredictable and dangerous. Cleanup bags are available for those who opt to stretch their pets here.

Golden West Park
At the end of Jennifer Court

(805) 473-4580

www.grover.org

FREE!

From Highway 101 take Oak Park Boulevard south. Turn right onto The Pike, right onto Lynn Street and right onto Jennifer Court.

This pocket park offers a bit of room to run, picnic tables, horseshoe pit and barbecues.

Grover Heights Park
Atlantic City Avenue at North 10th Street

(805) 473-4580

www.grover.org

FREE!

From Highway 101 take 4th Street south, turn left onto Atlantic City Avenue.

Lots of room to run, climb play structures and host a barbecue. The park includes horseshoe pits, barbecues, sand volleyball court, basketball court and lighted tennis courts.

☞ Hero Community Park
Farroll Road at South 16th Street

(805) 473-4580

www.grover.org

FREE!

From Highway 101 take Oak Park Boulevard south. Turn right onto Farroll Avenue.

The city's newest park, named for the family that owned a hog farm near this site, features ocean-themed play structures and some of the coolest new equipment around. While other cities lay waste to the age-old favorite merry-go-round, Grover Beach has added a new mini version that offers great physics lessons. Ask standing riders to huddle together toward the center post. Get them spinning, and then tell them to hold tight while they lean out simultaneously for an unexpected boost. The park also includes a basketball court, tennis court, horseshoe pits, barbecue areas and restroom.

Mentone Basin Park
Mentone Ave. between south 14th and 16th streets

(805) 473-4580

www.grover.org

FREE!

From Highway 101 take Oak Park Boulevard south. Turn right onto Mentone Avenue.

This large grassy park also has barbecue areas, and lighted basketball and tennis courts.

Ramona Garden Park & Community garden
993 Ramona Ave.

(805) 473-4580

www.grover.org

FREE!

From Highway 101 take 4th Street south, turn left onto Atlantic City Avenue, right onto 9th Street.

Features a gazebo, restroom, Ramona Garden Park Center (capacity 200 standing, 125 seated), an amphitheatre and grass for free roamers. It's a popular park for events like the city's annual Stone Soup Festival held in late summer.

The Grover Beach Community garden at 920 Brighton (adjacent to the park) provides residents opportunities to rent 6-foot-by-15-foot planter. Call for details and to reserve a plot.

South County Skate park
1750 Ramona Ave.

(805) 597-4725

www.grover.org/skatepark.htm

$

From Highway 101 take Oak Park Boulevard south, turn right onto Ramona Avenue.

This 13,234-square-foot park features pool-style action for inline skating and skateboards only. (No bicycles allowed.) The park is staffed by city parks employees and hosts special events throughout the year. Helmets, knee pads and elbow pads are required and are available for free one-day rentals. Call for current hours, class schedules and special event details.

OTHER ADVENTURES

Pismo State Golf Course
25 Grand Avenue

(805) 481-5215

www.pismogolf.com

$

From Highway 101 take 4th Street exit and head south. Turn right onto Grand Avenue.

This public 9-hole three par course is open 365 days per year from sunup to sundown. The putting and pitching green, water hazards, greens and roughs are one slice away from the dunes and only a few good swings from the Pacific Ocean.

Exploration Station
867 Ramona Avenue
(805) 473-1421
$

From Highway 101 take 4th Street south, turn left onto Atlantic City Avenue, right onto 9th Street and right onto Ramona Avenue.

This educational center in the city's old fire station offers revolving science exhibits designed for hands-on educational fun. The non-profit organization also offers field trips, special programs, clubs and courses some of which have included robotics and Lego clubs. Open Thursday, Friday and Saturday from 1 p.m. to 5 p.m.

The Village of Arroyo Grande is historic and quaint with locally owned shops and more than half a dozen restaurants, but Arroyo Grande also serves as a gateway to the Los Padres National Forest. The vast back country includes a variety of hiking, horseback riding, mule packing, mountain biking and off-highway-vehicle opportunities, campgrounds and a California condor monitoring station housed in an old fire lookout.

Chapter 6

Arroyo Grande

"Big ditch," Arroyo Grande's translation to English, doesn't do this Central Coast city justice. This valley 2 miles from the Pacific Ocean charmed even its earliest European settler, Francisco Zeba Branch, with its wild beauty. Today the city invites visitors interested in browsing, dining, picnicking and antiquing.

Branch acquired nearly 17,000 acres in the Arroyo Grande Valley after his first visit in 1832. His cattle dominated the land until 1864 when drought forced him to sell parcels to settlers.

"By 1876, there were 35 families and the farm-based community began to flourish," the City of Arroyo Grande reports. "A railway depot was established in 1882. In 1911 residents voted to incorporate the city of Arroyo Grande. From the beginning businesses were established along a road appropriately named Branch Street."

Nearly a century later that original shopping area remains the commercial and governmental hub of the city and is commonly called the Arroyo Grande Village. Residential neighborhoods stretch up Crown Hill, over neighboring hill and dale and west onto the flatlands.

The city's namesake "big ditch" also remains a central feature of the village. Heavy winter storms can turn Arroyo Grande Creek into a muddy, boiling rivulet, but most days it's an inviting trickle of water that generally divides the city's commercial district from its quiet old-town neighborhood.

ARTS

Clark Center for the Performing Arts

Arroyo Grande High School

(805) 489-9444

clarkcenter.org

Prices vary

From northbound Highway 101 take the Traffic Way exit and proceed straight toward town, then turn left onto Fair Oaks Avenue. From southbound Highway 101 take the Grand Avenue/Branch Street exit, turn east onto Branch Street, right onto Traffic Way, and then right onto Fair Oaks Avenue.

This theater, owned and operated by the Lucia Mar Unified School District, was built after a huge fundraising effort by local volunteers. It serves as a venue for local and international performers in one of two theaters: the 617-seat Forbes Hall and the 150-seat studio theater. Rules involving children are very strict. Check at the box office **in person** before purchasing any tickets for children. Children are banned from some shows, and even babes in arms are required to have tickets.

Fair Oaks Theatre

1007 E. Grand Ave.

(805) 489-2364

www.fairoakstheatre.net

$

From Highway 101 take the Grand Avenue exit and head west.

Known locally as the "dollar theater," Fair Oaks offers cheap seats (though no longer just a buck) for first run movies that are a little behind the times. If you missed it at the blockbuster theater but still want to catch it on the big screen, this is the place.

Regal Arroyo Grande Stadium 10 Theater

1160 W. Branch St.

(805) 481-7553

www.regmovies.com

$$

From northbound Highway 101 take the Oak Park Road exit. Turn right at the end of the ramp onto West Branch Street.

Stadium seating at this 10-screen theater may make it more attractive to the shorter set. The marquee regularly emphasizes Hollywood blockbusters.

LETTERS

Arroyo Grande Library

800 W. Branch St.

(805) 473-7161

www.slolibrary.org

FREE!

From Highway 101 take the Grand Avenue/Branch Street exit. Turn east onto Branch Street, then immediately left onto West Branch Street. The Library is in the South County Regional Center on the right side of the road.

From noon until 9 p.m. every Tuesday through Sunday, this branch of the San Luis Obispo County Library system provides access to, among other things, one of the most expansive children's libraries on the Central Coast. In addition to weekly preschool story time, this branch offers summer reading programs for children and adults alike as well as a winter reading program for adults. There are book discussion groups, monthly Saturday family events, and other special events held throughout the year. This branch is also home to one of the best children's librarians in the area. Seek her out for details on great books befitting any child's interest.

Doc Burnstein's Ice Cream Lab

114 W. Branch Street

(805) 474-4068

www.docburnsteins.com

FREE!

From Highway 101 take the Grand Avenue exit and turn east. (Grand Avenue becomes Branch Street immediately east of the freeway.)

Besides offering homemade ice cream during operating hours (noon 'til 9 p.m. daily), this shop in Arroyo Grande Village welcomes visitors to watch the ice cream making process and attend special events. Doc's Reading Lab, held every Tuesday from 3:30 p.m. to 4:15 p.m., is a free public reading event designed for young children. At 7 p.m. most Wednesdays, visitors are invited to take part in the Ice Cream Lab Show, an entertaining combination of history, myth, science and fun. Audience members help create a brand-new flavor which is put on sale over the following week.

HISTORY

☞ Heritage House Museum

126 Mason St.

(805) 489-8282

southcountyshistory.org

FREE!

From Highway 101 take the Grand Avenue exit and turn east, then turn right onto Mason Street.

This home, built in the late 1800s, has served in a variety of capacities as a single-family residence, duplex, Dr. Walter's Sanatorium, city daycare facility, and home to the city's parks and recreation department. Now completely renovated, the house serves as a visitors center and a museum including all sorts of interesting local artifacts including period clothing, photographs and household items. Be sure to continue out the back door to the barn with its antique tractors, agriculture equipment, a gazebo and gardens.

Open Saturdays noon to 3 p.m. and Sundays 1 p.m. to 4 p.m.

Odd Fellows Hall

128 Bridge St.

(805) 473-3231

southcountyhistory.org

FREE!

From Highway 101 take the Grand Avenue/Branch Street exit. Turn east onto Branch Street, then right onto Bridge Street.

In 1902, natural sandstone from a local quarry was artfully stacked and filled to form the home of the Independent Order of Odd Fellows. Its street-level storefront has served as a funeral parlor, an accordion studio and, most recently, an art gallery.

In 1985 this building, noted on the National Register of Historic Places, was acquired by the South County Historical Society which maintains it today as a public meeting space and art gallery. Generally open Friday and Saturday from 1 p.m. to 5 p.m.

Patricia Loomis History Library

134 S. Mason St.

(805) 489-8282

southcountyhistory.org

FREE!

From Highway 101 take the Grand Avenue/Branch Street exit. Turn east onto Branch Street, then right onto Mason Street.

The South County Historical Society maintains this publicly accessible collection of works pertaining specifically to California history with an emphasis on southern San Luis Obispo County. Future plans at the 1888 Ruby's house include reenactments and other family-friendly, educational events. Call for current hours and special events schedules.

Paulding House
551 Crown Hill Road
(805) 473-3231
southcountyhistory.org
FREE!

From Highway 101 take the Grand Avenue/Branch Street exit. Turn east onto Branch Street. Where Branch Street curves right around Crown Hill, take the lesser-traveled street straight ahead, Crown Hill Road.

A 250-year-old oak tree spans the front yard of this historic home which housed the city's first resident physician. In 1891, Dr. Edwin Paulding bought the two-year-old house in which he and his family made their home until donating it, along with all its contents, to the South County Historical Society in 1997. Artifacts include carvings made by Dr. Paulding and authentic Chumash Indian basketry.

Docents offer guided tours of this home by appointment. The house museum is open Saturdays from noon until 3 p.m.

Santa Manuela Schoolhouse
127 Short Street
(805) 489-8232
southcountyhistory.org
FREE!

From Highway 101 take the Grand Avenue/Branch Street exit. Turn east onto Branch Street, turn left onto Short Street.

This one-room schoolhouse was built in 1901 on property that is now under Lopez Lake. After 56 years as a school, two moves and a renovation, the structure now serves as home to South County Historical Society. The building and grounds are open for free tours Saturdays from noon to 3 p.m. and Sundays 1 p.m. to 4 p.m.

The grounds also include the barn annex which houses historic vehicles and other machinery, Heritage House (p. 94), gazebo and gardens.

NATURE

Biddle Regional Park
3500 Lopez Drive
(805) 781-5930
www.slocountyparks.com
FREE!-$

From Highway 101 take the Grand Avenue/Branch Street exit. Turn east onto Branch Street and follow it as it curves around Crown Hill. Turn right onto Huasna Road which becomes Lopez Drive. Continue about 5 miles.

If you're looking for a large, local park with ample shade and running room, this may just be the spot for you. This 47-acre, sycamore-shaded park is adjacent to Lopez Drive east of Arroyo Grande. When it's foggy at the beach, chances are good the sun has burned through for beautiful days here. The park includes playgrounds, ball fields, volleyball courts, horseshoe pits, a gazebo, restrooms and picnic areas, not the least of which is the large group barbecue area (by reservation) which can accommodate up to 500 guests. An entrance fee is charged when the kiosk is staffed.

Community Garden
1221 Ash Street
(805) 473-5474
arroyogrande.org
$$

From Highway 101 take Oak Park Boulevard south, turn left onto Ash St.
These public garden plots are available for rent from the city on a first-come, first-served basis. Walk through for a quick garden lesson or rent a plot of your own for a more thorough education.

Cypress Ridge Golf Resort
780 Cypress Ridge Parkway
(805) 474-7979
cypressridge.com
$$$

From Highway 101 take Grand Avenue west, turn left onto Halcyon Road, left onto Highway 1/Cienaga Street which becomes Mesa View Drive. Turn left onto Halcyon Road (again), right onto West El Campo Road and then left onto Cypress Ridge Parkway.
Cypress Ridge's 18-hole Peter Jacobsen course has been designated a signature sanctuary by Audubon International. The course is unique in its ability to enhance habitat and conserve wildlife but is in no way designed for junior golfers. This is a spot for budding champions with well-established skills.

Elm Street Park
1221 Ash St.
(805) 473-5474
arroyogrande.org
FREE!

From Highway 101 take the Grand Avenue/Branch Street exit. Turn west onto Grand Avenue and then left onto Elm Street.
This community park immediately adjacent to Soto Sports Complex (p. 104) offers volleyball standards, large grass area, barbecue areas, restrooms, nautical-themed play structures and Elm Street Off-Leash Dog park, (fivecitiesdogpark.org) the first official dog park in the South County. The park's community center (capacity 225) and group barbecue area (capacity 75) are available by reservation. Smaller barbecue facilities are available on a first-come, first-served basis.

The property also houses the city's parks department and childcare center. Swing by for preschool/kindergarten childcare programs and to learn about the city's recreational offerings.

Hart-Collett Memorial Park

201 Traffic Way

(805) 473-5474

arroyogrande.org

FREE!

From Highway 101 take the Grand Avenue/Branch Street exit. Turn east onto Branch Street, and then right onto Traffic Way.

Possibly the smallest park in the county, this triangular bit of grass surrounded by busy streets is dedicated to the memory of Harry Hart and Robert "Bob" Collett who were both long-time firefighters for the Arroyo Grande Fire Department. The park includes picnic tables and benches, grass and raised flowerbeds shaded by trees.

Health Fitness Park

834 Fair Oaks Avenue

(805) 473-5474

arroyogrande.org

FREE!

From Highway 101 take the Grand Avenue exit. Turn west onto Grand Avenue, left onto Halcyon Road and then left onto Fair Oaks Avenue.

A paved pathway leads visitors through a variety of exercise stations tucked between a housing development and Arroyo Grande Creek.

Heritage Park & Rotary Bandstand

205 Nelson Street

(805) 473-5474

arroyogrande.org

FREE!

From Highway 101 take the Grand Avenue/Branch Street exit. Turn east onto Branch Street, then right onto Traffic Way and left onto Nelson Street.

Take a toddler by a hand and lead her into the bandstand for free, innocent fun. Kids love to dance on the round stage, sing in a pretend microphone or simply run circles here. The park includes a large expanse of open grass and some shade trees all just steps from the city's historical museums and swinging bridge (p. 104).

Hoosegow Park

150 LePoint Street

(805) 473-5474

arroyogrande.org

FREE!

From Highway 101 take the Grand Avenue/Branch Street exit. Turn east onto Branch Street, left onto Nevada Street, then follow the curve to the right onto LePoint Street.

This pocket park overlooking Arroyo Grande Village is named for the tiny old city jail that was built around 1910 and is still standing (though usually vacant). There's a bit of grass large enough for a small game of catch or toddling or bubble blowing, and a bench for quiet contemplation. There are no restrooms.

☞ James Way Oak Habitat & Wildlife Preserve
James Way between La Canada and Stevenson Drive
(805) 473-5474
FREE!

From Highway 101 take Oak Park Boulevard east. Turn right onto James Way. The preserve is on the right.

This nature preserve seems unlikely as motorists quickly pass from shopping area to residential development, but the preserve offers a fantastic reprieve from all things city. Maintained trails lead through old growth oak forests where deer, fox, bobcats, rabbits and myriad birds are often seen. The windmill, water tank and surrounding garden are highlights.

Kingo Park
1501 Huckleberry Avenue
(805) 473-5474
arroyogrande.org
FREE!

From Highway 101 take Oak Park Boulevard south, turn left onto Ash Street and then turn left onto Courtland Street.

Another neighborhood pocket park with a play structure and picnic tables. Barbecues are also available for a fee.

☞ Kiwanis Park
Kiwanis Park opposite Ira's Bike Shop east of Bridge Street
(805) 473-5474
arroyogrande.org
FREE!

From Highway 101 take the Grand Avenue/Branch Street exit. Turn east onto Branch Street, right onto Bridge Street and left into the first parking lot.

The Bridge Street Bridge offers a good view of this park which includes picnic tables under the shade of old sycamore trees, and a fairly treacherous bank on the edge of Arroyo Grande Creek. The pathway down is relatively well maintained and easy, but there are no maintained paths in the park and no wheelchair access to the water. Public restrooms are available back up in the parking lot about one half block east from the park entry.

La Mesa Village Park

Bambi Court

(805) 473-5474

arroyogrande.org

FREE!

From Highway 101 take Traffic Way or Fair Oaks Avenue exit. Turn west onto Fair Oaks Avenue, left onto Valley Road, left onto Tiger Tail Drive and then right onto Bambi Court.

This pocket park offers a little room to run, but no restrooms or additional facilities.

Lopez Lake Recreation Area

10 miles east of Arroyo Grande on Lopez Lake Drive

(805) 788-2381

www.slocountyparks.com/activities/lopez.htm

$

From Highway 101 take the Grand Avenue/Branch Street exit. Turn east onto Branch Street, right onto Huasna Road which becomes Lopez Drive and continues 10 miles to the lake.

This man-made lake has served as southern San Luis Obispo County's inland recreational mecca for sport fishing, waterskiing, sailing, picnicking, hiking, canoeing and bird watching since 1969. In recent years mountain biking has been added to the list of things to do, as well as taking the plunge at Mustang Water slides (p. 106) which operates within the park's boundary.

When the lake is completely full, it offers 22 miles of shoreline and nearly 1,000 acres of lake surface. Still mornings make early glass for water skiers while afternoon winds assure a good ride for sailboarders. Regular rainbow

Hikers who make it to Duna Vista viewpoint on the Two Waters Trail are rewarded with 360-degree views from 1,178-foot elevation. There are benches here, but no shade. Head back down to the junction with Two Waters for an oak-shaded bench and breeze.

trout plants add to other frequent catches which include crappie, red-ear sunfish, bigmouth bass, small mouth bass and catfish. The park sponsors regular fishing days during which children are paired with fishing buddies who offer pointers with loaner rods and reels. The marina includes a launch ramp, ample parking, a food market, tackle shop and boat rentals.

The area also includes 354 campsites that vary from primitive to full hook ups for trailers and motor homes. Reservations are advised. Some camp restrooms include hot showers.

More than 15 miles of hiking, biking and equestrian trails are particularly popular during late spring when wildflower blooms peak. Perhaps the easiest hike in the park is the half-mile Marina Trail. It begins just inside the park entrance past the old barn. Another easy option is the 15-minute walk through the oaks out to Rocky Point, a popular fishing spot overlooking the lake's Arroyo Grande Arm. One of the most popular trails among mountain bikers is the Tuoski-Two Waters Trail-Dune Vista Trail loop off the lake's Wittenberg Arm. It features expansive 360-degree views which are particularly striking at sunrise and sunset. Hard-core climbers enjoy Wittenberg Trail which leads up the steep ridge to Hi Ridge Trail.

Visitors with a boat and responsible children might consider boating out the Lopez Arm, dropping their children and an adult guide at the Two Waters Trail, then boating peacefully around to the Wittenberg Arm to pick up the walkers at the trail's end.

For sunbathing, begin exploring the shore at Cove Beach off Grizzly Drive, then venture farther into the park for more privacy.

☞ Los Padres National Forest
Hi Mountain Road east of Arroyo Grande
(805) 925-9538
tinyurl.com/3bs2u8g
FREE!/$

From Highway 101 take the Grand Avenue/Branch Street exit. Turn east onto Branch Street, right onto Huasna Road which becomes Lopez Drive. Follow the road about 9 miles, then turn right onto Hi Mountain Road which continues 15 miles through private lands and forest and connects with Pozo Road.

The LPNF includes some 1.75 million acres in five counties including expansive holdings east of Arroyo Grande. This area, managed by the Santa Lucia Ranger District, includes miles of trails for hikers, bikers, off-road-vehicle enthusiasts and equestrians as well as several designated campgrounds.

Local highlights include Hi Mountain Condor Lookout (www.condorlookout.org) on the 3,198-foot crest of Hi Mountain Ridge. The old fire lookout has been transformed into a field research station staffed full-time in summer by student biologists who track the endangered California condor. The project,

supported by the Morro Coast Audubon Society, U.S. Forest Service, U.S. Fish and Wildlife Service, Ventana Wilderness Society and Cal Poly Biological Sciences Department, features a small interpretive center and expansive views over condor territory.

Garcia Ridge (junction Hi Mountain Road) is an off-highway-vehicle access road with 360-degree views stretching from the Pacific Ocean to Sierra Nevada Range. Experienced mountain bikers may enjoy this ride along the eastern ridge in late fall, winter or spring, but summer jaunts are not advised due to high heat. There is a picnic table near Balm of Gilead where a barricade blocks motorized vehicles. The old road otherwise offers nice travel.

Hi Mountain Lookout Road (junction Hi Mountain Road) is a graded dirt road generally passable by street-legal vehicles. It leads to Hi Mountain Campground, a primitive area that includes pit toilets but no running water, on to the condor lookout, and west along the ridge with its spectacular views. The 6-mile road ends abruptly after passing several abandoned mines and the Big Falls and Little Falls trailheads.

Parkside Park

401 N. Bakeman Lane

(805) 473-5474

arroyogrande.org

FREE!

From Highway 101 take Oak Park Road south, turn left onto Farroll Road, then left onto Bakeman Lane.

This small neighborhood park just over the fence from Soto Sports Complex provides locals quick access to a playground, picnic table, half-court basketball court and drinking fountains. No restrooms.

Rancho Grande Park

500 James Way

(805) 473-5474

arroyogrande.org

FREE!

From Highway 101 take Oak Park Road east, turn right onto James Way.

This large neighborhood park includes two play structures, a basketball court, horseshoe pits, barbecue areas and open lawn. Large group barbecue areas available by reservation can accommodate up to 60 guests and two additional barbecue areas can accommodate 30 guests each. Pedestal barbcues also located in the park are available on a first-come, first-served basis.

☞ Santa Lucia Wilderness

East of Arroyo Grande off Lopez Lake Drive

(805) 925-9538

tinyurl.com/3kwvweu

FREE!/$

From Highway 101 take the Grand Avenue/Branch Street exit. Turn east onto Branch Street, right onto Huasna Road which becomes Lopez Drive. Follow the road about 9 miles, then turn right onto Hi Mountain Road.

Since 1978 this 20,412-acre wilderness in Los Padres National Forest has provided recreational opportunities that today include hiking, camping, mountain biking and equestrian use.

There are already a number of fantastic books outlining trails in this area. See Resources at the end of this book.

Two local favorites in this expansive area include Big Falls (Upper Lopez Canyon, 9 miles from Hi Mountain Road) and Little Falls (Upper Lopez Canyon, 13.5 miles from Hi Mountain Road).

Because the falls are located in the wilderness, trail travel is limited to equestrian and foot traffic. But the road in from the end of the pavement to the trailheads makes a great mountain bike ride for experienced riders. This section of graded dirt road features multiple creek crossings which may be impassable during winter storm season or, for low-clearance vehicles, at any time of year.

Hike either of the two trails as they meander back and forth across year-round streams. Little Falls Creek offers cascades and some small falls. Big Falls Creek is just as its name implies. Swimming holes abound on both. (Do not swim under waterfalls. Debris varying in size from leaves to large boulders can and will fall from above at any time.)

Each hike can be done independently, but they make a great loop hike. Start at the Little Falls trailhead, hike 2.6 miles to Hi Mountain Lookout Road. Turn left at the graded dirt road and follow it about 2 miles. Near the road's end, the Big Falls Trailhead takes off to the right. Follow that trail 2.6 miles down to Upper Lopez Canyon Road for a 4-mile return along the graded dirt road and several more creek crossings.

Soto Sports Complex

1275 Ash Street

(805) 473-5474

arroyogrande.org

FREE!-$$

From Highway 101 take Oak Park Boulevard south, turn left onto Ash Street.
This large athletic park includes four lighted softball fields, one lighted
Babe Ruth field, two Little League fields and five lighted tennis courts. The
fields are converted to soccer and football configuration in the fall.

The Jaycee Room located in the park is home to the senior pool playing
group, which offers classes and recreational pool playing year round for a
minimal annual fee ($). Call 556-0169 for details.

☞ Strother Community Park

1150 Huasna Road

(805) 473-5474

arroyogrande.org

FREE!

*From Highway 101 take the Grand Avenue/Branch Street exit. Turn east
onto Branch Street and follow it as it curves around Crown Hill. Turn right
onto Huasna Road.*
Among the most family-friendly parks in the city, Strother Park includes
play structures, a ball field, basketball court, restrooms, horseshoe pits, grass
volleyball court and picnic areas including three large picnic areas adequate for
groups of up to 80 guests. The park extends down to Arroyo Grande Creek.

Terra de Oro Park

311 Oro Drive

(805) 473-5474

arroyogrande.org

FREE!

*From Highway 101 take the Grand Avenue/Branch Street exit. Turn east
onto Branch Street and follow it as it curves around Crown Hill. Turn right
onto Huasna Road, and then left onto Oro Drive.*
This small neighborhood park that has no restroom but does include play
structures and volleyball standards on a sand court.

☞ Village Green Gazebo, Gazebo Park
& Swinging Bridge

Olohan Alley and Short Street, directly behind City Hall

(805) 473-5474

arroyogrande.org

FREE!

From Highway 101 take the Grand Avenue/Branch Street exit. Turn east onto

Branch Street, right onto Bridge Street, then left into the first parking lot.

This grassy spot features a picturesque gazebo and the city's historic swinging bridge which offers a clear vantage point for viewing the creek. According to local history, the Short family built the bridge in early 1875 when they owned this section of land divided by the creek. The 171-foot-long bridge is now owned and maintained by the city. City officials are so proud of the bridge, which they claim to be the only one of its kind in California, they issue a wallet-sized "Lifetime Pass to the Swinging Bridge" to any interested party. Call 473-5400 for pass details.

OTHER ADVENTURES

Arroyo Grande High School Pool

Fair Oaks Road

(805) 474-3000

www.lmusd.org

$

From northbound Highway 101 take Traffic Way exit, then turn left onto Fair Oaks Avenue. From southbound Highway 101, take Fair Oaks Avenue west.

The high school opens its competition pool to the public for recreation swim and swim lessons during summer holiday. The 12-lane, 25-yard pool also offers two 1-meter diving boards, showers and locker rooms. School, year-round club and summer swim teams are all available here.

☞ Bitter Creek Western Railroad

2110 S. Halcyon Road

(805) 481-7353

bcwrr.org

FREE!

From Highway 101 take the Grand Avenue/Branch Street exit. Turn west onto Grand Avenue, left onto Halcyon Road and follow it out of town.

This private 7.5-inch gauge railroad includes 1.2 miles of main line with various sidings and two rail yards. Owner/hobbyist Karl Hovanitz maintains the 7-acre site for his entertainment and for the entertainment of his friends, but opens it to the general public regularly. Check the website for the current schedule.

Free rides take visitors past a variety of facilities including fourteen steaming bays, a hydraulic lift, turntable, car barn, three bridges, three trestles, four tunnels and six water sources.

Five Cities Swim School

425 Traffic Way

www.5citiesswimclub.com

(805) 481-6399

$-$$$

From southbound Highway 101 take the Fair Oaks exit, turn left at the top of the ramp, then right onto Traffic Way. From northbound Highway 101 take the Traffic Way exit and proceed straight ahead.

This privately owned indoor swimming pool is designed with the very young and very old in mind. The water is always very warm, and the windows typically are not vented enough to promote a breeze. There are plentiful toys in this 20-yard pool and a full schedule of recreational swimming, lap swimming, water aerobics as well as individual and small-group lessons. There are no lockers and the dressing room situation is less than ideal. Plan on a quick shower and tight squeeze in small shared space, or plan to shower and change elsewhere.

Kennedy Club Aquatic Programs

1299 James Way

(805) 481-2888

tinyurl.com/3lcjsqp

$$

From Highway 101 take Oak Park Boulevard inland, then turn right onto James Way.

This private fitness club makes its facilities available to non-members for a daily fee. The three-lane, 25-meter, outdoor pool is open to swimmers ages 10 and older for lap swimming. Reservations are highly recommended.

Mustang Water slides

Lopez Lake Recreation Area

(805) 489-8898

www.mustangwaterslides.com

$$-$$$

From Highway 101 take the Grand Avenue/Branch Street exit. Turn east onto Branch Street, right onto Huasna Road which becomes Lopez Drive. Follow the road 10 miles east, pay the toll to enter Lopez Lake Recreation Area, and then continue on to the slides.

From May through September the county's oldest waterslide park offers thrills for the entire family. Visitors hike uphill with mats to mount either of the two original slides for a 600-foot, wet, curvy, twisty ride to the final plunge. The addition of Poly Pools and Slides, three mini-slides leading from one wading pool to another, provides thrills for kids 9 and younger. In 2005, the park added Stampede, a 38-foot-tall half pipe. The adventurous hike up stairs for a plunge with up to three riders on a raft.

Four hot tubs provide a more relaxing retreat or a place to warm up between slide runs. The park also includes dressing rooms, lockers, and a snack bar. (No outside food or beverages are permitted, but there are picnic areas directly outside the water slide park.)

Turtle and Tortoise Rescue of Arroyo Grande

(805) 481-5222

Thomas-turtles@juno.com

FREE!

Call for directions.

Bob Thomas has turned his 5-acre property into a park-like setting that houses more than 300 turtles and tortoises representing more than 40 species. The facility provides shelter to unwanted animals, houses a captive breeding program and provides public education about the care and feeding of these creatures. The site is also home to more than 100 birds. One-hour group tours are available by reservation only April 15 through first of October. Minimum age: 8. Maximum group size: 16. Donations accepted.

Chapter 7

Oceano

Oceano is a community quite literally divided by the railroad tracks. To the west is the beach town, the resort town, a gateway to one of California's last remaining beaches open to motorized vehicles. To the east is a quiet bedroom community with a handful of restaurants, services and a melodramatic holdout.

The town is best known for its access to Oceano Dunes State Vehicular Recreation Area, the last beachfront off-highway recreational vehicle area remaining in California. Some 1 million visitors per year from around the globe, though most from the Central Valley and Southern California, bring motorcycles, quad runners, dune buggies and four-wheel-drive vehicles to the beach to challenge the steep dunes. Some stay in area hotels, but most camp by tent, trailer or recreational vehicle on the sand just a Frisbee toss from the Pacific Ocean.

From the birth of the automobile, people were allowed to drive the length of the beach stretching from Pismo Beach's white cliffs south to Devil's Slide in the Guadalupe-Nipomo Dunes Complex. The area was popular with picnickers, campers and, in the 1930s and 1940s, a group of free-thinking artists, hermits, writers and nudists who referred to themselves as Dunites.

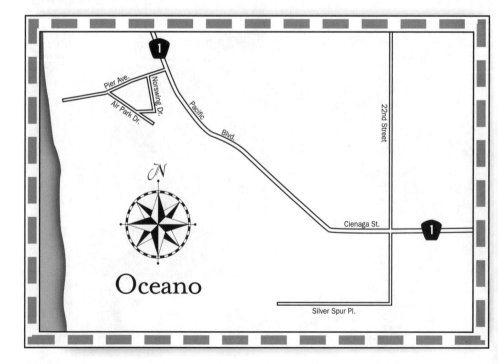

The city of Pismo Beach was first to block motorized traffic from its beaches in an effort to protect pedestrians and the tourist dollars they brought to the city. In 1987, the state fenced vehicles out of the southern 10 miles and 13,500 acres. The move was intended to protect the 1,400 known species of plants and animals living in the unique area.

In more recent years, oceanfront residents in Oceano have persuaded the state to further limit beach access and uses in the 3½-mile stretch of beach marked by numbered posts two through eight. Today the ramps at Pier Avenue in Oceano and Grand Avenue in Grover Beach provide motorists access to 1,500 acres of open sand dunes and beachfront property.

Pedestrians, however, are allowed on the entire stretch of sand, and horseback riding is allowed in many areas. Other area attractions include all-terrain vehicle rentals, biplane rides, and horse rentals for rides on the beach. Check telephone directories for current business listings.

ARTS

☞ **Great American Melodrama & Vaudeville Revue**
1863 Pacific Blvd. (Highway 1)
(805) 489-2499
americanmelodrama.com
$$

From the north, take Highway 101 south to Halcyon Road south 3 miles to its intersection with Highway 1. Turn right onto Highway 1. The melodrama is about 1 ½ miles west. From the south, take Highway 101 to the Los Berros Road/Oceano exit. Turn left onto Los Berros Road, cross under the freeway, then continue 5 miles to its intersection with Valley Road. Turn left onto Valley Road, then right onto Highway 1. The melodrama is about 2 miles west.

Boo as the dark-cloaked villain steals away a fair maiden. Cheer with gusto as her hero returns to save the day. Or will he?

Since 1975, this live theater has offered entertainment. An audience of strangers quickly gets acquainted thanks to cabaret-style seating. Players also serve as hosts and hostesses at the snack bar during intermission as the stage and costumes change from the first show to the ensuing vaudeville review. Unlike so many other area theaters, the melodrama welcomes audience participation in turn-of-the-20th-Century style.

LETTERS

Oceano Library
1551 17th St. (Oceano School)
(805) 474-7478
slolibrary.org
FREE!

From Highway 101, take Oak Park Boulevard south, turn right onto Wilmar, then left onto 17th Street.

This branch of the San Luis Obispo County Library system specializes in its bilingual collection. The library, which is open Tuesdays, Thursdays and Fridays offers a summer reading program for children. Stop by for information about additional special events.

HISTORY

Oceano Railroad Depot/Museum

1650 Front St

(805) 489-5446

www.oceanodepot.org

FREE!

From Highway 101 take 4th Street south, turn right onto Grand Avenue, left onto Highway 1/Pacific Boulevard which becomes Front Street.

This original Pacific Coast Line depot was built in 1904. It was completely restored prior to celebrating its centennial and today serves as a picturesque railroad museum and community center. Volunteers also maintain rolling stock. Hours vary. Call for latest schedule of special events.

NATURE

Oceano Memorial Park, Lagoon & Campground

540 Airpark Drive

(805) 781-5930

(805) 781-4900 for camping reservations)

www.slocountyparks.com/activities/oceano.htm

FREE!-$$

From Highway 101 take 4th Street south, turn right onto Grand Avenue, left onto Highway 1/Pacific Boulevard, right onto Pier Avenue, left onto Norswing, right onto Medel and right onto Airpark Drive.

This scenic park is popular for duck feeding and bird watching. Coots have nearly overrun other species of birds here, but provide fine entertainment for kids and may contribute more than their fare share to the lagoon's pungent aroma. New playground equipment across Norswing Street beckons children to swing, slide and climb below real and artificial trees. The park also includes grassy expanses, barbecue pits, picnic tables, basketball court, horseshoe pits and restrooms.

The related campground includes 22 camp sites each of which can accommodate four to six people. Full hook-ups are available, and showers are available for an additional charge.

Oceano Dunes State Vehicular Recreation Area

Pier Ave.

(805) 473-7220

www.ohv.parks/ca/gov/?page_id=1207

$

From Highway 101 take 4th Street south, turn right onto Grand Avenue. Continue straight onto the beach or turn left onto Highway 1/Pacific Boulevard, right onto Pier Avenue, then straight onto the beach.

This 1,500-acre sand playground is popular for off-highway vehicle use, on-beach camping and surf fishing. As the last remaining drive-on beach in California, and one of only a handful on the West Coast, this area can become quite busy with motorists who regularly travel from as far away as Arizona and Nevada. Keep kids close at hand.

The surf is also popular with local longboarders looking to escape the crowds and smaller waves farther north in Pismo Beach. Waves can be larger than up by the pier, but rip tides are also more common here.

Pismo Nature Center

Pier Ave. (inside Oceano Campground)

(805) 773-2147

www.ccnha.org/pismo

FREE!

From Highway 101 take 4th Street south, turn right onto Grand Avenue, left onto Highway 1/Pacific Boulevard and right onto Pier Ave.

This small museum offers a relatively active calendar and hands-on exhibits focused on the natural and cultural history of the area. The museum relies on its various gardens, including the Chumash Interpretive Garden, Dunes Interpretive Garden, and the Walk-through-nature Garden which represents five coastal habitats (dunes, riparian, coastal scrub, woodland and chaparral). The 1-mile Guiton trail encircles the lagoon where birding is particularly popular.

The museum and its nature store are open from 1 p.m. to 4 p.m. Wednesday and Friday through Monday from June 1 to Labor Day, and 1 p.m. to 4 p.m. Friday through Sunday during off season.

Pismo State Beach Oceano Campground
Pier Ave.
(800) 444-7275
www.slostateparks.com/oceano_campground
$$
From Highway 101 take 4th Street south, turn right onto Grand Avenue, left onto Highway 1/Pacific Boulevard and right onto Pier Avenue.

This 88-site off-beach campground provides a near-beach camping experience for a little less sand in your sandwiches. The campground is also home to the Pismo Nature Center (p. 111). A native plant garden, a trail around Oceano Lagoon, and a trail to the dunes are among the campground's hidden assets.

OTHER ADVENTURES
Oceano Community Center
1425 19th Street
(805) 474-3900
tinyurl.com/3qaxlhp
From Highway 101 take Oak Park Road south, turn right onto Wilmar, then left onto 19th Street.

This center, owned and operated by Lucia Mar Unified School District, provides gymnasium, kitchen and meeting room space for a variety of organizations. In addition to adult education programs held here, the facility regularly host public and private events. The grounds include lawn and landscaping, picnic tables and restrooms.

Chapter 8

Nipomo

Nipomo is a sprawling area spanning Highway 101 about 30 miles south of San Luis Obispo. The unincorporated community stretches from the curves of old Highway 1 across the wide expanse of the Nipomo Mesa and east to Temetate Ridge. It includes two popular golf courses (Black Lake and Cypress Ridge), a variety of eateries, a handful of shops and is home to thousands of commuters.

The area has long been a horse community, but a boom in development has reduced the accessible riding areas, limited trail access and brought increased traffic that threatens the safety of roadside horseback riders. However, many of the new large developments include public mixed-use pathways popular among horseback riders, walkers, joggers and cyclists.

When in Nipomo it is particularly important to be aware that many recreationist use roadside access, particularly in the many neighborhoods where sidewalks are nonexistent. Slow for horses and young cyclists, both of which can be very unpredictable in their courses of travel.

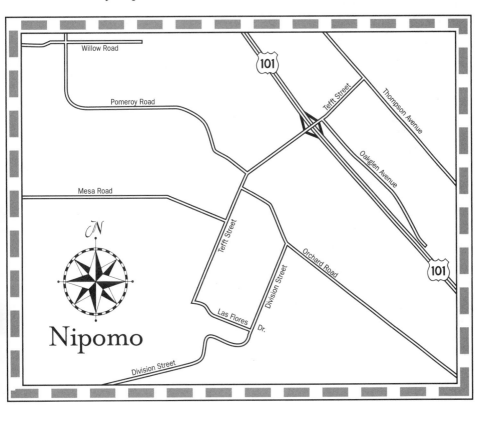

LETTERS

Nipomo Library

918 West Tefft St.

(805) 929-3994

slolibrary.org

FREE!

From Highway 101 take Tefft Street west, veer left at the Y intersection then turn right into the park.

Though on first approach this park-side branch of the San Luis Obispo County Library system appears small, it packs a wallop with a good collection of books, magazines, CDs, DVDs and other material, plus full access to the Black Gold Library System. This library has a tradition of providing entertaining story times for preschoolers as well as a lively calendar of events and a summer reading program. Call for current hours and events.

HISTORY

☞ Dana Adobe

6715 South Oakglen Ave.

(805) 929-5679

danaadobe.org

FREE!-$

From Highway 101 take Tefft Street east, then turn right onto Oakglen Ave.

La Casa de Dana, the oldest structure in Nipomo, is also California State Historical Landmark No. 1033. Construction on this historic home built on a 38,000 acre rancho began in 1839 and was completed in 1851 under the supervision of its owner, designer and chief resident Capt. William G. Dana of Boston, Mass. The famous Yankee sea captain, through his trading with the "Californios," interested the United States in expanding west and annexing California, according to Dana Adobe Nipomo Amigos, the nonprofit corporation organized to rehabilitate and care for the place. The ranch also served as the first stopping place south of San Luis Obispo along El Camino Real. In 1847 it became one of only four designated Pony Express exchange points for the state's first U.S. mail route.

Docent-led tours are generally offered from noon to 4 p.m. Saturdays and Sundays during spring, summer and fall. Winter hours vary. Call for current schedule. Educational group tours are available anytime by reservation.

NATURE

Black Lake Canyon Wetlands Preserve

Guadalupe Road/Zenon Way

(805) 544-9096

www.lcslo.org/black_lake.html

FREE!

From Highway 1 turn east onto Callender Road, turn right onto Sheridan

Road, then left onto Laguna Negra Lane and finally left onto Guadalupe Road.

This 140-acre portion of the canyon is home to at least two endangered plant species: marsh sandwort and Gambel's watercress. A well-established trail through oaks and eucalyptus is popular with local hikers, joggers and equestrians.

The Land Conservancy of San Luis Obispo County, which preserved the area, continues restoration efforts here. Plans for a trail system and other amenities are in the works.

Nearby Black Lake Ecological Area, across Highway 1, is closed to public access except by docent-led tours and special volunteer events. Call for details.

Miller Park

West Tefft Street at Carrillo Street

(805) 929-1133

ncsd.ca.gov

FREE!

From Highway 101, take Tefft Street east. Park at Olde Towne Plaza.

The community has plans to develop this vacant lot into a community park, complete with picnic tables, pedestrian and bike paths, a memorial rose garden and a gazebo.

Monarch Dunes Golf Club

1606 Trilogy Parkway

(805) 343-9459

www.monarchdunesgolf.com

$$$

From Highway 101, turn west onto Tefft Street, right onto Pomeroy and about 3 miles to Willow Road. Turn left onto Willow Road; continue about 2 miles to Via Concha onto which turn left. Continue another mile or so to Trilogy Parkway.

Three courses are planned for this development west of Nipomo. The first course to open was "The Old Course," an 18-hole par-71 course designed to feel like St. Andrew's in Scotland, complete with links-style holes, 35 bunkers and 5 lakes. The 12-hole Challenge Course includes five lakes, and tees which vary not only the hole distance, but its difficulty. Another nine-hole, executive course is planned for the development here, too.

☞ Nipomo Community Park

255 Pomeroy Road

(805) 781-5930

www.slocountyparks.com/facilities/communityparks.htm

FREE!

From Highway 101 take Tefft Street west, veer left at the Y intersection then turn right into the park.

This expansive park provides an array of activities, from romping on the ample lawn to exploring native outback, viewing wildlife or letting the dogs run wild in their own off-leash dog park.

Features include two play structures (developers were kind enough to leave wooden play structures in place for visitors enjoyment just a stone's throw from the newfangled structures), restrooms, basketball courts, volleyball courts, baseball fields, soccer fields, equestrian trails, bike paths, undeveloped areas, Nipomo Native Garden and Nipomo Botanical garden. Well-behaved dogs are welcome off leash in Nipomo Dog park, a dedicated space for canine companions, located at the eastern point of the park (near the T-ball field). Dog's people will find a picnic table and shade trees here.

Olde Towne Creekside Preserve

Behind Olde Towne Plaza
East Tefft St.
(805) 544-9096
FREE!

From Highway 101, take Tefft Street east. Park at Olde Towne Plaza.

This 2½-acre preserve located at the confluence of Nipomo Creek and Haystack Creek includes a very short, maintained loop trail with benches made of hay bales and plaster.

☞ Oso Flaco Lake Natural Area

West end of Oso Flaco Lake Road off Highway 1
(805) 473-7240
www.dunescenter.org/aboutus/ofl.html
$

Take Highway 1 to Oso Flaco Road. Turn west on Oso Flaco Road which ends at the parking lot.

This natural area offers easy foot access to the dunes (even with stroller). An entrance fee collected by State Parks qualifies visitors to walk the boardwalk over Oso Flaco Lake, through the dunes and out to a vast expanse of sand. Keep an eye out for cormorants drying their wings, ruddy ducks and white pelicans.

Although Oso Flaco Lake is under the general umbrella of Oceano State Vehicular Recreation Area, fees paid to enter the beach by car in Oceano do not translate to pedestrian passage here, or vice versa. Plan to pay separate fees

at each gate. Rules here are entirely different, too. No dogs, no horses and no camping are allowed at Oso Flaco, nor are campfires, vehicles, shooting, hunting, bicycling or collecting. Surf fishing, however, is a hit at the beach as are bird watching, kite flying and picnicking.

The non-profit Guadalupe Dunes Center (1055 Guadalupe St., Guadalupe; 805-343-2455) offers educational exhibits, docent-led walks, bird bingo, plant rubbings, scavenger hunts and more throughout the area.

OTHER ADVENTURES

Blacklake Golf Resort

1490 Golf Course Lane

(805) 343-1214

blacklake.com

$$-$$$

From Highway 101 take Los Berros Road north/west, turn left onto Pomeroy Road, right onto Willow Road, right onto Black Lake Canyon Drive and then left onto Golf Course Lane.

This 27-hole championship course offers three 9-hole layouts including lakes, canyons and ageless oaks, and also offers junior programs.

☞ Eufloria Flowers/Koch Mesa Nursery

885 Mesa Road

(805) 929-4683

eufloriaflowers.com

FREE!

From Highway 101 take Tefft Street west. Turn right onto Pomeroy Road, left onto Osage Street and then right onto Mesa Road.

This commercial grower welcomes the public to explore more than eight acres of greenhouses featuring more than 80 varieties of hybrid tea roses grown hydroponically. Guided tours are available by reservation. They offer peeks into the cultivation of long-stem roses that are sold to high-end florists throughout the United States and featured on parade floats during Pasadena's Rose Parade. Educational tours include discussion of Eufloria's practice of using beneficial insects to control pests throughout the greenhouses.

Private tours are available for groups of 15-30 people on the second Tuesday of each month between 8 a.m. and 11 a.m. by appointment; appointments must be made at least one week in advance. Additional tours dates may be possible depending on the season.

☞ The Luffa Farm

1457 Willow Road

(805) 343-0883

theluffafarm.com

FREE!

From Highway 101 take Los Berros Road north / west, turn left onto Pomeroy Road and then right onto Willow Road.

Visitors have been known to show up with fins, snorkels and a variety of other equipment to learn all about luffa, also known as loufa or loufah, that funky "sponge" found in countless showers. This quirky household item has multiple uses, however, and an often unexpected origin. The farm offers tours and, for groups with reservations, tea parties and catered lunches.

Santa Maria Speedway

Hutton Road north of Hwy 166/U.S. 101 interchange

(805) 922-2232

www.racesantamariaspeedway.com

$-$$

From Highway 101 take the Highway 166 exit and turn west. Turn right onto Hutton Road.

Plenty of noise, flying clay and speed abound at this 1/3-mile oval racetrack every Saturday night from April to mid-October. Stock, late model and sprint cars all make regular appearances for points races.

Chapter 9
Los Osos/Baywood Park

This growing community just across Morro Bay from the eponymous rock is a great jumping off point for outdoor adventures. The cool, coastal villages offer restaurants, shops and outdoor activities that vary from walks in preserved oak woodlands to a gnarly skate park. Park the car and take a walk through Los Osos to get a good look at its murals, the most prominent of which are along Los Osos Valley Road and 9th Street. Or park in the village of Baywood Park to pick up lunch at any of the fantastic spots, and enjoy on the dock or on public trails along the bay.

LETTERS

Los Osos Library
2075 Palisades Ave.
(805) 528-1862

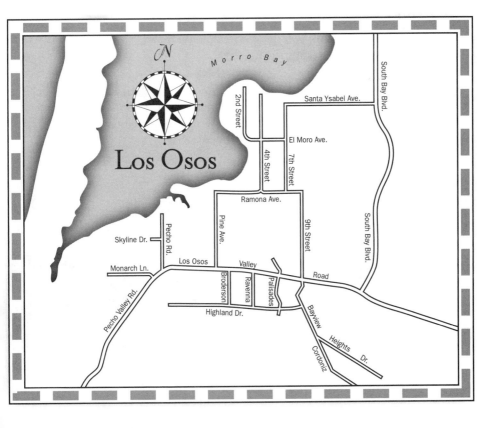

www.slolibrary.org/branch.htm
FREE!
From Highway 101 take Los Osos Valley Road west. In Los Osos, turn right onto Palisades Avenue.

Book discussion groups, weekly story times, monthly family events, summer reading programs for adults and children alike are always on schedule at this branch of the San Luis Obispo County Library system. Open Tuesday through Saturday, hours vary.

NATURE

Audubon Overlook
End of 4th Street
morrocoastaudubon.org
FREE!
From Highway 101 take Los Osos Valley Road west, turn right onto South Bay Boulevard, left onto Santa Ysabel Avenue then right onto Third Street, then turn onto dirt road on right and follow to small parking lot.

This easy-access public viewpoint a short walk from the Baywood Park Pier brings birding to everyone. Bring binoculars, snacks and a camera to fully enjoy this public place which includes benches, a shade structure, an interpretive sign and a fantastic bay view.

Baywood Park (Second Street) Pier
End of Second Street
www.losososbaywoodpark.org
FREE!
From Highway 101 take Los Osos Valley Road west, turn right onto South Bay Boulevard, left onto Santa Ysabel Avenue then right onto Second Street.

This short, quiet pier offers exquisite views of the Morro Bay estuary. It's also a good put-in for canoeists and kayakers.

☞ El Moro Elfin Forest
North of Santa Ysabel at the end of 11th through 17th Streets
(805) 528-0932
www.elfin-forest.org
FREE!

From Highway 101 take Los Osos Valley Road west, turn right onto South Bay Boulevard, left onto Santa Ysabel, then turn right on any street from 11th to 17th. Wheelchair access at 16th Street.

Few scenic walks with nature in San Luis Obispo County are easier than this one. A 4,000-foot, wheelchair-accessible, wooden boardwalk leads visitors on a loop tour of the 90-acre preserve that features diverse communities of flora and fauna and spectacular views of Morro Bay. Several side trails offer close-up looks at pygmy oaks, wildflowers and the habitat of more than 200 plant species, 110 kinds of birds, 25 species of mammals and 11 species of reptiles and amphibians. Poison oak also grows rampantly throughout the area; be sure you can identify it and keep your eyes peeled.

Volunteers from Small Wilderness Area Preservation (S.W.A.P.) lead walks through the forest the third Saturday of each month. Walks leave promptly at 9:30 a.m.

El Moro Linear Parkway
South Bay Boulevard to 12th Street via El Morro Ave.
(805) 781-5930

FREE!

From Highway 101 take Los Osos Valley Road west, turn right onto South Bay Boulevard and right onto El Morro Avenue.

A paved, gently winding path provides a nice, long pedal for young cyclists, stroller-friendly walk for families, or simple stretch for birders and sun worshippers alike. The trail's eastern terminus is just across South Bay Boulevard from Los Osos Middle School; its western end at 12th Street near Baywood Elementary School. There are no services along the route, no restrooms, and very little shade.

☞ Los Osos Oaks State Natural Reserve

1 mile south of Los Osos off Los Osos Valley Road

(805) 772-2694

www.parks.ca.gov/?page_id=597

FREE!

From Highway 101 take Los Osos Valley Road west about 7 miles.

This 85-acre reserve, with its spooky gnarled trees, dappled shade, plentiful bird life and historic past, would be a great place for a child's first hike. Keep children close, however, as poison oak thrives here. The reserve offers easy-to-navigate, dirt trails through ancient sand dunes and groves of centuries-old oak trees.

The trails, which are off limits to bicycles, are not stroller- or wheelchair-friendly. They are not paved and are too narrow, too sandy or too muddy at various points for wheeled vehicles of any sort. The trails pose little challenge for foot traffic. Some fallen trees have been notched to make way for pedestrians. Limbs have been cut off others to clear the way, and bridges have been constructed across spots that apparently are frequently damp or muddy.

Highway noise can drown out the sounds of nature at the outset, but the twisted, thriving old oaks that shelter visitors are captivating. Further into the reserve, the whoosh of passing cars diminishes, leaving visitors to enjoy the sound of rustling leaves and birdsong. About 25 yards past the parking lot, the trail diverges into three paths: one to a Chumash midden, or dump for domestic waste; one to a bluff overlooking Los Osos Creek; and yet another through the grove and on toward the back of the reserve. There are also several well-traveled, though unofficial, trails on which it is easy to roam. Watch for trail signs and wide beaten paths.

According to state parks, the reserve is home to several species of lichen found nowhere else.

Los Osos Community Park

2180 Palisades Ave.

(805) 781-5930

www.slocountyparks.com

FREE!

From Highway 101 take Los Osos Valley Road west, turn right onto Palisades Avenue.

Los Osos Valley School, built in 1872, has been the focal point of this park since the mid 1970s. Today the park also features tennis courts, play structures and restrooms, lawn. A barn and a group barbecue area are available by reservation.

The park is also home to Los Osos Skate park, a 17,000-square-foot, concrete skate park featuring kidney-shaped pool, mini-corner, flat panel, grinding rail, sloped rail, pocket, square bowl, mini-bowl, extension, waterfall and fun box. Safety rules apply, including mandatory helmet use. Open noon to 5 p.m. Monday through Friday and from 10 a.m. to 5 p.m. weekends.

Monarch Grove
West end of Monarch Lane
FREE!
From Highway 101 take Los Osos Valley Road west, turn right onto Monarch Lane then left onto Inyo Street.

This 18-acre protected grove is home to thousands of over-wintering Monarch butterflies. Trails lead to neighboring state park land and neighborhoods.

☞ Montaña de Oro State Park
7 miles south of Los Osos on Pecho Valley Road
(805) 772-7434
www.slostateparks.com/montana_de_oro
FREE!
From Highway 101, take Los Osos Valley Road west and continue through San Luis Obispo, through Los Osos and directly into the park.

For great adventures with nature, head to this 8,000-acre state park off the beaten path. Regulars make it a point to return for the peace of inland valleys, peaks and meadows or the raucous crashing of waves against sand, rock and bluff. The park offers spectacular views, whether visitors are interested in the long sand spit that separates Morro Bay from the ocean, the rugged bluffs further south, the wildflowers of inland valleys, or the sprawling branches of California live oak trees along the slopes. Wildlife also abounds throughout the park, from black-tailed deer to dolphin, coyotes to sea lions, hawks to oystercatchers. The best chance to see inland creatures is during the early morning hours. Take the easy walk along Bluff Trail or head up to one of the peaks.

The only man-made luxuries at Montaña de Oro are pit and portable toilets, occasional benches, picnic tables, barbecue stands and an information center. The true luxuries here are the opportunities to spot wildlife, camp between scenic shoreline and rolling hills, commune with nature, draw wildflowers, explore tide pools, and build forts from driftwood.

According to the Natural History Association of San Luis Obispo Coast, the land was used largely for grazing sheep until 1892. Then Alden B. Spooner, Jr., leased, and later purchased, the land around Islay Creek. Among other agricultural uses, he developed a creamery. Goods were transported to and fro via coastal steamers that tied up along the wharf at the southern end of

Spooner's Cove. His northern neighbor, Alexander S. Hazard, also farmed and ran a dairy. It was Hazard who planted hundreds of eucalyptus trees still growing along Pecho Valley Road at the north end of the park. Hazard had hoped to market the long straight lumber as the need for timber increased, but the stringy wood was not suitable for building. In 1965, the State parks system purchased the land from its last private owner, Irene McAllister.

The wharf, warehouses and many of the agricultural buildings are long gone. Much of the land has returned to its natural state. All that remains of the Hazard and Spooner legacies are the trees, skeletons of the Islay Creek barn and milldam, and the **Spooner Ranch House**, now used as an information center/museum. A nearby **botanical garden** names all the species you're likely to see while exploring the park.

Today, typical Montaña de Oro views include a red-tail hawk floating on thermals high above trails to **Alan Peak, Oats Peak** and **Valencia Peak**, then swooping toward grassland atop the white bluffs. Fifty yards west, a brown pelican glides inches above the Pacific Ocean, watching for fish amongst waves set to crash against jagged Monterey shale and flow into

endless tide pools where sea anemone, hermit crabs and sea stars abound.

Most trails are maintained, many remain relatively rugged, with steep climbs and weather-beaten culverts. Favorites for hiking with young children include the **Bluff Trail** (relatively stroller friendly), **Coon Creek Trail** (not stroller friendly) and the beach at **Spooner's Cove**. For a rugged, stroller-free hike that offers a diversity of fauna and terrain without extreme elevation changes, park in the dirt lot near Camp Keep, follow **Bloody Nose Trail** to its northern terminus, then cross the road and continue down sandy **American Canyon** to the beach. Follow the beach south to fantastic tidepooling (low tide), then back onto the bluff to follow **Dune Trail** across **Hazard Canyon Trail** and back to your starting point.

The **tide pool at Quarry Cove** is ideal for watching sea stars and anemones. **Islay Creek Road** and the **Ridge Trail** are among local mountain bikers' favorites. The oaks and chaparral up **Rattlesnake Flats** calls to horseback riders. **Hazard Canyon Reef** lures surfers to tempt fate

Montana de Oro State Park welcomes hikers, bikers and horses on most of its trails. Check maps for trail designations. Cyclists yield to pedestrians; everyone yields to horses.

in the quest for one excellent ride.

Point Buchon Trail, a 3-mile bluff-top trail just north of park boundary

on PG&E property, is open for docent-led walks Thursdays through Sundays, 8 a.m. to 5 p.m. April through October and from 8 a.m. to 4 p.m. November through March. Access is limited to 275 hikers per day and reservations are encouraged (tinyurl. com/6kkoud9). From the check-in booth at the far end of Pecho Road, the easy trail leads about 1.5 miles to Buchon Point. From there, the trail becomes more rugged as it continues to Crowbar Canyon near Lion Rock.

The park's information center, open weekends throughout the year and daily during summer months, offers protection from the cool coastal breeze that blows nearly constantly off the Pacific. Docents at the center can answer questions about park history and wildlife. Park rangers also offer educational nature talks throughout the summer months.

While experienced surfers are often found riding the waves along the park, swimming anywhere along the shore of Montaña de Oro is not advisable. The water is fraught with heavy currents, the bottom quickly drops to deep water, and there are no lifeguards on duty.

Poison oak flourishes throughout the park. No dogs are allowed on trails, though service dogs are welcome in other areas of the park. **Camping** is allowed only in designated sites including 50 family campsites off Islay Creek, a handful of primitive hike-in sites and Horse Camp, an area specifically designed to house horses and up to 50 people.

☞ Morro Dunes Natural Preserve

(805) 772-2560

www.slostateparks.com/montana_de_oro

FREE!

Though accessible by boat from Morro Bay, the easiest way to reach this stretch is: from Highway 1 take South Bay Boulevard south, turn left onto Los Osos Valley Road which becomes Pecho Valley Road. Once inside Montaña de Oro State Park, turn right onto Sand Spit Road and park, then start walking.

This extension of Montaña de Oro State Park stretches 7 miles along the sand spit that protects Morro Bay from the ravages of the sea. This stretch of sand is best for people who are not interested in sharing the beach with others. There are, however, tradeoffs: no services, no restrooms, no lifeguards, dangerous surf, stiff breezes and often fog.

The long spit of sand is little more than a quarter mile across at its widest point. The smooth sandy western side rises quickly into sand dunes that drop drastically on the east side onto the muddy banks of the bay.

With Morro Rock in site and only a quarter mile in width it seems silly to consult a map, but a quick once over will demonstrate how perception of distance changes drastically when there are no buildings, cars, people or trees to offer scale.

This march through soft sand is not an easy one if the end of the spit is the goal, but it's a fantastic place to meander, pick up rocks and ocean detritus, fly a kite or just watch the waves.

Morro Dunes Ecological Reserve – Bayview Unit

South of Highland drive

(707) 944-5500

www.dfg.ca.gov/lands/er/region3/morrodunes.html

FREE!

From Highway 101 take the Los Osos Road exit and head west. Turn left onto Bayview Heights and access the preserve at Calle Cardoniz, or turn right onto Highland Avenue and hop on trailheads south on Palisades, Ravenna, Broderson and Alexander avenues.

This 237-acre reserve maintained by the U.S. Fish & Wildlife Service is the result of a joint effort of a variety of local organizations including the Trust for Public Lands. Eventually, the trust intends to protect a 1,000-acre habitat and trail corridor connecting Morro Bay State Park and Montana de Oro State Park.

For now the reserve includes myriad trails that crisscross the hillside offering fantastic views of the Pacific Ocean, Morro Bay, Morro Rock, and points north. The trails are largely sandy and there are no services. Hikers and horseback riders are welcome. No motorized vehicles are allowed.

Sea Pines Golf Course

1945 Solano St.

(805) 528-5252

seapinesgolfresort.com

$-$$

From Highway 101 take Los Osos Valley Road west, turn right onto Pecho Road, left onto Skyline and continue straight to the resort.

This nine-hole executive golf course also offers a driving range, putting greens, and a chipping area, all with breathtaking views of Morro Bay, the estuary, sand spit, Morro Rock and points beyond.

Sweet Springs Nature Preserve

600 block of Ramona Avenue

www.morrocoastaudubon.org/sweet.htm

FREE!

From Highway 101 take Los Osos Valley Road west, turn right onto South Bay Boulevard, then left onto Ramona Avenue.

This 24-acre preserve offers a very short hike that even the youngest of

travelers can manage. Dirt paths are well maintained, and bridges and boardwalks protect vegetation, including tons of poison oak. Turtles are often spotted in the ponds, and plentiful wildlife is there for the viewing along the salt marsh and, ultimately, Morro Bay. Bring binoculars, picnic or snack, jacket and camera.

Chapter 10

Morro Bay

The city by the bay is nearly as entertaining as the bay itself. Activities include dining, shopping, park play, feeding seals at the aquarium, watching wildlife in the bay, whale watching, playing chess on the giant chess board, sport fishing, kayaking, biking, skating, kite flying, underwater tours, dinner cruises, brunch cruises, exploring the estuary, golfing, miniature golfing, camping, surfing and simply relaxing on the long, sandy beach.

Expect morning and afternoon fog which often remains thick throughout the day in the hottest summer months. Also expect cold water and be prepared for unpredictable currents at all area beaches.

Morro Bay Recreation and Parks Department manages and maintains several parks that cater to families with children. All are free to the public for typical day use, but permits are required for special events. The department also rents equipment on a daily basis including horseshoe, badminton, bocce and volleyball sets. Call 772-6200 for details.

Word is out that the Morro Bay Harbor Patrol and U.S. Coast Guard offer great field trips on a limited basis, and certainly there are other hidden treasures throughout the community. We've included, here, publicly accessible spaces that are generally available.

ARTS

Art Center Morro Bay
835 Main Street
(805) 772-2504
morrobayartassociation.org
FREE!
From Highway 1 take Morro Bay Boulevard west, and then turn right onto Main Street.
The Morro Bay Art Association offers regularly scheduled classes for children and adults, Art in the Park on Memorial Day and Labor Day weekends. It also operates this small gallery featuring works by local artists. Open daily noon until 4 p.m.

The Bay Theater
464 Morro Bay Blvd.
(805) 772-2444
$
From Highway 1 take Morro Bay Boulevard west.
A one-screen movie theater featuring Hollywood blockbusters.

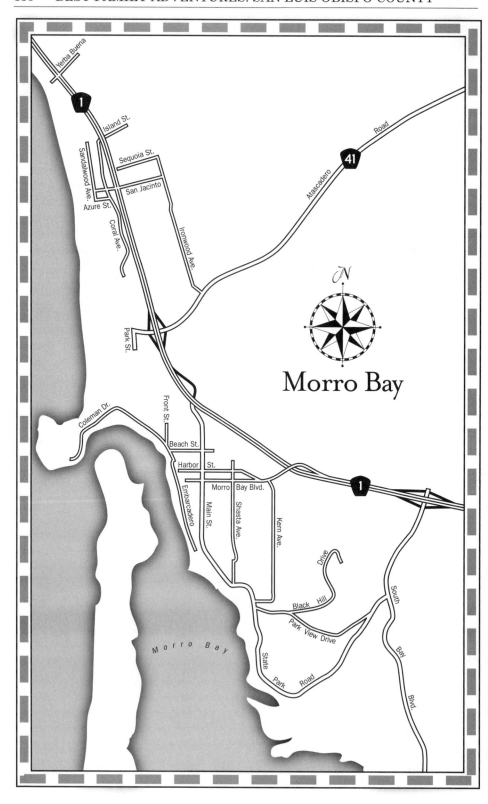

LETTERS
Morro Bay Public Library
625 Harbor Street

(805) 772-6394

www.slolibrary.org

FREE!

From Highway 1 take Morro Bay Boulevard west, then veer right onto Harbor Street.

This branch of the San Luis Obispo County Library system offers book discussion groups, mystery readers' group, a monthly meet-the-author series, summer reading programs for children and adults alike and weekly preschool story time. Open Tuesday through Saturday. Call for current hours and special events schedule.

NATURE
Anchor Memorial Park
Embarcadero at west end of Dunes Street

(805) 772-6278

www.morro-bay.ca.us

FREE!

From Highway 1 take Morro Bay Boulevard west, turn right onto Main Street, left onto Harbor Street, right onto Embarcadero, then left onto Dunes Street.

This tiny park, also referred to as Dunes Street Park, offers picnic benches, Rock views, and access to an observation deck immediately south.

Azure Street Coastal Access
FREE!

From Highway 1 turn left onto San Jacinto Street, left onto Sandalwood Avenue and right onto Azure Street to the parking lot at its end.

A small parking lot at the end of the street provides parking for those willing to take an easy walk through the dunes to the Morro Strand State Beach/Atascadero Beach. This is also the northern access to Cloisters Open space and restrooms are available here.

Bayshore Bluffs Park
Bayshore Drive

(805) 772-6278

www.morro-bay.ca.us

FREE!

From Highway 1 take Morro Bay Boulevard west, turn left onto Main Street, then right onto Sandpiper Lane (through Bayshores Village development).

This quiet, little-known, 3.2-acre patch of grass offers picnic tables, individual barbecues, restrooms, benches and fantastic bay views. Walk along the paved pathway under the arched cypress to find stairs that lead to the shore. Kayaks and non-motorized boats can be launched from this beach.

Beachcomber Drive Coastal Access
FREE!

From Highway 1 turn left onto San Jacinto Street, right onto Sandalwood Avenue, jog left onto Sienna Street and right onto Beachcomber Drive.

Watch for signs indicating public walkways between beachfront homes to less-crowded stretches of Morro Strand State Beach.

☞ Centennial Parkway
Embarcadero Road & Front Street

(805) 772-6278

www.morro-bay.ca.us

FREE!

From Highway 1 take Morro Bay Boulevard west, turn right onto Main Street, left onto Harbor Street then left onto Front Street.

This tiny park across the street from the public restrooms features the city's Giant Chess Board. The 16-foot square concrete board is available for play. Call weekdays to reserve the 18-20 pound chess pieces or join the Morro Bay Chess Club in play most Saturdays at noon.

The park also includes picnic tables and benches. The prominent Centennial Stairway connects the embarcardero with the business district up on the bluff.

☞ Cerro Cabrillo Area
Access from South Bay Boulevard or Turri Road

(805) 772-2560

www.parks.ca.gov

FREE!

From Highway 1 take South Bay Boulevard South. Two turn offs on the east side of the road mark the trailheads.

This extension of Morro Bay State Park encompasses acres of native plants, Cerro Cabrillo, Tiki Head and miles of trails accessible to hikers and mountain bikers alike. The eight mapped trails include Park Ridge, Live Oak, Portola View Point (elev. 329 feet), Quarry, Canet, Crespi, Chumash, Chorro and Cerro Cabrillo (elev. 911 feet). The area is aflutter with birds including a plethora of raptors who no doubt feast on the bountiful rabbits. Coyotes are also regularly seen here and the area is known to be a mountain lion habitat, though they have seldom been seen.

The Park Ridge Trail offers the easiest walk for young hikers or cyclists with some off-pavement experience. Quarry Trail offers more elevation change, but remains moderately strenuous as it leads away from the noise of the city, past the long-since-abandoned quarries below an aptly named rock formation known as Tiki Head and eventually to the park boundary fence. Live Oak Trail provides access to the trail that climbs to Portola Viewpoint.

Among the most diverse trails in the park is Crespi Trail. The single-track trail named for Father Juan Crespi who passed through the area in 1769 rises and falls with the contours of Cerro Hutash before dropping into an oak grove. Older children with plenty of off-pavement experience may enjoy this route.

☞ Cloisters Park
Coral Avenue
(805) 772-6278
www.morro-bay.ca.us
FREE!
From Highway 1 take San Jacinto Street west, turn left onto Coral Avenue
Expansive park includes play structures, group and individual barbecue areas, restrooms, walking trails and beach boardwalks. Open turf areas give way to protected dunes through which paved trails dotted with interpretive signs lead to the beach.

Coleman Park
Coleman Road
(805) 772-6278
www.morro-bay.ca.us
FREE!
From Highway 1 take Morro Bay Boulevard west, turn right onto Main Street, left onto Beach Street, right onto Embarcadero which becomes Coleman Drive and follow it to its end.
A timeless park that provides beach access, swings, picnic tables, restrooms and benches adjacent to the dunes and just a stone's throw from Morro Rock.

Del Mar Park
Ironwood Avenue
(805) 772-6278
www.morro-bay.ca.us
FREE!
From Highway 1 turn east onto San Jacinto Street, then left onto Ironwood Avenue.
This evolving park has been home to a BMX track and roller hockey rink in its day. Lasting features include play structures, picnic tables, restrooms, barbecues, basketball and volleyball courts, trails, benches, a horseshoe pit and loads of grass. A soft-court tennis complex is in the works.
The park is also home to Jodi Giannini Family Dog park, a fenced, off-leash area that offers separated small- and large-dog areas. Friendly, vaccinated, socialized dogs are welcome.

Heron Rookery Preserve
(805) 772-2560
FREE!
From Highway 1 exit Morro Bay Boulevard and turn west. Turn left onto

Kern Avenue which becomes State Park Road.
Eucalyptus and cypress trees provide roosting and nesting sites for cormorants, egrets and herons. Visitors can view lively brooding behavior in the spring.

Lila H. Keiser Park
Park Street/Atascadero Road
(805) 772-6278
www.morro-bay.ca.us
FREE!
From Highway 1 take the Atascadero Road/Highway 41 exit, then turn west onto Atascadero Road and left onto Park Street.
This 10-acre sports park behind the city's three famous stacks includes baseball and softball diamonds, soccer fields, horseshoe pit, picnic tables, individual and group barbecue areas, a restroom, play structures and benches.

Mariner Park
Embarcadero Road
(805) 772-6278
www.morro-bay.ca.us
FREE!
From Highway 1 take Morro Bay Boulevard west, turn right onto Main Street, left onto Harbor Street then left onto Embarcadero.
This tiny park serves to provide public access to the bay and its fishing opportunities. The park also has benches and picnic tables.

Monte Young Park
South Street/Shasta
(805) 772-6278
www.morro-bay.ca.us
FREE!
From Highway 1 take Morro Bay Boulevard west and then turn left onto Shasta Avenue.
This neighborhood park includes tennis courts, play structure, restroom and picnic benches.

Morro Bay City Park
Morro Bay Blvd/Harbor St.
(805) 772-6278
www.morro-bay.ca.us
FREE!
From Highway 1 take Morro Bay Boulevard west.
This is a triangular park bordered on two sides by busy streets, but there's room to run kids on the grass or play a pickup game of basketball

or shuffleboard. Also includes picnic tables, individual and group barbecue areas, play structure and restroom.

Morro Bay Golf Course
State Park Road
(805) 782-8060
centralcoastgolf.com
$$-$$$
From Highway 1 exit Morro Bay Boulevard and turn west. Turn left onto Kern Avenue which becomes State Park Road.

This 18-hole course located within Morro Bay State Park offers junior rates, lessons, pro shop and driving range all overlooking the scenic bay.

Morro Bay State Park
(805) 772-2560
www.parks.ca.gov/?page_id=594
FREE!

From Highway 1 exit Morro Bay Boulevard and turn west. Turn left onto Kern Avenue which becomes State Park Road.

This 2,700-acre park features trails, marina, boat launch and boat rentals, camping, an 18-hole golf course and other amenities.

A relatively short and easy walk to the top of Black Hill east of the golf course affords expansive views of the coastline from Montana de Oro to San Simeon and well inland.

There are no services at the trailhead, so use the restroom elsewhere and pack water, lunch, binoculars and a camera.

The park's marina offers a café, human-powered boat rentals and views. It's a fun place to watch little sailboats come and go.

Morro Bay Sub Sea Tours
699 Embarcadero
(805) 772-9463
www.subseatours.com
$$
From Highway 1 take Morro Bay Boulevard toward the bay, turn left on

Market Street, and right onto Pacific Street.

Climb aboard a banana-yellow boat and head into the harbor for a view of the underwater life in the bay. Stay topside for views of otters, sea lions, seals and other bay fauna, or climb below decks to view kelp forest life through the windows. The 45-minute tours run daily throughout the year. From Jun through September, trips depart on the hour from 10 a.m. to 4 p.m. Winter months (October to May) bring one trip on weekdays (1 p.m.) and three trips on weekends (1 p.m. – 3 p.m. on the hour). Children 3-12 climb aboard for a reduced rate and children 2 and younger ride free.

The company also offers kayak rentals.

Morro Bay Estuary National Preserve
Can be viewed from Morro Bay State Park Marina or Sweet Springs Nature Preserve in Los Osos
(805) 772-3834
www.mbnep.org
FREE!

From Highway 1 exit Morro Bay Boulevard and turn west. Turn left onto Kern Avenue which becomes State Park Road and leads past the marina.

This highly protected 800-acre salt marsh located within Morro Bay State Park is generally available only for observation from afar. Bring binoculars and lunch to enjoy myriad waterfowl and shorebirds living throughout the tidal slough. For an estuary education, stop by the Morro Bay Estuary Nature Center (p. 140).

☞ Morro Rock Nature Preserve & Beach
Coleman Drive
FREE!

From Highway 1 take Morro Bay Boulevard west, turn right onto Main Street, left onto Beach Street, right onto Embarcadero which becomes Coleman Drive and follow it to its end.

Most visitors eventually find their way to Morro Rock, the city's 576-foot-tall landmark and namesake. The gigantic 20-million-year-old outcropping juts from the ocean at the mouth of the bay. It's one in a chain of nine lava plugs that extend east past San Luis Obispo. While others are popular among hikers (like Bishop Peak in San Luis Obispo), no climbing or hiking is allowed on Morro Rock. It's dangerous, and it's also a sanctuary for the rare peregrine falcon and other fowl.

Waves and dangerous currents once protected the rock, sometimes referred to as "The Gibraltar of the Pacific," from all sides. According to various local historians, early written references to the landmark date back to 1542 when explorer Juan Cabrillo took note of it.

Today, California State Historical Landmark No. 821 is accessible by car, bicycle or on foot via the World War II era causeway at the end of Embarcadero. Visitors often sport binoculars in hopes of catching a glimpse of the endangered peregrine falcons that nest high in the crags, and the otters that raft in the ocean eddies below.

The jetty offers protection from wind and surf along the beach north of the road. It's a good place to look for shells and rocks at low tide, but the current can be strong here.

The beach on the north side of the rock offers epic surfing for the experienced. Summer waves are typically small, but winter boomers combined with the rip tide alongside the rock make this a winter spot for experts. Lifeguards have historically been stationed here during summer months. No open fires or fireworks are allowed on the beach, and some areas are closed seasonally to protect Snowy Plover nests.

☞ Morro Strand State Beach/Atascadero Beach
(805) 772-2560
www.parks.ca.gov
FREE!
From Highway 1 turn west onto Atascadero Road to reach the most southerly stretch of this beach. See also Studio Drive Coastal Access, Azure Street Coastal Access, Beachcomber Drive Coastal Access, and Morro Strand State Beach/Atascadero Beach.

Morro Strand State Beach is divided into two sections. The southern section, sometimes referred to as Atascadero Beach, stretches from Atascadero Road north to Yerba Buena Street. The northerly stretch of sand runs from 24th Street in Cayucos to south of Chaney Avenue. There are, however, no lines in the sand for the entire section of sandy beach that stretches from Morro Rock to the bluffs north of Cayucos Pier.

The area is known for its fairly gentle waves and views of Morro Rock. A fairly steady ocean breeze makes this and northern neighbor Morro Strand State Beach popular among kite enthusiasts, windsurfers, kite-skiers and kite-surfers. Local surfers come here when it's too crowded at Morro Rock or in fall and winter months when the waves here hollow out.

At low tide it is possible to walk via this beach from Morro Rock to the bluffs north of Cayucos Pier. The three-mile stretch of beach between 24th Street in Cayucos and Yerba Buena in Morro Bay is particularly popular for wind sports: kite sailing, kiting, and windsurfing. But it isn't always windy. Swimming and surfing are also favorites along this long sandy stretch.

Expect morning and afternoon fog which often stretches clear through the day in the hottest summer months. Also expect cold water and be prepared for unpredictable currents at all area beaches.

☞ Museum of Natural History
Morro Bay State Park
State Park Road
(805) 772-2694
www.slostate parks.com/natural_history_museum
$

From Highway 1 exit Morro Bay Boulevard and turn west. Turn left onto Kern Avenue which becomes State Park Road.

One of the most beautiful views of Morro Bay is hidden behind a great big rock. Not Morro Rock, but a miniature morro that conceals this museum from the park's main thoroughfare. The museum, opposite the

campground and down the road from the golf course, is an underutilized treasure along the bay.

The museum itself is quite small, but a 2002 renovation greatly improved the collection and presentation. More than 25 displays, many of them hands-on, emphasize local fish, birds, Chumash people indigenous to the Central Coast, and local geology.

What the museum lacks in quantity it makes up for in quality, staff and special programs. Every weekend, there are puppet shows, story hours, kids' cinema and special hands-on activities for children as well as docent-led walks.

Open 10 a.m. to 5 p.m. daily except Thanksgiving, Christmas and New Years Day.

North Point Natural Area
Toro Lane
(805) 772-6278
www.morro-bay.ca.us
FREE!
From Highway 1 turn west onto Yerba Buena Street then immediately right onto Toro Lane.

As its title suggests, this 1.3-acre public space has not been covered in turf but left in its natural state. A bluff-top trail provides a quick retreat from civilization and offers ocean views and beach access. A stairway leads from the parking lot to a beach which offers fascinating tidepools at low tide.

Studio Drive Coastal Access
FREE!
From Highway 1 turn west onto Studio Drive.

Public access to Morro Strand State Beach is available on marked pathways between homes near cross streets of Rapf, Mayer, Thalberg, Del Mar, El Sereno, Gracia and Juanita avenues. Parking is extremely limited, but the area is prime for long walks and good surf.

☞ Tidelands Park
South end of Embarcadero
(805) 772-6278
www.morro-bay.ca.us
FREE!
From Highway 1 take Morro Bay Boulevard west, turn left onto Main Street, right onto Beach Street, right onto Pacific Street and left onto Embarcadero.

Children at heart are invited to play roles on a wooden ship in the park's sea of sand overlooking the bay. The nearby boat launch provides added interest. Facilities at this 2-acre park also include restrooms, picnic tables, and individual and group barbecue areas.

OTHER ADVENTURES

The Embarcadero

Embarcadero from Tidelands Park to Front Street

(805) 772-4467

FREE!

From Highway 1 take Morro Bay Boulevard west, turn right onto Main Street, left onto Beach Street and continue to Embarcadero.

Though the Embarcadero has its fair share of shops featuring postcards, T-shirts and other memorabilia, the percentage of art studios and specialty stores is on the rise. It is also home to kite shops, restaurants, boat charter companies, a mom-and-pop aquarium, nature center, giant chess board, bay viewing platforms and outdoor dining as well as Tidelands Park, a great place for kids to run.

Morro Bay Aquarium

595 Embarcadero

(805) 772-7647

www.morrobay.com/morrobayaquarium/

$

From Highway 1 take Morro Bay Boulevard west, turn left onto Main Street, right onto Beach Street, right onto Pacific Street and left onto Embarcadero.

Though not expansive or particularly time consuming, this small 40-year-old aquarium includes little tanks of sealife specimens as well as pools filled with vociferous seals and sea lions. For a small fee, visitors can feed the animals rehabilitating here after being found sick, injured or abandoned.

Morro Bay Estuary Nature Center

601 Embarcadero, Suite 11 (upstairs)

(805) 772-3834

mbnet.org

FREE!

From Highway 1 take Morro Bay Boulevard west, turn left onto Main Street, right onto Beach Street, right onto Pacific Street and left onto Embarcadero.

The center strives to educate the public about the past, present and potential future of the 2,300-acre Morro Bay Estuary (p. 136). Exhibits offer insights into the estuary and watershed. Hands-on displays offer tips for identifying local birds and other wildlife. The center also provides docent-led workshops for school groups with advance reservations. Open daily 10 a.m. to 6 p.m. (10 a.m. to 5 p.m. January and February).

Morro Fleece Works

1920 Main Street

(805) 772-9665

www.morrofleeceworks.com

FREE!

From Highway 1 take Main Street east.

This specialty business scours, picks, cards and roves wool from llama, alpaca and other wool-bearing animals. Batts and felt sheets are also made here. Tours are available by appointment only. Groups preferred. Open Monday through Friday and by appointment.

Morro Bay Teen Center & Skate park

231 Atascadero Road

(805) 772-6212

www.morro-bay.ca.us

FREE!

From Highway 1 take the Atascadero Road exit and head west.

The recreation center located near Morro Bay High School is also home to the city's skate park. Knee pads, elbow pads and helmets are required in the park which is open during recreation center hours: daily after school and on Saturdays; closed some school holidays; open 1 p.m. to 7 p.m. Monday through Saturday during summer break.

Chapter 11

Cayucos

This tiny, sunny, quiet, funky beach town on Highway 1 between Morro Bay and Cambria is an ideal place to beach with kids. The wide, flat sands are only steps away from ice cream parlors and taquerias - a blessing for anyone with hungry children (or hungry adults). Southern exposure means Cayucos is likely to see fog burn off earlier than Morro Bay - another important consideration in choosing beaches.

The charm of Cayucos is that it hasn't changed in years. The population remains at about 3,000. Old homes just keep getting better. Old shops continue to provide good food and entertainment. And the beach retains its beauty and natural peace.

Everything in Cayucos is within walking distance, so just pick a spot, park the car, unload the family and go. Keep your eyes peeled for public art which is displayed in the forms of murals, sculptures and random acts of art in unexpected places.

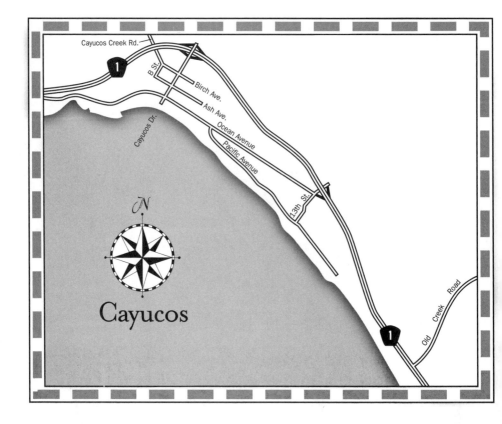

ARTS
Cayucos Art Association Gallery
10 Cayucos Drive
(805) 995-2049
cayucosarts.org
FREE!
From Highway 1 take the Cayucos Drive exit and continue west to the end of the street.
Local artist show their works in this pierside gallery that rotates its exhibits every six weeks. Paintings, photographs, sculptures and crafts are all included. There are also bins of artwork, cards and crafts for sale. Open Tuesdays through Sundays from 1 p.m. to 4 p.m.

LETTERS
Cayucos Library
310 B Street
(805) 995-3312
slolibrary.org
FREE!
From Highway 1 take Cayucos Drive west, and then turn left onto Ocean Avenue.
This branch of the San Luis Obispo County Library system offers preschool story times weekly, youth summer reading programs and special programs for teens. Open Tuesdays through Thursdays.

NATURE
☞ Cayucos Pier
West end of Cayucos Drive
(805) 781-5930
www.slostateparks.com/cayucos_state_beach/
FREE!
From Highway 1 take the Cayucos Drive exit and continue west to the end of the street.
The 125-year-old Cayucos Pier is a popular spot for pedestrians and fishermen alike. Benches along both sides of the gently swaying pier offer visitors picturesque views of sand, surf and seagulls. Below, body boarders and surfers wait for the next big wave.

Cayucos Skate Park
North Ocean Avenue
(805) 995-0856
FREE!

From Highway 1 take the Cayucos Drive exit and continue west to the end of the street.

A 10,000-square-foot concrete skate park has long been in the planning stages across Highway 1 at the proposed Norma Rose Park, but until then, Cayucos enjoys a giant wooden bowl ramp with a 90-degree elbow corner. The 5,400-square-foot, well-used park is free for all. Helmets are required.

☞ Cayucos State Beach

West end of Cayucos Drive

(805) 781-5930

www.slostateparks.com/cayucos_state_beach

FREE!

From Highway 1 take the Cayucos Drive exit and continue west to the end of the street.

The 10-mile stretch of sand that begins in Morro Bay includes great climbing rocks midbeach, then turns to tide pools at its northern end. On shore, driftwood serves as the medium for artists and architects. At the hand of visitors, it becomes shade structures for parents, teepees for children or stick people who occupy sandcastles.

A good collection of playground equipment near the pier includes full-size slides, swings, jungle gyms and a smaller toddler set. Restrooms and public showers are at the base of the pier, and kayak and surfboard rentals are available nearby.

Though the most obvious access to the beach is downtown at the pier, there are a number of marked public access pathways between homes along Pacific Avenue near 12th, 9th, 3rd and 1st streets. Head down the steep 24th Street stairs to hit a hot surfing spot, sometimes called Studios.

Coastal Viewpoint
290 Pacific Avenue
FREE!
From Highway 1 take 13th Street exit, turn west onto 13th Street, then right onto Pacific Avenue
This public viewpoint offers expansive views of Estero Bay and its miles of sandy beaches and coastal bluffs.

☞ Estero Bluffs State Park
West of Highway 1 from North Ocean Street to Villa Creek
(805) 772-7434
www.slostateparks.com/estero_bluffs/
FREE!
Very large dirt pullouts along the coastal side of the highway mark this relatively little known 355-acre public open space. Some highlights of this property include incredibly serene coves, seals, sea lions, otters, driftwood, tide pools, herons, egrets and 9 miles of trails along bluffs.

The beach at Villa Creek typically is loaded with driftwood ideal for a day of creating with kids. The same beach is ideal habitat for snowy plover, so some sections of the park are fenced off during nesting season.

The largest parking area is north of Cayucos along Highway 1, but the bluffs can also be accessed legally from the north end of North Ocean Avenue.

Hardie Park
B Street & Birch Avenue
FREE!
From Highway 1 take the Cayucos Drive exit, head west, then turn right onto Birch Avenue.
This grassy park has plentiful swings, play structures for big kids and a fenced in play structure area for smaller ones. There's also a large covered picnic area, barbecue, tennis courts and a restroom.

Hardie Park & Pool
Birch Avenue and "B" Street
(805) 781-5930
www.slocountyparks.com/facilities/pools.htm
FREE! - $
From Highway 1 take the Cayucos Drive exit, head west, then turn right onto Birch Avenue.
This grassy park has plentiful swings, play structures for big kids and a fenced in play structure area for smaller ones. There's also a large covered picnic area, barbecue, tennis courts and a restroom.

Just across the street is the community's pool. It's open Memorial Day to Labor Day. Call for current hours and class offerings.

Harmony Headlands State Park
West of Highway 1 near Harmony
(805) 772-7434
FREE!
From Cayucos, continue north on Highway 1 about 5 miles to a small (10-car) dirt parking lot on the west side of the highway.
This 784-acre former ranch property is now operated as a largely undisturbed natural area replete with native flora and fauna. From the parking lot, the park offers a 1-mile trail west through the marine terrace to coastal bluffs. Morning visitors may see mule deer grazing or coyotes out for a morning snack. Otters, sea lions and seals are often seen lounging in the coves or fishing just offshore. The park is also home to several particularly sensitive plant and animal species includ San Luis Obispo morning glory, San Luis Obispo owl's clover, compact cobwebby thistle and adobe sanicle, California red-legged frog, southwestern pond turtle.

The park is open for day-use hiking from 6 a.m. until sunset daily. There are no amenities or services at the park, though future plans call for expansion of the trail system and the addition of restrooms, picnic areas and interpretive signage.

Norma Rose Park
Bay Avenue
(805) 781-5930

FREE!

From Highway 1 take 13th Street east, turn immediately right onto Cabrillo Avenue.

Locals have big plans for this park wedged between the east side of Highway 1 and the Cayucos Cemetery. Amenities will include turf, paths, basketball courts, picnic areas, an off-leash dog park, restrooms and a 10,000-square-foot cement skate park complete with pool and other obstacles.

Old Creek Road

FREE!

From Highway 1 turn east onto Old Creek Road.

This scenic drive past Whale Rock Reservoir also serves as a great ride for experienced road cyclists. It's particularly attractive when the wildflowers are out (late spring), as the hills turn golden (early summer) and when the colors change (late fall). While the area is also beautiful in mid-summer, heat makes it a killer ride that is best delayed until cooler weather prevails.

The rural road meanders along Willow Creek before heading up and past the reservoir, then on to the ridge and eventually across Highway 46. Here the road changes names to Santa Rosa Creek Road. The route also turns somewhat treacherous here. The steep, rough pavement has proven tough to maintain, so riders must watch for swells, dips and extreme cracks.

The lower portion of the road offers a relatively easy, peaceful and seldom-traveled road to Main Street in Cambria.

Paul Andrew Park

Ocean Avenue & 3rd Street

(805) 781-5930

FREE!

From Highway 1 take the 13th Street exit, turn toward the beach, then turn right onto Ocean Avenue.

This county park with an ocean view stretches one narrow city block from Ocean Avenue to Pacific Avenue. It includes long patch of lawn as well as play structures and picnic tables.

Whale Rock Reservoir

Old Creek Road

(805) 995-3701

www.slocity.org/utilities/sources.asp#Whale

$

From Highway 1, turn east onto Old Creek Road.

This reservoir was built in 1961 to serve as a water source for San Luis Obispo. The result: a scenic reservoir surrounded by serene landscape and offering breathtaking views of the Pacific Ocean. It's an inexpensive spot, but there are plenty of restrictions: no body contact with the reservoir water, no boats, no live bait, dogs must be on leash.

The 2 miles of shoreline trail is actually an old dirt road that is open to bicyclists and hikers from 7 a.m. to 4 p.m. Wednesdays through Sundays beginning the last Saturday in April and running through Nov. 15. There is no winter access.

Shoreline fishing is allowed with a California fishing license. Regular piscine sightings include steelhead trout, western sucker, catfish and blue gill. Facilities also include picnic tables at each end of the trail, outhouses and garbage cans.

OTHER ADVENTURES

The Abalone Farm

Highway 1

(805) 995-2495

www.abalonefarm.com

FREE!

Call for appointment and directions.

For more than 40 years this business venture has enjoyed a spectacular view of Estero Bay from its bluff-top location hidden behind rolling hills west of Highway 1. The largest and oldest producer of California red abalone in the U.S. opens its doors by reservation only for group educational tours from May to September. Visitors meander from one outdoor tank to another while a guide explains the history of the business and the system that provides fresh seawater for the marine snails that can grow up to 12 inches across and fetch more than $100 per pound.

Chapter 12

Cambria

Cambria, a traditionally artsy community both exposed to the ravages of the Pacific Coast and nestled in the wooded rolling coastal hills, is a community divided by Highway 1. The western portion offers supreme ocean views, coastal access and hikes. The eastern portion offers shops, restaurants, parks and historic points of interest.

The beaches here are, largely, fantastic places to hunt for the perfect rock. That was Grandma Ruth Poore's favorite part. "The rocky beaches have this special sound when the tide rolls out from the rocks," she said. "I love that sound."

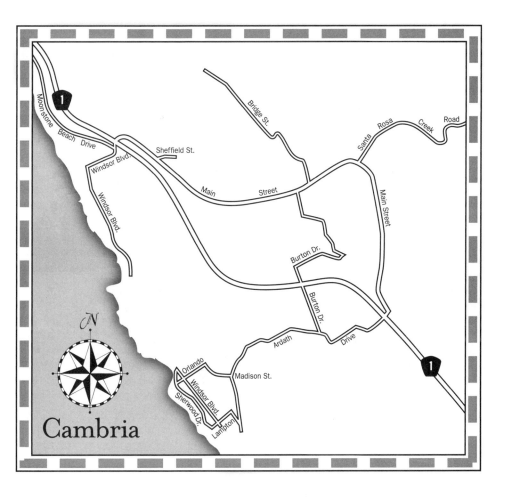

ARTS

Allied Arts Association Schoolhouse Gallery

880 Main St.

(805) 927-8190

artistsofcambria.com

FREE!

From Highway 1 turn east onto Main Street.

Local artists show their works throughout the year in the historic Santa Rosa Schoolhouse. Exhibits, open Friday through Sunday year round, include a variety of media and moods. The association also sponsors several public events throughout the year including a Home Tour, Spring Music Competition, Pinedorado Art Show and Reception and the Petals and Palettes Garden and Art Show. The association also includes a theater arts group.

Pewter Plough Playhouse

824 Main St.

(805) 927-3877

pewterploughplayhouse.org

$$$

From Highway 1 turn east onto Main Street.

For nearly three decades community players have gathered on stage here to present their best with six productions each year. A monthly readers' theater is free and open to the general public. (It also seeks readers regularly.) Call or check online for current schedule.

LETTERS

Cambria Library

900 Main Street (2043 Main St. in 2014)

(805) 927-4336

www.slolibrary.org

FREE!

From Highway 1 turn east onto Main Street.

In addition to basic library services, this branch of the San Luis Obispo County Library system maintains three artists on staff. They create and maintain inspired diplays which change regularly. Additional library services include preschool story time every Thursday at 10:15 a.m., and summer reading programs for children and adults. This branch is open Tuesday through Saturday.

HISTORY

Cambria Historical Museum

Guthrie-Bianchini House

2551 Center Street

(805) 927-2891

www.cambriahistoricalsociety.com
FREE!
From Highway 1 turn east onto Main Street.
If it's local history you're after, this is your ultimate stop. Located in the community's Historic Center Park (p. 152), this volunteer-driven museum features artifacts of local history including a relatively vast archive of local lore. Topics include all things Cambria as well as documents and articles related to Piedras Blancas Lighthouse, the construction of Highway 1 and the sinking of the Montebello.

The museum and its gardens are open Friday through Sunday 1 p.m. to 4 p.m. and Monday 10 a.m. to 1 p.m. The grounds are also available for special events. Call for rental details.

Joss House/Cambria Chinese Temple
2264 Center Street
(805) 927-2866
www.greenspacecambria.org/creekside_menu.htm
FREE!
From Highway 1 turn east onto Main Street.
The oldest Chinese temple in Southern California rests on this quiet city center lot and the heart of Historic Center Park. The temple was a focal point of Cambria's Chinese district at the turn of the 19th Century when immigrants harvested seaweed and abalone and worked in the area's mercury mines. The structure and surrounding park space are wheelchair accessible and include interpretive signs.

NATURE

Andy's Garden
Guildford Drive at Worcester Drive
FREE!
From Highway 1 turn west onto Windsor Boulevard and then left onto Worcester Drive..
This privately owned and maintained corner park welcomes public use. It offers tree-shaded lawn, garden, aviary and benches a short walk from the beach.

Cambria area coves
FREE!
From Highway 1 turn west on Ardath Drive. Turn right onto Randall Drive, then left onto Lampton Street, then right onto Sherwood Drive.
Like other coastal communities, Cambria offers public access to beaches even in private neighborhoods. Watch for marked pathways between homes along Sherwood Drive near its intersections with Harvey and Drake streets.

Cambria Coastal Viewpoint
Harvey/Sherwood Dr.

From Highway 1, turn west on Ardath Drive. Turn right onto Randall Drive, then left onto Lampton Street, then right onto Sherwood Drive.

A nice place for a quick stop or a long break with fantastic Pacific views.

Cambria Community Park
Rodeo Grounds Road

(805) 927-6223

www.cambriacsd.org

FREE!

From Highway 1 take Main Street east, turn right onto Burton Drive, then right onto Rodeo Grounds Road.

This proposed 17½-acre park on a portion of East Fiscalini Ranch is still in the works, but plans call for play structures, paths, soccer/baseball fields, picnic grove, restrooms and an area dedicated for dog use.

Cambria Dog Park
2700 block Main Street

(805) 927-7229

www.slodoggies.com/dogparks.html

FREE!

From Highway 1 turn east onto Main Street. The park is near the intersection of Main Street and Santa Rosa Creek Road.

Local dog walkers have personalized this small fenced park at the edge of town. A shade structure, benches, chairs and tables offer respite for weary dog owners while their canine companions roam free, take a drink, share a dog toy and sniff to their little hearts' content. It's run by volunteers, so feel free to pick up a rake or shovel and pitch in, or to adopt the park for a family, club or Scout project.

Cambria Historic Center Park
Bridge Street at Centre Street

(805) 927-6223

www.cambriacsd.org

FREE!

From Highway 1 turn east onto Cambria Road, right onto Main Street then right onto Bridge Street.

More than 3-acres of public space in the east village offers open space and gardens but is largely tasked with preserving the community's history. In addition to gardens and a nature walk along Santa Rosa Creek, the park includes Cambria Historical Museum at the Guthrie-Bianchini House, White House shops, and the Joss House, home of the oldest Chinese temple in Southern California.. Additional plans for this park include a gazebo, a pedestrian bridge to Tin City, and a patio gallery.

Cambria Pines Lodge Organic Herb & Produce Gardens
2905 Burton Drive
(800) 445-6868
cambriapineslodge.com/garden.htm
FREE!
From Highway 1 take Main Street east to Burton Drive.
This privately-owned lodge welcomes visitors onto its 25 acres of gardens including a manicured herb garden and a certified organic vegetable garden that supplies the property's restaurant.

Chelsea Lane Reserve
Chelsea Lane
(805) 927-2866
www.greenspacecambria.org
FREE!
From Highway 1, turn inland onto Weymouth Street, left onto Brighton Lane, then right onto Chelsea Lane.
This pocket park is one of several open spaces protected for public enjoyment and preservation of Monterey pine trees and related habitat. Includes a bench for passive enjoyment of this otherwise unimproved park.

Dorking Avenue Reserve

Dorking Avenue

(805) 927-2866

www.greenspacecambria.org

FREE!

From Highway 1, turn west onto Ardath Drive, left on Emerson Road, then left onto Dorking Avenue.

This neighborhood reserve held by Greenspace, The Cambria Land Trust, for public enjoyment and preservation of Monterey pine trees and related habitat. No facilities.

Emerson Road Reserve

Emerson Road

(805) 927-2866

www.greenspacecambria.org

FREE!

From Highway 1, turn west onto Ardath Drive, then left on Emerson Road.

This neighborhood forest reserve protected by Greenspace, The Cambria Land Trust, offers public enjoyment and preservation of Monterey pine trees and related habitat. No facilities.

☞ Fiscalini Ranch Preserve

Windsor Drive

(805) 927-6223

www.cambriacsd.org

FREE!

From Highway 1 take either Windsor Drive west to its terminus at the north edge of the open space or turn west on Ardath Drive. From Ardath, turn right onto Madison, left onto Orland Drive, then right onto South Windsor Drive which terminates at the south end of the open space.

To access the eastern parcel from Highway 1, turn inland on Cambria Road, right onto Main Street, right onto Burton Drive and right onto Rodeo Grounds Road.

This 430-acre open space that divides the northern and southern coastal neighborhoods offers neighbors and visitors a peaceful escape from the developed world. A dozen trails crisscross the property and provide access to five stands of Monterey pine covering 65 acres, additional stands of coastal live oak, seabluff scrub, grassland, wetlands, marshes and coastal scrub.

Among the most family friendly is the 1-mile Bluff Trail along the blufftop marine terrace which offers views as far north as Piedras Blancas Light Station, beyond crashing waves to the horizon, or inland to tree-covered rolling hills. For a different perspective, take the Santa Rosa Creek Trail from the end of Rodeo Grounds Road to Highway 1 and back again. Along the way, observant hikers may notice stream bank stabilization efforts including built-in trout habitat devices.

Take binoculars and have a seat on any of the benches along the route. A quick peek and you're likely to see otters, seals, sea lions and, in season, whales. Spend more time on the property, especially in the early morning hours, and you may see deer, bobcats, skunks, raccoons or even red-legged frogs.

The area is popular for hikers, joggers and dog walkers. Bicycles are allowed on designated trails only. Equestrian use of the park is limited to groups by permit. No single equestrian use is allowed. Open dawn to dusk. Watch out for the bone-chilling coastal breeze. Bring a windbreaker.

Henry Kluck Memorial Trail
Fern Drive
(805) 544-9096
www.lcslo.org/black_lake.html
FREE

From Highway 1, turn south onto Burton Drive, then right onto Fern Drive. This ¾-mile, rough, dirt footpath connecting Fern Drive to Ardath Drive via Camborne Place meanders through Fern Canyon Preserve. There are lots of Monterey pines, ferns, oaks and even a seasonal creek, but no facilities.

Hillcrest Drive Reserve
Hillcrest Drive
(805) 927-2866
www.greenspacecambria.org
FREE!

From Highway 1, turn east onto Cambria Road, left onto Main Street, right onto Cornwall Street, then right onto Hillcrest Drive.

This publicly accessible reserve held by Greenspace, The Cambria Land Trust, is densely vegetated. While available for public use, there are no facilities here.

Joslyn Recreation Center
950 Main Street
(805) 927-3364
www.joslynrec.org
$$
From Highway 1 turn east onto Main Street.
This center focuses on recreation for the over-18 set, but adults are welcome
to bring younger guests along for a spot of lawn bowling during weekend
play. The facility also offers bridge, table tennis, bingo, couples dance club,
shot clinics, mature driving courses and a variety of special interest groups
including fishing, gardening, poker and a writers' workshop.

Lampton Cliffs Park
At the intersection of South Windsor Boulevard and Lampton
Street
(805) 781-5930
www.slocountyparks.com
FREE!
*From Highway 1 turn west onto Ardath Drive. Turn right onto Randall
Drive, then left onto Lampton Street and continue west to the park.*
For a seriously out-of-the-way rocky escape, seek out this tiny beach bound
by coastal bluffs with nothing but rough seas, jagged rock tidepools and
nearly guaranteed privacy. This 2.2-acre park has gone through multiple
renovations thanks to the waves that pound the cliffs here. The latest
incarnation includes a well-maintained loop trail atop the bluff and stairs to
a rocky beach below. The beach is only accessible at low tide, so check your
tide table before heading out if beach access is critical to your visit.

Leffingwell Landing Day-use Area
Moonstone Beach Drive
(805) 927-2020
www.parks.ca.gov/?page_id=590
FREE!
*From Highway 1 turn west onto Moonstone Beach Drive and proceed north
across bridge and then left into the park.*
Leffingwell Landing in San Simeon State Park north of Moonstone Beach
is a grassy bluff top featuring Monterey pines, picnic benches, barbecue grills
and restrooms. Families play in the sandy beach below, enjoy picnics in the
grass, and watch seals on nearby rocks.

Linn's Original Farm Store
6275 Santa Rosa Creek Road
(805) 927-1499
www.linnsfruitbin.com

FREE!

From Highway 1 turn east onto Main Street, then east onto Santa Rosa Creek Road. Continue several miles along this paved, narrow, country road lined with oak and sycamore trees.

The farm store that kicked off the Linns' restaurant experiment continues to offer the same great pies, jams and other goods it has since 1977. But kids will be most interested in the grassy spot under an ancient sycamore next to an inviting creek.

The Linns welcome families to picnic here. Open 10 a.m. to 6 p.m. daily throughout the summer, then 10 a.m. to 4 p.m. weekends during winter months.

Margate Avenue Reserve

Margate Avenue

(805) 927-2866

www.greenspacecambria.org

FREE!

From Highway 1, turn inland onto Burton Drive, then left onto Margate Avenue.

Like many of the other Greenspace (Cambria Land Trust) protected spaces, this neighborhood forest is open to public use, but there are no facilities. The system of pocket parks and neighborhood forests are designed to preserve Monterey pine trees and related habitat.

Marjorie Place Reserve

Marjorie Place

(805) 927-2866

www.greenspacecambria.org

FREE!

From Highway 1, turn west onto Ardath Drive, right onto Ernest Place, left onto Malvern Street, and left onto Marjorie Place.

A neighborhood forest reserve held by Greenspace, The Cambria Land Trust, offers public enjoyment and preservation of Monterey pine trees and related habitat. No facilities.

☞ Moonstone Beach

Moonstone Beach Drive

(805) 927-2020

www.parks.ca.gov/?page_id=590

FREE!

From Highway 1 turn west onto Windsor Boulevard then immediately right onto Moonstone Beach Drive. Moonstone beach extends from Chatham Lane north about ¼ mile.

The beach is named for its rough sand – or shall we say smooth rock – and is known best for its tide pools, bluff-top boardwalk and frequent visits from seals, otters and local surfers. My grandmother, Ruth Poore, always loved this beach for the treasures hidden among the teeny, tiny rocks. "Sometimes you can find some that look like jade, sometimes those that are white like moonstones. To me it is a treasure," she said.

While surfers enjoy the swell at the southern end of Moonstone Beach, the currents along this stretch of the North Coast are hazardous for swimmers, young waders and pets. Bring binoculars for closer views of seals, otters and surfers. There are restrooms at the southern end of the beach.

The 1¼-mile boardwalk begins just south of Leffingwell Landing and generally follows the bluff south to the dirt parking area just north of Windsor Drive. It is wide enough for strollers and wheelchairs and there are no major inclines.

Nottingham Bluff
Nottingham Drive
(805) 927-2020
www.parks.ca.gov/?page_id=590
FREE!
From Highway 1 turn west onto Windsor Boulevard then right onto Bristol Street which becomes Nottingham Drive.

This 3-acre bluff-top open space, bordered by Dorset Street on the north, Worcester Street on the south, is part of the expansive San Simeon State Park (p. 162) lands. The area includes dirt pathways and a picnic bench, ocean views and highly sketchy access to potentially dangerous coves.

Pocahontas Garden/Wilton Drive Reserve
Between Wilton Drive and Burton Drive
(805) 927-2866
www.greenspacecambria.org
FREE!
From Highway 1, turn inland onto Burton Drive.

This publicly accessible parcel owned by Greenspace, The Cambria Land Trust, is home to Cambria Community garden which offers a few raised beds for rent to interested gardeners.

Quail Hill Reserve
Pineridge Drive
(805) 927-2866
www.greenspacecambria.org
FREE!
From Highway 1 turn westward onto Ardath Drive, turn sharply left onto Pineridge Drive and cross Ellis Avenue twice.

This natural open space located near the end of Pineridge Drive on Lodge Hill is preserved by Greenspace, Cambria Land Trust. It provides room to wander and ponder, and picnic benches.

Santa Rosa Creek Road
FREE!
From Highway 1 turn east onto Main Street the continue east onto Santa Rosa Creek Road.

This rural road that leads from Cambria to Highway 46 offers a scenic setting for motorists and experienced cyclists alike. This road less traveled is particularly scenic for wildflower tours (late spring) and autumn colors.

The road that takes off east from Main Street offers a relatively easy ride, but it's narrow, so only recommended for more experienced cyclists. Santa Rosa Creek Road begins a steady climb that turns into an outright challenge toward the top complete with rough pavement, swells, dips and cracks.

Across Highway 46 the road is called Old Creek Road. Enjoy spectacular views from the ridges before plummeting back down toward Willow Creek, Whale Rock Reservoir and eventually Cayucos.

Shamel Park
5455 Windsor Blvd.

(805) 781-5930

www.slocountyparks.com

FREE!
From Highway 1 turn west onto Windsor Boulevard.

This 6-acre county park is bordered on the west by the Pacific Ocean and on the northeast by Santa Rosa Creek. The park offers beautiful ocean and inland views, lawn, playground, horseshoe pits, barbecue, restrooms, and public swimming pool.

Shamel Park Pool
5455 Windsor Blvd.

(805) 781-5930

www.slocountyparks.com/facilities/pools.htm

$

From Highway 1 turn west onto Windsor Boulevard.

This county-operated pool offers public swimming from Memorial Day Weekend to Labor Day. Call ahead for hours.

Sheffield Street Reserve
End of Sheffield Street

(805) 927-2866

www.greenspacecambria.org

FREE!
From Highway 1 take Cambria Road, turn left onto Main Street, right onto Cornwall Street and right onto Sheffield Street.

This publicly accessible open space is designed to protect native Monterey Pine. No facilties.

Skate Park
1000 Main Street
(805) 927-7776
FREE!
From Highway 1 turn east onto Main Street.
Helmets are required for skaters of all ages at this free park. Riders 12 and under must also wear pads. From 10 a.m. to dusk, riders are invited to enjoy the features that include a 50-foot-by-100-foot half pipe and a pyramid.

Sterling Forest Preserve
Pineridge Drive between Ellis crossings
(805) 927-2866
www.greenspacecambria.org
FREE!
From Highway 1 turn westward onto Ardath Drive, turn sharply left onto Pineridge Drive and cross Ellis Avenue.
This Monterey pine preserve is a Greenspace-owned public space. No facilities.

Strawberry Canyon Preserve
Burton Drive
(805) 927-2866
www.greenspacecambria.org
FREE!
From Highway 1 turn south onto Burton Drive, then park near the Kay Street intersection.
Two parcels preserved by Greenspace, The Cambria Land Trust, provide public access to a beautiful, relatively easy, single-track path through the woodlands. The 16-acre property also includes benches along the way.

Wales Triangle Reserve
West end of Wales Road at St. James Road
(805) 927-2866
www.greenspacecambria.org
FREE!
From Highway 1 turn south onto Burton Drive, right onto Ardath Drive, left onto Benson Avenue, right onto Bixby Road which becomes Wales Road as it circles the park
This Greenspace/Cambria Land Trust property is maintained as a natural space offering trees and local flora. No facilities.

OTHER ADVENTURES
Covell's Pines by the Sea Ranch
5694 Bridge St.

(805) 927-3398

www.covellscaliforniaclydesdales.com

$$$

From Highway 1 turn east onto Main Street, then north onto Bridge Street.

This 2,000-acre ranch is home to Covell's California Clydesdales, the largest private breeder of Clydesdale horses in the Western United States. The large, peaceful horses made famous by a certain American beer company roam in 100-acre meadows overlooking the Pacific Ocean.

Jim Covell has been raising Clydesdales since 1978. He moved his operation to Cambria from Southern California in 1998. Today the working ranch with a history of turning out award-winning teams offers tours to groups of four or more by appointment only.

Nitwit Ridge (aka Nitt Witt Ridge)

881 Hillcrest Drive

(805) 927-2690

$

From Highway 1, turn east onto Main Street, then left onto Sheffield, left onto Cornwall and then right onto Hillcrest Drive.

For many, this structure behind chain-link fencing will seem like nothing but a pile of garbage loosely connected by smears and plops of cement. For others, Arthur Harold Beal's lifelong construction project and home may seem resourceful, even innovative.

Once the city's junk man, Beal, aka Tinkerpaw, called this block home from 1928 to 1989. He used toilet seats as picture frames, perhaps as much for political commentary as utility. Magazine wallpaper, plentiful outhouses and a cascading fountain made of sinks and bathtubs offer glimpses of his artsy side.

Locals differ over what the future should hold for this home made of pipe, beer cans, abalone shells, bottlecaps and other castoffs. For now, it's a registered California State Historical Landmark (No. 939) as a notable 20th Century folk art environment. Public tours are available by appointment only. Footing throughout is sketchy and there are many hazards throughout the structure, so keep a very short leash on children.

Chapter 13

San Simeon & Coastal Points North

This world-famous stretch of scenic Highway 1 is home to one of the country's most-visited tourist attractions: Hearst Castle. It also includes countless coves, sandy beaches, and historic points of interest. Bring binoculars for viewing plentiful wildlife, a picnic and jackets; brisk ocean breezes often blow along this stretch.

Written directions for each entry are unnecessary since all publicly accessible properties are directly off Highway 1.

ARTS

Hearst Castle Theater
Hearst Castle Visitors Center
Highway 1 about 7 miles north of Cambria
(805) 927-6811

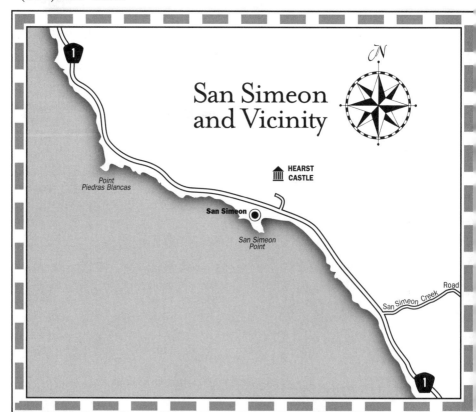

www.hearstcastletheater.com

$

This theater features the largest screen on the entire Central Coast. It's cinematic offerings include regular showings of "Hearst Castle: Building the Dream." Movies start hourly at 8:15 a.m. off season, more regularly during high season. The theater has also been used for special showings of other giant-screen presentations.

The lobby features exhibits highlighting county history and art. Access to the lobby exhibits is free.

HISTORY

Hearst Castle

Highway 1 about 7 miles north of Cambria

(805) 927-6811

www.hearstcastle.com

$$-$$$

Make reservations at least 10 days in advance if you're planning to tour this 90,000-square-foot home atop rolling coastal mountain foothills overlooking the San Simeon coastline.

It doesn't take a love of architecture, theater, sculpture, tapestry or wine to enjoy William Randolph Hearst's dream home. In fact, Hearst Castle, with its 56 bedrooms, 61 bathrooms, 41 fireplaces, 19 sitting rooms, three pools, tennis courts and zoo, seems a bit much, to say the least.

If the sight of all this development sickens the heart of some visitors, a stop in the sitting room of Casa del Mar holds the cure: a view that lifts the soul. Golden waves of grassland flow down the rolling foothills to sweeping views of the San Simeon coastline and Pacific Ocean. It's a view that has gone largely unchanged since George Hearst, William Randolph Hearst's father, began acquiring the land in 1865.

These days thousands of visitors each year pull off scenic Highway 1 into the ample parking lot at the castle's visitors' center. They meander through the gift shops, past the snack bar and Hearst Castle Theater to take bus rides up the hill. Once atop "La Cuesta Encantada" – the enchanted hill, as William Randolph Hearst called it – well-schooled castle docents provide a walking history of the property and its key players. They all have the details of their walking lectures down pat, but they are also open to questions, and seem to know all of the answers.

No single tour covers the entire 127-acre residential property. Instead, the hilltop estate is divided into four daily tours. Some cover portions of the large house, Casa Grande, while others focus on the wine cellar and gardens or the smaller Casa del Mar where W.R. Hearst spent his final days. All tours include stops at the absolutely magnificent 104-foot-long Neptune Pool. An self-guided Gardens & Vistas tour gives visitors relatively free rein over the grounds late afternoons Tuesday through Thursday, June to September.

The Hearst family enjoyed the property for more than half a century as a relatively rugged campsite where canvas tents atop platforms provided the peak of luxury. It wasn't until after 1919 when William Randolph inherited the 250,000-acre estate from his mother, Phoebe Apperson Hearst, that big changes began on the hill. It was then that the younger Hearst contracted with Julia Morgan for the construction of something a bit more comfortable.

George Hearst built his fortune in mining and ranching. Docents report that Hearst hoped his only child would take over those lucrative businesses, but William Randolph was only interested in taking over the family's newspaper – *San Francisco Examiner.*

Young Hearst built that single holding into a media empire that helped fund his 28-year love affair with the mountaintop project. Throughout construction, Hearst lived on the hill and served as editor-in-chief of his growing newspaper and magazine empire. Docents point out the desks at which Hearst read each publication when the ink was hardly dry – one at the foot of his enormous bed; another in the 4,000-plus-book library; others offering scenic views with a simple lift of his chin.

It is little wonder the property was so loved not only by Hearst, but also by visitors. Consideration was given not only to creating a picturesque, inviting atmosphere in the development of well-tended gardens, but Hearst and Morgan aspired to appeal to the artist, athlete and entertainer in each of his guests. He commissioned replicas of great sculptures and the construction of elaborately decorated swimming pools, complete with semi-private dressing rooms.

It is also little wonder that by the late 1930s Hearst's bankroll began to diminish and work on the castle project came to a standstill. In 1957, the Hearst Corporation deeded the castle and adjacent property to the State of California, and today it is one of the largest of 5,000 historic "house museums" in the country.

The Hearst Corporation presented the property to the state in 1958 as a memorial. It has since been designated California State Historic Monument No. 6405.

Hearst Castle Visitor Center
Highway 1 about 7 miles north of Cambria
(800) 444-4445 (reservations)
www.hearstcastle.com
FREE!
Located on the marine terrace well below William Randolph Hearst's castle is a large visitors center. Docent-led tours leave from this center, but it also serves as a free informational center with views of the castle, picnic areas and hugely overpriced, mediocre food. This is also the staging area for docent-led tours of Piedras Blancas Light Station (next entry).

☞ Piedras Blancas Light Station
15950 Cabrillo Highway (Highway 1)
www.piedras blancas.gov
(805) 927-7361
$

The lighthouse, now under the jurisdiction of the U.S. Bureau of Land Management, served as a beacon to ships passing this rocky coastline from 1875 until 1949 when a storm damaged the lantern room and its original Fresnel lens. The lens was removed, the tower capped and a rotating beacon placed on its top. The station was completely automated in 1975. A two-story Victorian-style home that served as the first keepers' residence was later moved to Cambria to serve as a private home.

The only way to access the lighthouse and the point now is via docent-led tours on Tuesday, Thursday and Saturday throughout the year (except federal holidays). Reservations are only required for groups of 10 or more visitors. The 2-hour tours depart at 9:45 a.m. from Piedras Blancas Motel 1½ miles north of the lighthouse. The walks include discussions about the lighthouse, its purposes and people. Botany is also frequent topics of discussion as is area wildlife, including migrating whales which can be seen from this point that juts out into the Pacific Ocean.

The unpaved pathways are fairly easy, but wear sturdy shoes and always be prepared for cool coastal breezes. Free to children 5 and younger.

Sebastian Store
San Simeon Road
(805) 927-3307
www.ohp.parks.ca.gov
FREE!
The oldest store building along the county's north coast still stands, though half a mile from its original location which was at Whaling Point. The store was built in the 1860s, and moved to its present location in 1878. Today the store and related café offer convenience items for visitors as well as a full kitchen and a storied menu. Kitchen opens at 11 a.m. Wednesdays through Sundays.

NATURE
California Coastal National Monument Discovery Center
William Randolph Hearst Memorial State Beach
5 miles south of Hearst Castle on Highway 1
(805) 927-2145
Montereybay.noaa.gov/vc/cdc
FREE!

In January 2000, the entire length of California's coastline was designated the California Coastal National Monument in an effort to preserve islands, rocks, exposed reefs and pinnacles. The Discovery Center provides public education about the shore and waters extending 12 nautical miles into the Pacific Ocean.

Hearst - San Simeon State Park
5 miles south of Hearst Castle on Highway 1
(805)927-2035
www.parks.ca.gov/?page_id=590
FREE!

A conservation deal with Hearst Ranch at the turn of the 21st Century added 949 acres to this, one of the oldest state parks in the system. The new portion— 13 miles of coastline stretching from San Simeon to San Carpoforo Creek just south of the county line — expanded the park to 2,280 acres. Nearly half a dozen entry points are planned for development in coming years including a turnstile at Arroyo Laguna Seca, a popular windsurfing area. Other access points may include Lone Palm Drive, San Simeon Acres, Arroyo de la Cruz and San Carpoforo Creek. There are rumors that a coastal trail will stretch the entire distance.

Until then, take advantage of the trails, campgrounds and breathtaking scenery throughout the established park areas including: **Santa Rosa Creek Natural Preserve**, 40 acres of forests and wetlands; **San Simeon Natural Preserve**, 365 acres of wetlands; and **Pa-nu Cultural Preserve**, a 13.7-acre archeological site dated to 5,580 years ago. The most accessible route is the 3.3-mile trail through San Simeon Natural Preserve and Washburn Campground. It includes views, benches and interpretive signs.

Drive north of the village of San Simeon to discover **Pico Cove**. A very small dirt parking lot about a quarter mile north of San Simeon provides docent-led access to the trailhead for ½ mile of rugged, largely unmaintained, blufftop trails overlooking Pico Cove. Access to the protected beach below is hazardous at best.

Further north, and immediately south of **Ragged Point**, is a fantastic stretch of sand with beautiful coastal views. State parks plans include developing legal, docent-led access to this previously privately held land and some 2 miles of trails, including two, ¼-mile trails connecting the beach to trailheads at Highway 1. Ragged Point itself also offers self-guided trail access ranging from the easy loop through the landscaped bluff to the treacherous trail down to the cove north of the point.

Camping is also available in this expansive park at **San Simeon Creek Campgrounds** (115 sites for tents or RVs up to 35 feet, flush toilets, coin-op showers, dump station, pay phones) and **Washburn Campground** (primitive campground 1 mile east of Highway 1, chemical toilets, water spigots, dump station). Check with park staff for junior ranger programs, docent-led hikes and regularly scheduled campfire programs.

Pico Avenue Coastal Access
Pico Avenue
FREE!
From Highway 1 turn west onto Pico Avenue
This long sandy stretch is also known for its tide pools.

☞ Piedras Blancas elephant seals
Point Piedras Blancas, 11.7 miles north of Cambria on Hwy 1
elephant seal.org
(805) 924-1628
FREE!
A pair of two-ton elephant seal bulls lunge toward each other. Their bodies slam together, emitting a dull thud. Before backing away, they bite savagely at each other's neck as they battle for the harem resting a dozen feet away on shore. Wind-whipped waves crash on sand and rock, threatening

the infant seals that are born unable to swim. Some mother seals encourage their babies to move further inland while others struggle to push their sinking babies back to shore. A few others continue in a fruitless search for those seal pups already washed too far out to sea.

January marks birthing season at Piedras Blancas elephant seal rookery. Visitors to this stretch of sand just north of San Simeon can witness first hand the circle of life, for better or worse.

That elephant seals continue to exist is a miracle in itself, docents gleefully explain to visitors. The animals, sought for their blubber, were hunted nearly to extinction as the 19th Century drew to its close. Docents say that in 1908, Smithsonian scientists found eight elephant seals on an island off the coast of Mexico. Thinking these were the last of the species, they slaughtered the animals and shipped the remains to the museum for research and display.

Jump ahead to a morning in 1990. A marine biologist researching otters along the Central Coast stepped out for his morning walk along the bluffs only to discover more than a dozen elephant seals on shore. Those allegedly extinct giants of the sea not only had survived but had made a comeback.

Today, an estimated 7,000 elephant seals stop at Piedras Blancas each year on their trek between San Nicholas Island off Los Angeles and the Farallon Islands north of San Francisco. They mate here, bear their pups here, molt and learn life lessons here.

Onshore, elephant seals look like large, inanimate blobs of blubber. They spend most of their onshore time resting or nursing their young. Spend a bit more time and you'll see they flip sand onto themselves and each other to keep cool or express nervousness; hear their strange calls to each other; and see them head out to sea to fish, fight or play.

While they appear unable to move quickly on shore, elephant seals can in fact charge quite quickly and forcefully with little or no notice. In years past, uneducated visitors have attempted to place their children on and next to the hulking beasts for photos – a dangerous proposition for man and beast. Fences have been erected to help human visitors keep their distance. Wooden boardwalks provide relatively safe viewing.

From the inland side of the fence, the docents drop tidbits of information as they walk from visitor to visitor. The female elephant seals are generally only about one-third the weight of their 3,000 to 5,000 pound male counterparts. Babies are 60 pounds at birth and unable to fish or swim. They nurse onshore for three weeks, by which time they have grown to some 200 pounds. The mothers then simply swim away, leaving the babies to learn to swim and fish on their own. Pups remain at the beach through March nursing, weaning, learning to swim and feed before beginning their own migration.

☞ W.R. Hearst Memorial State Beach
5 miles south of Hearst Castle on Highway 1
www.slostateparks.com/hearst_memorial
(805) 927-2020
FREE!

Hearst Memorial State Beach was home to William Randolph Hearst's own private pier from whence he stocked his famous hilltop estate. The beach and bay are well protected by San Simeon Point, which makes the area ideal for kayakers.

Hearst's previously private south-facing hideaway protected in its little cove is superb for families. Stretch out on the sand, have a picnic in the grassy park, or grab a rod and take a walk on this 795-foot public pier for a bit of fishing. No license is required, though all fishing regulations are in effect. The area is nice for long walks on the beach, tide pooling, kayaking in the bay and body boarding.

For a more energetic adventure, take the 1.5-mile San Simeon Point trail. The trailhead, at the west end of the parking lot and just above the west end of San Simeon Cove's sandy bits, leads to a relatively easy, dirt path through a forest of cedar, eucalyptus, cypress and Monterey Pine to dramatic San Simeon Point. Bring binoculars during whale migration for some great views. No dogs, picnics, fires, bicycles, motorized vehicles or alcohol are allowed on the point trails.

This park is open daily until sunset. Restrooms are available.

Chapter 14

Santa Margarita

You might not know it to look at little Santa Margarita today, but in the late 18th Century, this community was integral to the California mission system. In 1878, church officials decided this spot between Mission San Luis Obispo de Tolosa and Mission San Miguel was just the place for Santa Margarita de Cortona assistencia, a mission-like facility designed to indoctrinate area Chumash people while extending the church's ranching lands. Mexican independence in 1822 led to secularization of the mission system, and in 1841 the land was granted to Joaquin Estrada. Today, the remaining adobe walls of California State Historical Landmark No. 364 stand protected inside a large barn at private Rancho Santa Margarita.

Fifty years later Santa Margarita was in the limelight again. From 1889 to 1894, this was the end of the line for the northern half of the state's coastal rail system. Real estate speculators tried to cash in on the Cuesta Grade tunneling and bridge project which eventually linked northern and southern California and returned Santa Margarita to rurality.

Today, the small town off Highway 101 just north of Cuesta Grade is a stepping off point for backcountry adventures, whether on foot, on horseback, via off-highway vehicle or family van. A handful of locally owned businesses provide gas, food and other basic services. Don't expect any old chain standbys here anytime soon.

LETTERS

Santa Margarita Library
9630 Murphy Ave.
(805) 438-5622
slolibrary.org/branch.htm

FREE!

From Highway 101 turn east onto Highway 58 toward Santa Margarita, turn right onto Yerba Buena Avenue, left onto I Street, then left onto Murphy Avenue.

This branch of the San Luis Obispo County Library system is open from noon to 6 p.m. Tuesday through Thursday. Staff provides preschool story time at 11:30 a.m. Thursday and there are summer reading programs for adults and kids alike. This library also offers summer special events.

NATURE

Blue Sky Gardens
19505 Walnut Ave. (Garden Farms)
(805) 438-5801
www.blueskygardens.sanityonline.com
FREE!
Hwy 101 to Santa Margarita exit. After passing through Santa Margarita

continue 1 mile to Linden. Turn left onto Linden, then follow the posted signs.

This family-owned farm welcomes picnickers to enjoy its lawn or stop by to visit the animals. It also offers special events and pick-your-own fruits and vegetables in season including: blackberries, apples, tomatoes, pears and cherries in June and July; pumpkin patch, corn made and haunted house in October. Fresh eggs are also on sale and farm animals are available for viewing.

The owner said she does her best to keep the place organic. No sprays are used on berries, and all weeding is done by hand or by rototilling.

Lazy Arrow Outdoor Adventures

9330 Camatta Creek Road

Between Santa Margarita and California Valley/Carizzo Plain

(805) 238-7324

lazyarrowadventures.com

$$$

From Highway 101 take the Highway 58/Santa Margarita exit. Continue on Highway 58 east out of town, through Calf Canyon and past La Panza Road. Turn left onto Shell Creek Road, then right onto Camatta Creek Road.

The 32,000-acre Camatta Ranch offers cattle drives semi-annually, fishing, tours, camping, guesthouse accommodations, barbecues, horseshoes, all by reservation.

Railhead Arena

2750 I Street

(805) 467-3535

$$$

From Highway 101 take the Santa Margarita exit and proceed east toward town. Turn right onto Wilhelmina and follow the road as it curves left and becomes I Street.

The Railhead Riders maintain this arena on leased property. The arena is open for use by members (membership is $100 per year/family; $75 for individuals) on weekdays and odd weekends, and gymkhanas are held here on the second Saturday of every month. There is no fee to watch.

Rinconada Mine Trail

Connecting Highway 58 to Hi Mountain Ridge

Tinyurl.com/3charzb

FREE!

From Highway 101 take the Highway 58/Santa Margarita exit. Continue on Highway 58 east out of town. Continue straight onto West Pozo Road. The trailhead is on the right past Las Pilitas Road.

A strenuous trail to the old Rinconada Mine site offers a good starting or ending point for a full day's adventure for big kids and their adult chaperones. Hike, bike or ride horseback 2 miles up the well-maintained, steep, rugged trail to the ridge. Return via the same trail to the car or turn left on the ridge road and travel 7 miles to Hi Mountain Condor Lookout. Or drop down the other side into picturesque Upper Lopez Canyon via Big Falls or Little Falls trails (no bicycles allowed on these trails). Another option is to make a loop ride of it by traveling up the Rinconada Trail, east along the Hi Mountain Lookout fire road, then north along Hi Mountain Road to Pozo with a paved return to the trailhead.

Santa Margarita Community Forest

2000 block of H St.

(805) 543-9319

www.smcf.org

FREE!

From Highway 101 take the Highway 58/Santa Margarita exit.

Local residents have worked since 1996 to preserve and augment the trees and native plants throughout Santa Margarita. An easy trail through a small park adjacent to the school offers a brief education about common native plants complete with signage. Go online for a copy of the group's tree walk map (www.smcf.org/tree_walk).

Volunteers also work with local schools on various woodland ecological projects.

☞ Santa Margarita Community Park

Corner of H Street and Estrada Avenue/Highway 58

(805) 781-5930

www.slocountyparks.com/facilities/communityparks.htm

FREE!

From Highway 101 take the Highway 58/Santa Margarita exit.

Don't be fooled by the view from Highway 58. What appears to be a tiny roadside park is actually a surprisingly large park for such a small town. Amenities include Western-themed play structures, a restroom, sandbox, swings, gazebo, a bridge over a seasonal creek, a large turf area, picnic area and large barbecue pit

☞ Santa Margarita Lake Regional Park

4695 Santa Margarita Lake Road

(805) 788-2397; Marina Store (805) 438-1522

www.slocountyparks.com/activities/santa_margarita.htm

www.slocountyparks.com/facilities/pools.htm (pool info)

$

From Highway 101 take the Highway 58/Santa Margarita exit. Continue on Highway 58 east out of town. Continue straight onto West Pozo Road, then left onto Santa Margarita Lake Road.

Though most notable for its lake, a key source of water for San Luis Obispo, the 7,100-acre park includes campgrounds, a pool and trails available for hikers, mountain bikers and equestrians. Though no body

contact with the water is allowed, the lake is available for boating and fishing. A pool provides for refreshing dips Memorial Day to Labor Day.

The lake was created in 1941 by the construction of Salinas Dam as a water source for Camp San Luis Obispo. In 1957 the park opened for boating and fishing. Camping is now available, too, including 60 sites in four campgrounds (Coyote, Roadrunner, Grey Pine and Osprey) where showers and flush toilets are available.

Santa Margarita Natural Area, the primary hiking, biking and horseback riding area, is at the east end of the lake. Take West Pozo Road 8 miles east. Turn left on River Road. The entrance is on the left 2 miles down. This is also the trailhead to the park's two primitive camping areas, Sapwi and Khus, which are available for boat-in or pack-in camping.

There are several trails in the park. We particularly enjoy the Rocky Trail, a moderately strenuous, largely single-track, out-and-back trail through oak forest along the lake's western shore. Over the course of 1.8 miles, it climbs just 300 feet in elevation to a wide spot from which talk folks may view Salinas Dam and the rest of us enjoy 360-degree views of rural San Luis Obispo County. Vaca Flat provides a relatively easy, 2.6-mile, multi-use route with restrooms along the way. Nearby Grey Pine Trail offers a 3.7-mile, moderately strenuous loop for equestrian and pedestrian use. This route incorporates higher elevations, more single track and offers a few cutoffs for early return to your starting point.

An additional trail system accessible from River Road (east of the main park entrance) offers more solitary routes. Sandstone Trail is a moderately strenuous, multi-use, 5.4-mile out-and-back along the lake's southeastern shore. Blinn Ranch Trail is an 18-mile, moderately strenuous, out-and-back route along the lake's northern shore. It offers multi-use access the Sapwi

Trail which hosts the boat-in/pack-in Sapwi and Khus camping areas. Blinn Ranch Trail also provides access to the very strenuous, 5.6-mile Falcon Trail which climbs up Cold Canyon, meanders among the northern peaks and ridges, then descends back down to Blinn toward the dam.

☞ Wildflower romp on Shell Creek Road
FREE!

From Highway 101 take the Highway 58/Santa Margarita exit. Continue on Highway 58 east out of town, through scenic Calf Canyon and past La Panza Road. Turn left onto Shell Creek Road.

Some of the most spectacular wildflower viewing in San Luis Obispo County can be found up this rural road north of Los Padres National Forest. The meadows and hillsides explode into a natural bouquet of native flowers. Take the drive in late spring for best viewing.

Tidy tips are among the wildflowers that about in eastern SLO County.

Chapter 15

Points East: Pozo & Carrizo Plain

Downtown Pozo, such that it is, passes in the blink of an eye. The town, if you can call it that, is only a block long and a block and a half deep if you include the California Department of Forestry Fire Department around the corner from the main street. Atop a nearby hill, an abandoned schoolhouse keeps watch over the crossroads and tavern.

Pozo offers a wrinkle in the fabric of normalcy: mountain bikers and dirt bikers rub shoulders, little old men out for a Sunday drive play horseshoes with long-haired motorcyclists, children run in the sun or stretch out in the shade of very old oak trees. It's little known, but worth a stop.

Further east, the Carrizo Plain is one of San Luis Obispo County's least traveled, most natural remaining places. The 50-mile-long narrow valley is bordered on the east by the Temblor Range and San Andreas Fault and on the west by the Caliente Range. It is home to expansive ranches, secluded homes and Carrizo Plain National Monument.

The peace of the valley is timeless, but some of the best seasons to visit are winter for raptor and sand hill crane viewing and late spring when the valley explodes into a bouquet of wildflowers. Though the valley is expansive, there are no services: no gas stations; no restaurants. Restrooms are available seasonally at the Goodwin Education Center (p. 179). Plan accordingly.

LETTERS

Simmler Public Library
13080 Soda Lake Road
(805) 475-2603

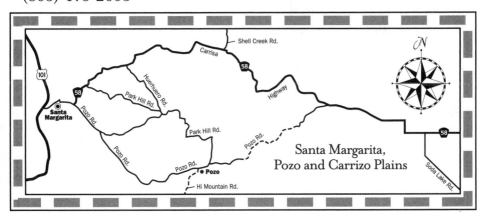

slolibrary.org/branch.htm

FREE!

From 101, take the Santa Margarita/Highway 58 exit and head east through town. Just past downtown Santa Margarita, turn right across the railroad tracks and follow Highway 58 about 35 miles to California Valley. Turn south onto Soda Lake Road.

You never know when you might run out of reading material, or just need a quiet break for the family. The county library system provides for such times, even in communities as remote as this.

This small branch of the San Luis Obispo County Library system offers summer reading programs for kids and limited hours year round.

NATURE

Caliente Ridge/Caliente Peak

Selby Road & Caliente Ridge Road

(661) 391-6000

www.blm.gov/ca//bakersfield/calientemtn.html

FREE!

From Highway 58 turn south onto Soda Lake Road and continue about 15 miles. Turn west onto Selby Road and follow the dirt road about 5 miles to the locked gate at the ridge.

This rural ridge offers plentiful quiet saddles and peaks with views spanning as far east as the Sierra Nevada and west to the Sierra Madre. Traffic is minimal here due to extreme off-the-beaten-path location, but the ridge is readily accessible via a well-maintained dirt road.

Once parked along the ridge, take a rugged stroller, mountain bike or hike along the ridge as it dips and rises 8 miles east to Caliente Peak, the highest peak in San Luis Obispo County. Reaching the peak is not for the average youngster, but keen teens may be able to tackle it. The ridge offers loads of beautiful picnic spots, birding opportunities and family photo ops.

☞ Carrizo Plain National Monument

Btwn. Hwy. 166 and wy. 58, both sides of Soda Lake Road

(805) 475-2131 (seasonal)

tinyurl.com/6o72qv

FREE!

From 101, take the Santa Margarita/Highway 58 exit and head east through town. Just past downtown Santa Margarita, turn right across the railroad tracks and follow Highway 58 about 35 miles to California Valley. Turn south onto Soda Lake Road.

The 250,000-acre monument was set aside in 2001 after generations of families farmed and ranched in this remote valley that separates the coast from the central valley. It is home to more than half a dozen species of unusual, endangered or threatened animals including: San Joaquin kit fox, the California condor, the blunt-nosed leopard lizard, the giant

kangaroo rat, the San Joaquin antelope squirrel, the longhorn fairy shrimp and the vernal pool fairy shrimp. The list of plants growing in the valley is huge, but unusual, rare and endangered specimens found here include: astragalus, spiny-sepaled button celery, pale-yellow layia, forked fiddleneck, Jared's peppergrass, Lost Hills crownscale, San Joaquin bluecurls, Hoover's eriastrum, cottony buckwheat, temblor buckwheat, hollisteria, gypsum-loving larkspur, oval-leaved snapdragons, stinkbells, Kern tarplant, California jewelflower, Hoover's wooly-star and San Joaquin woolythreads (source: BLM Bakersfield office).

The valley is riddled with archaeological remnants of Chumash, Yokuts and Silanan tribes who called this valley home. The most publicized is **Painted Rock**. From Highway 58, travel south on Soda Lake Road 14 miles to the **Goodwin Education Center** on Painted Rock Road. The center is open December through May, Thursday through Sunday from 9 a.m. to 4 p.m. Access to the rock is limited: self-guided tours by permit only July 16 through the end of February; closed March 1 to July 15 except to guided tours provided by center staff mid-March through May. Climbing on, touching or otherwise defacing the rock and its artwork is prohibited, as are bicycles, dogs, horses or any other pets.

For a long scenic drive in good weather, take the 70-mile Soda Lake, Elkhorn Plain, and Seven Mile roads loop. These roads are unpaved and the clay from which they are carved is dangerously slippery when wet. In good weather, they provide sufficient surface for most street vehicles and provide access to some of the monument's official points of interest. Stops on the loop include Goodwin Center and Painted Rock as well as:

Soda Lake Boardwalk – *About 9 miles south of Highway 58 on the east side of Soda Lake Road.* A short dirt path leads to a wooden boardwalk that extends along the oft-squishy banks of one of the largest remaining natural alkali wetlands in California.

Soda Lake Viewpoint – *About 9 miles from Highway 58 turn right onto the dirt spur road.* The road circles around the back of Overlook Hill where there is ample parking. A short uphill hike on a dirt path leads to a saddle between two low peaks. The splendid view of the valley includes the Soda

Lake Boardwalk almost directly across Soda Lake Road. For more expansive views, continue north or south along the ridge trail to its termini where additional information signs are posted.

Wallace Creek – *From Highway 58, turn right on Seven Mile Road. Continue about ½ mile, then turn left onto Elkhorn Road and continue south about 4 miles to a clearly marked parking area.* Interpretive signs along this easy, ½-mile out-and-back trail explain how and why Wallace Creek shifted 30 feet in a single day as the San Andreas Fault over which it passes moved in a massive quake. The dirt trail is not stroller friendly but does include a child-friendly mellow climb.

The monument welcomes recreational activities including mountain biking, hiking, road biking, birding, horseback riding and wildlife viewing. Campers are also welcome. There are 12 primitive camp sites offering picnic tables, fire pits and portable toilets but no potable water at Kern County Land Company (KCL) Ranch 10.4 miles south of Goodwin Center. Selby Ranch offers 13 primitive sites, portable toilets, no water and no shade up Selby Road about 8/10-mile south of Goodwin Center. Open camping is allowed generally in the foothills and mountainous areas.

Hi Mountain Road
(805) 925-9538

Tinyurl.com/3bs2u8g

FREE!/$

From Highway 101 take the Santa Margarita exit and proceed east through town. Turn right onto Highway 58. About 2 miles out of town the road splits. Don't follow Highway 58 left, but continue straight onto Pozo Road.

Across the headwaters of the Salinas River is a well-established dirt road through Los Padres National Forest. The area includes trails, dirt roads, four-wheel-drive trails, motorcycle trails, campgrounds and a California condor lookout. See entry for Los Padres National Forest in the Arroyo Grande chapter (p. 101) for more details. An Adventure Pass (p. 9) is required in this area.

Pozo/La Panza Off-highway vehicle Area
(805) 925-9538

Tinyurl.com/3o8llot

$

From Highway 101 take Highway 58 east. Continue well out of Santa Margarita. At the Y, continue straight onto Pozo Road, and continue past the Pozo Saloon.

As motorcycle and four-wheel-drive roads and trails become increasingly scarce on the Central Coast, this area becomes more popular. More than 44 miles of trails lead adventurers into the forest, along ridges and to more remote trailheads for backcountry getaways. The Pozo/La Panza area of the Santa Lucia Ranger District includes 18,867 acres of wild space. An Adventure Pass (p. 9) is required..

Camping is available at Turkey Flat and Navajo Flat, though there are

other smaller sites throughout this recreation area. Trails include the relatively flat La Canada Trail along a riverbottom to the experts-only Stair Steps challenge along Pine Mountain Road.

A sturdy fence keeps motorists along Pine Ridge out of Machesna Mountain Wilderness, home of Castle Crags, a nesting site for the endangered California condor. But the abandoned road makes for an exceptionally pleasant and lengthy hike along the ridge and through Coulter pine forest.

OTHER ADVENTURES

Pozo Saloon
90 West Pozo Road
(805) 438-4225
www.pozosaloon.com
FREE!

From Highway 101 take Highway 58 east. Continue well out of Santa Margarita. At the Y, continue straight onto Pozo Road.

To feel this rural community's heartbeat, stop by the saloon. Despite its name, the popular establishment is quite family friendly with good barbecue, cold drinks for all ages, indoor seating and outdoor dining under expansive oak trees. Summer weekends bring live music to the back deck and concerts are held with increasing frequency.

Chapter 16

Atascadero

Once a small town serving cowboys in northern San Luis Obispo County, Atascadero is a growing family-friendly community. Coastal mountain ranges protect this and other North County communities from the Pacific's marine layer, bringing much warmer summer weather than in communities in the south county or along the coast.

ARTS

Galaxy Colony Square Theatres
6917 El Camino Real
(805) 466-8437
$

From northbound Highway 101 take the Highway 41/Morro Road exit, turn right at the end of the ramp onto Highway 41, then left onto El Camino Real. From southbound Highway 101 take the Traffic Way exit, turn left onto Traffic Way, then right onto El Camino Real.

This new theater offers stadium-style seating, 10 screens, 3-D potential and a VIP Lounge for customers 21 and over.

Envisions Gallery
5975 Traffic Way
(805) 466-5850
FREE!

From Highway 101 take the Traffic Way exit and proceed east.

In 2010, this gallery opened its doors to provide local and international artists a venue for their works. The commercial gallery offers paintings, photographs, glass works, pottery, jewelry and bronze works as well as mixed media.

The ARTery
5890 Traffic Way
(805) 464-0533
FREE!

From Highway 101 take the Traffic Way exit and proceed east.

This commercial frame shop that celebrates art in all of its forms – from traditional to downright odd – also houses a gallery which offers four art shows each year.

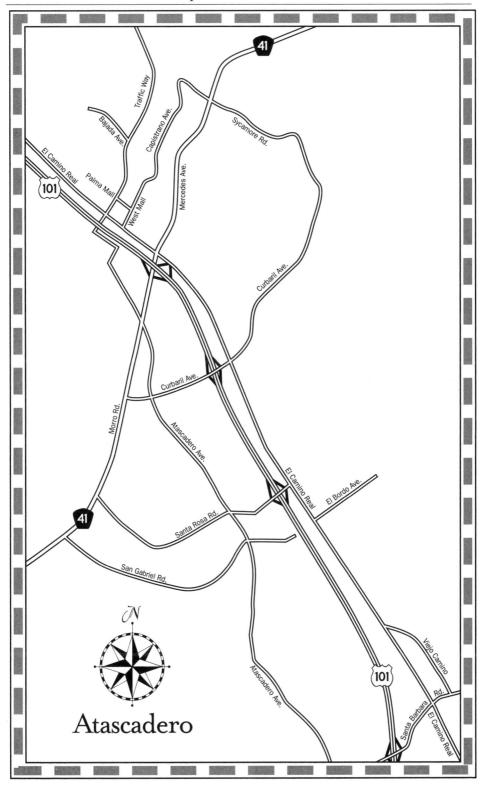

LETTERS

Atascadero – Martin Polin Regional Library

6850 Morro Road (6555 Capistrano Ave. from 2013)

(805) 461-6161

slolibrary.org/branch.htm

FREE!

From Highway 101 take the Highway 41/Morro Road exit. Turn west onto Morro Road.

Active supporters of this branch of the San Luis Obispo County Library system have helped raise funds to move this library to a larger location in 2013. Meanwhile, in addition to the books, magazines, CDs and DVDs available on free loan, the branch offers monthly family programs, a book discussion group the first Tuesday of each month, summer reading programs for adults and children alike and preschool story time Wednesday and Thursday. The library is open Tuesday through Saturday.

HISTORY

Atascadero Administration Rotunda

6500 Palma Ave

(805) 461-5000

www.atascadero.org/?page_id=2786

FREE!

From northbound Highway 101 take the Highway 41/Morro Road exit, turn right at the end of the ramp onto Highway 41, then left onto El Camino Real, then right onto East Mall Road and then left onto Palma Ave.. From southbound Highway 101 take the Traffic Way exit, turn left onto Traffic Way, then right onto Palma Avenue.

Northeast of the city's sunken garden, just off El Camino Real is one of Atascadero's most historical structures. The rotunda, built from 1914 to 1918 of reinforced concrete and locally produced brick, has served as the headquarters for Edward G. Lewis' model community, Atascadero Colony as the town was originally known. The building has also served as a private school for boys, a veterans' memorial building, county offices and city offices. The site was named California State Historical Landmark No. 958 before it was heavily damaged in the 2003 Paso Robles earthquake, leaving the Atascadero Historical Museum which it houses closed indefinitely. (For museum updates, call 466-8529.)

Estrada Adobe

3805 Traffic Way

(805) 461-5000

From Highway 101 take the Traffic Way exit and proceed east.

At publication time, this 5.7-acre, city-owned property was closed to public access, but the city has plans to develop a historic park around this home, among the first adobe structures in North County. Meanwhile, the city is working with the Atascadero Native Tree Association to protect, preserve and restore the property. In future, it may be open for public tours and recreation.

Amigos de Anza and Paso Robles Trails Association

Multiple accesses

(805) 461-5000

www.nps.gov/juba

FREE!

Pick up a trail guide from Atascadero, Paso Robles and San Luis Obispo chambers of commerce or Atascadero Recreation Department to begin exploring the route traveled by Juan Bautista de Anza in 1775-76. He led 30 soldiers and their families along this trail in search of a route to the San Francisco Bay. Today, the city welcomes visitors to explore more than 5 miles of trail along the Salinas River by foot, bicycle or horseback. No motorized vehicles are allowed, no fires, no camping.

There are two key trailheads: County Maintenance Yard, 6805 Sycamore; Wranglerette Arena, 7785 Aragon. Since the total length of the trail is more than 1,000 miles, the parks service offers an online junior ranger program. For more information go to www.anzajuniorranger.org.

NATURE

Anza Arena

1405 N. Ferrocarril Road

www.atascadero.org

FREE!

From Highway 101 take Santa Cruz Road east, turn left onto El Camino Real and right onto Ferrocarril Road.

This public equestrian arena includes ample parking for trucks and trailers and provides access to the Juan Bautista de Anza Trail. The arena is regularly used for practice and gymkhanas.

Atascadero High School Swimming Pool

1 High School Hill

(805) 470-3472

tinyurl.com/3cx51re

$

From Highway 101 take Traffic Way exit, turn west onto Traffic Way/Santa Lucia Road, immediately left onto Ardilla Road, then right onto Atascadero Mall which becomes High School Hill Road.

The high school's pool is sometimes used for summer lessons and recreational swimming through the city recreation department.

Apple Valley Park

1980 San Ramon Road

(805) 461-5000

www.atascadero.org

FREE!

From Highway 101 take Del Rio Road west, then turn left onto San Ramon.
This open space offers room to run or throw around the Frisbee. A well-maintained, tree-lined path is a fun spot for young tricyclists and bicyclists to get in some miles, and there are shaded picnic benches. No restrooms.

☞ Atascadero Lake Park

9305 Pismo Avenue

(805) 461-5000

tinyurl.com/3m2eoxh

FREE!

From Highway 101 head west on Highway 41/Morro Road.
The namesake of this 25-acre park is open year round for rowing, paddling and fishing, but no swimming. Large play structures, swings, sand volleyball court, and wooded lawns provide active entertainment. The park also boasts multiple picnic areas, large barbecue pits, restrooms, a gazebo, and a public wading pool that is open summers only. (tinyurl.com/3cx51re)

The park is a popular place for parties, but reservations are required to ensure access to a group area. The city also hosts free public concerts in the park every Tuesday evening during summer months. The neighboring Charles Paddock Zoo (p. 190) is an added attraction. Kayaks are available for rent during spring weekends and all summer.

Colony Park
5599 Traffic Way
(805) 461-5000
www.atascadero.org
FREE!
From Highway 101 take Traffic Way exit, and turn east onto Traffic Way.
This is a 3-acre park adjacent to Colony Park Community Center & Pavilion (p. 187) offers two softball fields, a children's play area with structures, a full basketball court and a half court as well as restrooms.

Colony Park Community Center & Pavilion
5599 Traffic Way
(805) 470-3472
www.atascadero.org
FREE!
From Highway 101 take the Traffic Way exit and proceed east on Traffic Way.
This 17,250-square-foot public facility includes gymnasium, arts and crafts room, dance and exercise rooms, meeting room, teen center and café. The center is adjacent to Colony Park (p. 187) and a planned swimming complex on two additional acres.

Chalk Mountain Golf Course
10000 El Bordo Rd.
(805) 466-8848
chalkmountaingolf.com
$$-$$$
From Highway 101 take the Santa Rosa Road exit and turn east. Turn right onto El Camino Real, then left onto El Bordo Avenue.
This 18-hole public golf course offers year-round play, a driving range, club rental, cart rental, an onsite golf pro and full restaurant. Oak trees line the narrow fairways of this hilly course bordering Heilmann Regional Park (p. 187).

Happy Grapes
13005 Salinas Road
(805) 462-0347
FREE!
From Highway 101 take Santa Barbara Road west. Turn right onto El Camino Real, left onto Santa Clara Road, then left onto Salinas Road.
Pick your own Thompson seedless grapes at this farm that opens to the public September and October weekends.

☞ Heilmann Regional Park
9400 El Bordo Avenue

(805) 781-5930

www.slocountyparks.com/facilities/regionalparks.htm

FREE!

From Highway 101 take the Santa Rosa Road exit and turn east. Turn right onto El Camino Real, then left onto El Bordo Avenue.

Although the park is well signed, visitors are unlikely to happen upon this expansive stretch of green that is hidden from the main drag by a neighborhood, hill and dale. But this park is well worth seeking out.

The oak-studded rolling hills of this 37-acre park adjacent to Chalk Mountain Golf Course (p. 186) host a flying disc golf course, lighted tennis courts, Heilmann Off-leash Dog park (461-5749), play structures, swings, restrooms and spraying jets of cool water that invite visitors to splash throughout the hot summer months. The park also includes three main trails including: Blue Oak Trail, an easy, 1.3-mile multi-use trail; Jim Green Trail, a 1.7-mile, moderately strenuous trail that connects hikers and equestrian users to the park from neighborhoods to the north; and a stretch of the 5.8-mile-long Juan Bautista de Anza Trail, an easy multi-use trail.

Hidden Springs Tree Farm

3202 Monterey Road

(805) 466-2220

FREE!

From Highway 101 take the San Anselmo Road exit. Turn west onto San Anselmo Road, then right onto Monterey Road.

This family-owned tree farm offers locally grown fruits and vegetables, snacks and other refreshments daily most of the year. Trees go on sale the first Saturday after Thanksgiving.

Kennedy Club Fitness Center Pool

3534 El Camino Real

(805) 466-6775

www.kennedyclubs.com/Atascadero

$$

From Highway 101 take the Del Rio Road exit east, then turn right onto El Camino Real.

Although this fitness club promotes membership, it also provides public access to its aquatic facilities for a fee. The club offers a youth swim team, water polo team, springboard diving lessons and water safety courses including lifeguard training. It is also available for lap swim.

Paloma Creek Park

11665 Viejo Camino

(805) 461-5000

www.atascadero.org

FREE!

From Highway 101 take the Atascadero Road/Santa Barbara Road exit. Turn east onto Santa Barbara Road. Jog slightly left across El Camino Real and continue east on Santa Barbara Road, then turn left onto Viejo Camino.

This 23-acre neighborhood park offers a picnic area, play structures, soccer fields, two lighted softball fields, little league fields, horseshoe pits, a large barbecue pit, and restrooms. It also includes Miles Wemp Arena, a public equestrian arena.

Stadium Park

Capistrano Avenue at Hospital Drive

(805) 461-5000

www.atascadero.org

FREE!

From Highway 101 take the Highway 41/Morro Road exit. Turn east onto Highway 41, then left onto Capistrano Avenue. Park in the dirt lot at Hospital Drive, then follow the footpath under Highway 41.

This natural amphitheatre in the middle of town offers 5 acres of natural space to explore and several established trails. The Marj Mackey Trail is a relatively easy jaunt from the park entrance into the natural amphitheater/bowl. From the bowl take either the moderately strenuous Blue Oak Trail, or cowboy up for a tougher adventure with a view on Pine Mountain Loop Trail. No restrooms.

Sunken Gardens Park

6500 block El Camino Real

(805) 461-5000

www.atascadero.org

FREE!

From Highway 101 take the Traffic Way exit, turn east onto Traffic Way, then right onto El Camino Real.

The 2-acre park in front of the city's rotunda building offers plenty of room to play tag, enjoy a fountain and view public art, but its proximity to a major thoroughfare may deter families with small children.

OTHER ADVENTURES

Beatie Skate Park

5493 Traffic Way

(805) 461-7606

www.atascadero.org

FREE!

From Highway 101 take Traffic Way east four blocks.

The only indoor skate park in San Luis Obispo County features modular ramps, a lounge area, a small concession stand, and restrooms. Pads, signed waiver forms, and helmets with straps are required for skaters of all ages. The park is generally open during the school year from 3 p.m. to 6 p.m. Monday through Friday, 10 a.m. to 3 p.m. Saturday and 1 p.m. to 4 p.m. Sunday. Call for extended summer hours and skate camp offerings.

Charles Paddock Zoo

9305 Pismo Avenue

(805) 461-5080

www.charlespaddockzoo.org

$

From Highway 101 head west on Highway 41/Morro Road.

For decades this five-acre zoo adjacent to Atascadero Lake Park has given children an up close and personal view of animals from forests, deserts, mountains and farms. With about 100 animals, relatively small enclosures and a bit of running room, the zoo is fine for small children, but is less exciting for bigger kids.

The zoo hosts special events throughout the year including zoo camps and holiday events. Call 47-3172 for current programs, camps and children's workshops.

Chapter 17

Templeton

Tucked off today's beaten path is an old-town community made up of residents who know how to get things done. Though small in population, the community is home to amenities often not found in cities twice its size. Special events cater to locals and, as such, are the place to be when you're looking for neighbors. Friends and family picnic in droves during the tremendously successful summer concert series, and the Independence Day parade has traditionally been one of the most family-friendly in the county.

Templeton was established by the West Coast Land Company in 1886 as a real estate investment to be parceled off and resold. Its locale on the end of the Southern Pacific Railroad line helped establish the heart of the community, and some of those early structures still stand today. When the rail cut its way through to San Luis Obispo, Templeton became another small, quiet town along the line, but that's precisely what we like about it.

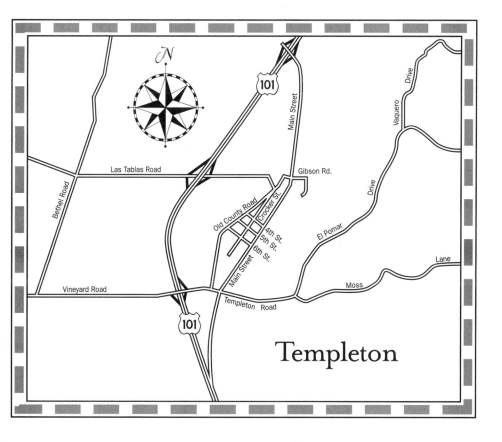

ARTS
Templeton Performing Arts Center
1200 Main Street

(805) 434-5855

www.tusdnet.k12.ca.us/pac

FREE!-$$$

From Highway 101 take Vineyard Road east, then turn right onto South Main Street.

This 340-seat theater offers public performances by theater arts students at Templeton High School and arts organizations throughout the area. Call for current program, prices and rules regarding young children.

LETTERS
Templeton Bookmobile
Templeton Park

(805) 788-2145

FREE!

Templeton has been without a library since 1977, but an active support group is working toward rectifying that matter. Meanwhile, the San Luis Obispo County Library Bookmobile swings into town most Saturdays during Templeton Farmers' Market. After picking up the fresh, locally grown fruits and vegetables, stop in the bookmobile to order books, magazines, recorded stories, movies and music for delivery, or peruse the collection available on hand.

HISTORY
Templeton Historical Museum
309 Main St.

(805) 434-0807

www.templetonmuseum.com

FREE!

From Highway 101 take the Vineyard Road exit. Proceed east on Vineyard Road, and then turn left onto Main Street.

The Templeton Historical Museum Society operates this non-profit museum that focuses specifically on the lives and times of Templeton area residents. The original museum is operated in the Horstman house (circa 1920). An 1886 Southern Pacific Railroad warehouse building houses large equipment including antique cars, trucks and buggies. Docents open the library to walk-in company most Fridays through Sundays from 1 p.m. to 4 p.m. and for school tours and special events by reservation. The site is ADA accessible and facilities include public restrooms.

NATURE

Tom Jermin Sr. Community Park

300 block of South Bethel Road

templetoncsd.org

(805) 434-4900

FREE!

From Highway 101 take the Las Tablas Road exit and turn west onto Las Tablas Road, then left onto South Bethel Road.

This 5-acre community park offers running space including a soccer field, restrooms, playground with structures, open turf and basketball hoops.

Chesebrough Farm

790 Moss Lane

(805) 434-0843

chesebroughfarm.com

FREE!

Exit Highway 101 at Vineyard and head east. When Vineyard curves sharply left and becomes El Pomar, continue straight onto graded-dirt Moss Lane and continue a mile and a bit to the farm.

This working cow-calf operation on a century-old farm is open to the public daily in October from 10 a.m. to 6 p.m. The Chesebroughs welcome visitors to look at fields in different stages of cultivation, growth and harvest, the refurbished barn (including original milking stanchions), vintage machines, big tractors, farm stand and pumpkin patch. Call ahead to arrange guided tours which are available only during the off season.

Duveneck Memorial Park

490 Vaquero Drive

(805) 781-5930

www.slocountyparks.com

FREE!

Exit Highway 101 onto Vineyard and head east as it becomes Templeton Road then El Pomar. Turn left onto Vaquero Drive.

This 81-acre property, donated by the family of Bernard H. (Barney) and Elizabeth (Liz) Duvenek, is slated to become a park, most likely with an emphasis on agricultural education. No opening date has been scheduled. Call for current developments.

Evers Sports Park

East end of Gibson Road

(805) 434-4900

www.templetoncsd.org

FREE!

From Highway 101 take the Las Tablas Road exit and turn east onto Las Tablas Road. Turn left onto Old Country Road, then right onto Gibson Road.

This 8-acre park includes baseball, softball and T-ball fields, soccer fields, concession stand, and restrooms, all under lights.

Hollyhock Farms

200 Hollyhock Lane

(805) 239-4713

hollyhock-farm.com

$

From Highway 101 take the Vineyard exit and turn east onto Vineyard. Veer left onto El Pomar Road and continue about 4 miles to Hollyhock Lane. Turn left onto the lane and continue another mile to the farm.

Visitors are invited to watch organic farming in action, pick floral bouquets June through December or enjoy an overnight farm stay by reservation any time. The farm includes 80 chickens, Jacob sheep and organic-farming education. A farmstand also offers seasonal fruits and vegetables throughout the growing seasons. Tours of the farm by visitors age 10 and older are available by appointment.

Jack Creek Farms

4665 Jack Creek Road

(805) 239-1915

jackcreekfarms.com

FREE!

From Highway 101 turn west onto Highway 46 and continue 6 miles.

This fifth-generation family farm grows pumpkins, heirloom tomatoes,

There are loads of agricultural education opportunities in Templeton.
Jack Creek Farm offers hands-on activities for children and farm-fresh foods seasonally.

antique apples and other produce and offers pick-your-own flowers and olallieberries from late June through mid-November. Families are welcome to use the picnic tables and children's play area, visit farm animals and view antique farm machinery.

The farm holds several annual public events. In August, Kids Day offers children of all ages the opportunity to churn butter, press cider, and try their hands at washboards among other traditional farm skills. September brings the Harvest Festival complete with its Old-Fashioned Threshing Bee. Heirloom tomato tasting is also held in September. October brings the Pumpkin painting workshop. Refer to the website for the latest offerings.

Templeton Community Center

601 S. Main Street

(805) 434-4900

templetoncsd.org

FREE!

From Highway 101 take the Vineyard Road exit. Proceed east on Vineyard Road, and then turn left onto Main Street.

This 2,525-square-foot building is a hub of activity. The property includes the town's skate park (p. 197) and a community garden (p. 196). The facility's meeting rooms are available for public use by reservation.

Templeton Community Garden

601 S. Main Street

(805) 434-4900

templetoncsd.org

$$

From Highway 101 take the Vineyard Road exit. Proceed east on Vineyard Road, and then turn left onto Main Street.

Residents of Templeton are invited to adopt any of the 8-foot-by-20-foot garden plots behind the Community Center (p. 196). The plots are available March 1 until mid-December, then are left to rest in winter months.

☞ Templeton Park

Sixth Street and Crocker Street

(805) 434-4900

templetoncsd.org

FREE!

From Highway 101 take the Vineyard Road exit. Proceed east on Vineyard Road, and then turn left onto Main Street.

This good old-fashioned city center park features an entire city block of fun for the family: plenty of grassy space for throwing a ball or playing tag, play structures, swings, a gazebo, picnic tables, large barbecue pit and restrooms. A public pool (p. 197) in the park offers free swimming during the hot summer months, thanks to local Lions Clubs that help fund pool operation. A fire department located directly across the street from the park will serve as an added bonus for families whose kids just can't get enough of those big ol' trucks.

Templeton Park Pool
6th and Old County Road in Templeton Community Park
(805) 781-5930
slocountyparks.com/facilities/pools.htm
FREE!

From Highway 101 take the Vineyard Road exit. Proceed east on Vineyard Road, turn left onto Old Country Road.

The Lions Club adopted the pool in recent years, ensuring the plunge's future and providing free swimming for all. Open Memorial Day to Labor Day.

Templeton Skate Park
599 Main Street
(805) 434-4900
templetoncsd.org
FREE!

From Highway 101 take the Vineyard Road exit. Proceed east on Vineyard Road, and then turn left onto Main Street.

Helmets and pads are required at this free, 10,000-square-foot concrete park featuring rails, half pipes and two bowls. Hours vary with the local school schedule. Basically, if school's in session, the park is closed. During summer hours the park is generally open from sun up to sundown.

Templeton Youth Center
599 Main Street

(805) 434-4829

templetoncsd.org/cm/youth_center

$

From Highway 101 take the Vineyard Road exit. Proceed east on Vineyard Road, and then turn left onto Main Street.

The recreation department runs this after-school and summer child care facility for a fee. Programs include arts and crafts, sports, games, field trips and computer access.

Vineyard Park
Semillion Lane at Vineyard Drive

(805) 234-4437

$

From Highway 101 take the Vineyard Road exit. Proceed east on Vineyard Road, turn left onto Old Country Road.

The community has plans for this largely undeveloped park on Templeton's west side. At press time, the paved parking lot provided access to the west end of a paved, dedicated bike path that runs ¼ mile west along Vineyard Road. The park itself is home to the ¾-acre Vineyard Dog park, a fenced facility designed specifically for canines and their human companions. Facilities at the dog park include two separate areas, shade trees, picnic tables, benches, dog toys and, during summer months, dog wading pool. For dog park details, go to www.vineyarddogpark.org.

Chapter 18

Paso Robles

Many people still think of Paso Robles as a dusty cow town, home to the California Mid-State Fair, kids in cowboy hats and jeans, but little more. In fact, Paso Robles is in the middle of a revival complete with upscale restaurants and shops, a growing art community, and renovation of some of its historic places.

Images of cowboys, cattle and working horses permeate the 200-year-old Central Coast city, from Cowboy Café to Western Art Gallery and on toward the fairgrounds. Look closer and you'll find a wine bar, museums, haute cuisine, a renovated park and revived downtown event calendar.

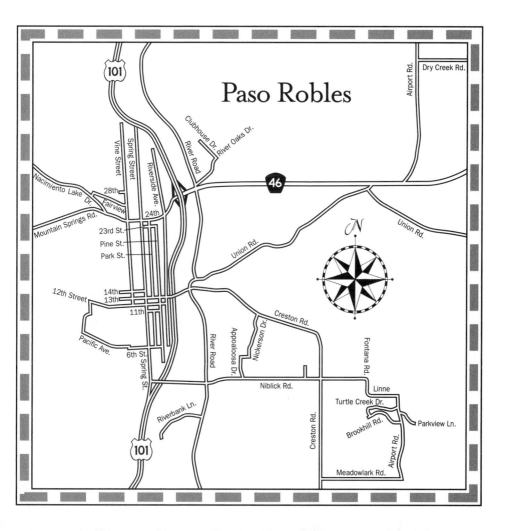

ARTS

Park Cinemas
1100 Pine St.
(805) 227-2172
www.parkcinemas.com
$$

From northbound Highway 101 take the Spring Street exit and proceed north on Spring Street. Turn right onto 10th, then left onto Pine Street. From southbound Highway 101 take the Riverside Ave./Pine Street exit and proceed north onto Pine Street.

A nine-screen movie theater offering all the latest Hollywood has to offer.

LETTERS

Paso Robles City Library
1000 Spring Street
(805) 237-3870
www.prcity.com/government/departments/library/
FREE!

From Highway 101 southbound take the Pine Street exit. Turn left onto 10th Street then right onto Spring Street. From northbound Highway 101 take the Spring Street exit and proceed straight to the library.

The library offers toddler story time, preschool story time, Homework Helpers tutoring program and Grandparents and Books Program. Open Mondays through Fridays from 10 a.m. to 8 p.m., Saturdays 10 a.m. to 5 p.m. Closed Sundays and national holidays.

Paso Robles City Library Study Center
3600 Oak Street, Suite 101
(805) 237-4743
www.prcity.com/government/departments/library/
FREE!

From Highway 101 take Exit 232 and proceed south on Spring Street.

This facility includes tables, chairs and a few computers for student use after school. While no tutors are employed here, students are welcome to bring in their own tutors. Open Monday through Wednesday from 2:30 p.m. to 5:30 p.m.

HISTORY

Carnegie Library
800 12th Street
(805) 238-4996
www.pasorobleshistoricalsociety.org

FREE!

From Highway 101 turn west onto 13th Street, then left onto Spring Street.
This historic stone structure listed in the National Register of Historic Places was built in 1908 and housed the city's library for 90 years. When the city moved the library to more modern digs, the Paso Robles Historical Society took over this space in the middle of Paso Robles City Park (p. 206). In addition to exhibits of locally significant artifacts and art, the museum houses historical and genealogical records for public reference.

Estrella Adobe Church

Airport Road 2.5 miles
north of Highway 46
(805) 467-3357
rios-caledoniaadobe.org/
index_files/Page433.htm

FREE!

From Highway 101 turn east onto Highway 46, then left onto Airport Road.
This adobe, built in 1878, was the first Protestant church in northern San Luis Obispo County. The grounds are open to the public, but there are no public amenities. Although the 75-seat adobe is available for special events by reservation, its doors are not generally open to the public. One exception is the annual memorial service held each May to honor the pioneers.

☞Estrella Warbirds Museum

4251 Dry Creek Road
(805) 227-0440
ewarbirds.org
$

From Highway 101 turn east onto Highway 46, turn left onto Airport Road, then right onto Dry Creek Road.
More than 300 volunteers have developed this private museum of historic aircraft, military machinery and war-era memorabilia ranging from pictures to uniforms. An onsite reference library of some 5,000 books documents American involvement in wars around the world. It is also home to the 8,000-square-foot Woodland auto display.

The museum was named after the World War II U.S. Army Air Corps P-38 training base once situated on the adjacent Paso Robles Municipal

Airport. Estrella Warbirds operates on land leased from the city and most of the aircraft on display are on loan from the U.S. Naval Museum in Pensacola, Florida.

The official hours are Thursday through Saturday 10 a.m. to 4 p.m. and Sunday noon to 4 p.m., but weekday tours are available by appointment at least two weeks in advance, and special events are also scheduled occasionally throughout the year.

Young people are welcome to take part in most aspects of the organization, including aircraft renovation, and the public is welcome at the squadron's regular dinner meetings. Dinners typically include museum updates and guest speakers. Call 467-3521 for reservations.

☞ Paso Robles Pioneer Museum

2010 Riverside Ave.

(805) 239-4556

www.pasoroblespioneermuseum.org

FREE!

From southbound Highway 101 take the 16th Street exit, turn right onto Riverside Road. From northbound Highway 101 turn east onto 24th Street, then turn left onto Riverside Road.

Spending an entire afternoon in and around the museum adjacent to Pioneer Park should be no problem for most families given this nonprofit's extensive collection of Americana.

The entrance hall features exhibits displaying life as it was: a print shop, bank, sporting goods store, creamery, gun shop, post office, hospital, mercantile and cattle camp. There's plenty of taxidermy, exhibits about area mining efforts and the historic Geneseo Schoolhouse which houses an exhibit of early American public schooling.

The museum claims its barbed wire collection is the largest in the Western U.S. It hangs on a wall in the neighboring building which also houses a fine collection of vintage carriages, buggies, cars and trucks including a 1911 Maxwell.

Open afternoons Thursday through Sunday and by appointment.

NATURE

Alpacas at Crossroads Ranch

2950 Old Ford Road

(805) 237-9640

crossroadsranch.openherd.com

FREE!

From northbound Highway 101 take Spring Street to Niblick Road, then turn right onto Creston Road and left onto Branbrit/Old Ford Road. From southbound Highway 101, take Pine Street, turn left onto 4th Street, left onto Spring Street, left onto Niblick Road then right onto Creston Road and left onto Branbrit/Old Ford Road.

This family-owned alpaca farm offers up-close-and-personal

experiences with the hypo-allergenic, fleece-bearing beasts of burden. The owners offer a variety of classes and workshops throughout the year, and alpaca fleece products are on sale in the fiber barn.

☞ Barney Schwartz Park

2970 Union Road

(805) 237-3991

www.prcity.com/government/departments/recreation/facilities

FREE!

From Highway 101 take Highway 46 east. Turn right onto Union Road which splits immediately south of Highway 46. Take Union Road to the left.

This 40-acre modern sports park includes four baseball/softball diamonds, four soccer/football fields, a lake, group picnic areas, two concession stands, three large play structure areas, a small lake and loads of walking paths. No wading is allowed in the ponds, but toe-dipping and fishing are welcome as are remote-controlled watercraft.

Casa Robles Park

600 Palomino Circle

(805) 237-3991

www.prcity.com/government/departments/recreation/facilities

FREE!

From Highway 101 northbound exit onto Spring Street, turn right onto Niblick Road, then left onto Appaloosa Drive. From Southbound Highway 101 exit at Pine Street, turn left onto 4th Street, left onto spring Street, left onto Niblick Road and left onto Appaloosa Drive.

This is a quarter-acre park with a play structure and a bit of grass.

Centennial Park

600 Nickerson Drive

 (805) 237-3988

www.prcity.com/government/departments/recreation/facilities

FREE!

From Highway 101 turn east onto Highway 46, then right onto River Road, left onto Creston Road and right onto Nickerson Drive.

This 16-acre park includes a gymnasium with basketball court, wading pool, two large group barbeque areas, grassy picnic areas, an amphitheatre, restrooms, walking paths, two playgrounds, two outdoor half-court basketball courts and four lighted tennis courts. There is also an outdoor pool that operates June through August.

Franklin Hotsprings & Paintball Park

3015 Creston Road, Paso Robles

(805) 712-5372

www.franklinhotsprings.com

$

From Highway 101 take the Niblick Road exit in Paso Robles. Turn east onto Niblick Road, and then right onto Creston Road and continue about 2.3 miles to the lakes on the south side of the road.

Franklin Lake Aquaculture Farm is a privately owned hot springs and recreation resort offering opportunities to dip into a mud-bottom pool that is maintained at 100.1 degrees by nature, fishing in a private lake (no license required), space to run remote control boats and plenty of room for paintball on a designated field of play. The hot springs pool is open daily from 8 a.m. to midnight and occasionally operates on the honor system (just deposit payment on your way to the pool area). The paintball park, open weekends, offers paintball equipment rental and sales.

Harris Stage

5995 North River Road

(805) 237-1860

harrisstagelines.com

$$$

From Highway 101 turn east onto Highway 46, then left onto North River Road.

This private ranch specializes in the training of horses, but also hosts private events and activities including riding and driving lessons, horse-drawn vehicles for hire (chariots, carriages, hay wagon rides, chuck wagon, stagecoach), parties and school field trips. The ranch also holds cowboy and cowgirl day camps for children ages 7 and up, and overnight camps for children ages 10 to 18. There are also two- and three-day clinics for adults with focuses on horsemanship, driving, and riding.

Hunter Ranch Golf Course

4041 Highway 46 East

(805) 237-7444

www.hunterrranchgolf.com

$$$

From Highway 101 take Highway 46 east to the course.

A public/private 18-hole course offers junior lessons, driving range, four putting greens, mini-executive three-hole practice course, golf shop, group barbecue facilities, and The Grill at the clubhouse. The facility also offers private and group lessons.

Larry Moore Park

155 Riverbank Lane

(805) 237-3991

www.prcity.com/government/departments/recreation/facilities

FREE!

From southbound Highway 101 take the 4th Street/Pine St. exit, turn left onto 4th Street, left onto Spring Street, then left onto Niblick Road, then right onto South River Road and right onto Riverbank Lane. From northbound Highway 101 take the Spring Street exit, turn right onto Niblick Road, right onto South River Road and right onto Riverbank Lane.

This 21-acre open space includes plenty of running room, public restrooms and picnic tables. The park is also the southern trailhead for the Salinas Parkway Trail.

LencoPark

Niblick Road at Appaloosa Lane

(805) 237-3991

www.prcity.com/government/departments/recreation/facilities

FREE!

From southbound Highway 101 take the 4th Street/Pine St. exit, turn left onto 4th Street, left onto Spring Street, then right onto Niblick Road. From northbound Highway 101 take the Spring Street exit, turn left onto Niblick Road.

This small neighborhood park is a grass area which serves as a retention basin for winter storm runoff. There are no additional facilities.

The Links Course of Paso Robles

5151 Jardine Road

(805) 227-4567

www.linksgolfcourseofpasorobles.com

$$$

From Highway 101 take Highway 46 east, and then turn left onto Jardine Road.

Play 9 holes or 18 at this par-72 course that features a Scottish-style course and offers junior rates.

Mandella Park

300 Fairview Lane

(805) 237-3991

www.prcity.com/government/departments/recreation/facilities

FREE!

From Highway 101 take the Highway 46/24th Street exit and head west. Turn right onto Fairview Lane.

A quarter-acre open area is more a green space than a park. There are no amenities here.

☞ Meridian Vineyard

7000 Highway 46 East

(805) 226-7133

www.meridianvineyards.com

FREE!
From Highway 101 take Highway 46 east.
While primarily a wine making facility with wine tasting for adults, Meridian Vineyard also features one of the most beautiful public herb gardens in the area. Families are welcome to bring their own picnics and frolic under the oaks, explore the garden or simply enjoy a peaceful day out.

Mount Olive Company
3445 Adelaida Road
(805) 237-0147
www.mtoliveco.com
FREE!
From Highway 101 take the Highway 46/24th Street exit and head west. Veer left onto Adelaida Road.
This certified organic farm turns out seasonal fruits and vegetables including strawberries, olives and more than a dozen types of sprouts from alfalfa to wheatgrass. Free range chickens help keep down pests, and also provide fresh eggs. Fruit orchard and worm farming tours led by super friendly staff are available by appointment 10 a.m. to 7 p.m. Thursdays through Sundays for groups of 10 or more visitors. An organic lunch menu, bakery and deli are also featured at the company store where all products grown here are also for sale.

Oak Creek Park
301 Cedarwood Drive
(805) 237-3991
www.prcity.com/government/departments/recreation/facilities
FREE!
From Highway 101 northbound take Spring Street, turn right onto Niblick Road, then right onto Creston Road. From southbound Highway 101 take Paso Robles Street exit and proceed straight, turn right onto Creston Road.
This 10½-acre park south of Sherwood Park includes a three-quarter-mile lighted walking path, playground, and three small barbecue/picnic areas. No restrooms.

☞ Paso Robles City Park
Bounded by Spring, 11th, 12th and Pine streets
(805) 238-3991
tinyurl.com/664nc3g
FREE!
From Highway 101 turn west onto 13th Street, then left onto Spring Street.
While Paso Robles evolves and upgrades, 4.8-acre City Park maintains

its hold on our attention with its wooded walks, play structures, historic Carnegie Library and works of art in the Western Art Museum. The park also offers horseshoe pits, picnic tables, a gazebo and restrooms.

The city sponsors free twilight concerts in the park throughout the summer. Other annual events that call this park home include Pioneer Day, Mid-State Fair Pancake Breakfast, Trading Day, Paso Robles Wine Festival, car shows and 4th of July festivities.

Paso Robles Event Center (aka Mid-State Fairgrounds)

2198 Riverside Ave.

(805) 239-0655

midstatefair.com

FREE!-$$$

From Highway 101 turn west onto 24th Street, then left onto Riverside Ave.

This 40-acre facility hosts the California Mid-State Fair each July/ August and other special events throughout the year including agricultural exhibitions, equestrian events, concerts and trade shows. Call for current offerings.

Paso Robles Golf Club

1600 Country Club Drive

(805) 238-4722

www.centralcoast.com/pasoroblesgolfclub

$$

From northbound Highway 101 take the Spring Street Exit, then turn east onto Niblick Road. From southbound Highway 101 take Pine Street, turn left onto 4th Street, left onto Spring Street, then left onto Niblick Road. From Niblick Road, turn right onto Country Club Drive.

This 6,215-yard, 18-hole, par-71 golf course offers public play, pro shop, restaurant, bar, lounge, banquet hall, reduced junior rates and incentives for frequent golfing. Carts available.

Paso Robles Municipal Pool

528 30th Street

(805) 237-3984

www.prcity.com/recreation/aquatics/

$

From Highway 101 turn west onto 24th Street, right onto Spring Street, then left onto 28th Street.

The city's central pool facility offers one outdoor pool open through summer months and a smaller indoor pool open year round. The city offers various programs including swimming lessons, springboard diving lessons and water safety instruction. Call for current hours and offerings.

Pioneer Park & Pioneer Skate Park

2030 Riverside Drive

(805) 237-3991

www.prcity.com/government/departments/recreation/facilities

FREE!

From southbound Highway 101 take the 16th Street exit, turn right onto Riverside Road. From northbound Highway 101 turn east onto 24th Street, then turn left onto Riverside Road.

This park comprises nearly 7 acres and includes a lighted softball field, a full basketball court, playground, restrooms, large barbecue area and Pioneer Skate park. Helmets and pads are required at the 10,500-square-foot concrete park that features a quarter pipe and rails. Like the park in which it is housed, the skate park is open daily from dawn to dusk.

Paso Robles Public Trail System

(805) 237-3991

www.prcity.com/recreation

FREE!

From Highway 101 turn west onto 24th Street, right onto Spring Street, then left onto 28th Street.

Walking the loop around City Park or the trails in Turtle Park might give some people the kick they need, others may be more attracted to the city's trail offerings that exist outside park settings.

Some trails serve as neighborhood connectors, like **Almendra Court Trail** which connects Crown Way with Union Road via a less-than- ¼-mile, paved path. Others serve as commuter trails that run parallel to existing roads, like **Charolais Trail** which runs more than 2 miles from Creston Road to Larry Moore Park (p. 204) largely in parallel with Charolais Road. **Union Road Trail** offers paved, off-street riding for more than a mile from 13th Street to Kleck Road. **Water Tank Loop** covers nearly 2 miles of pavement parallel to Rolling Hills Road, Golden Hill Road, onto the sidewalk at Creston Road, then back to Rolling Hills Road. (To avoid shopping center traffic, cut the loop short by passing through the its back parking lot and reconnecting at Rolling Hills Road.)

For a more natural experience, head to **Snead/Rambouillet Trail**. The route connects Snead Street with Rambouillet Road, St. Andrews Circle and Oxen Street via more than a mile of oak-shaded trail featuring several seasonal creek crossings. Or take the **Salinas Parkway Trail** (River Walk) as it meanders more than 1½ miles from Larry Moore Park to River Drive north of Navajo Avenue.

The city even offers a designated dog path: **Centennial Park Trail** provides a gentle stroll under the oaks connects Lana Street and Andrea Circle to Centennial Park at Nickerson Drive and serves as a nice stretch for very young mountain bikers in training. Extend the ride/walk to nearly 1 mile each way by beginning at Lana, crossing Nickerson Drive, then continuing to Mohawk Court.

☞ The Ravine Water Park

2301 Airport Road

(805) 237-8500

www.ravinewaterpark.com

$$

From Highway 101 take the Highway 46 exit and proceed east on Highway 46, then turn left onto Airport Road.

The north county's first large water park is a family-friendly, 15-acre facility that offers picnic areas, a wave pool, 9,000-square-foot interactive kiddie pool, lazy river, two 325-foot-long flume water slides and two extreme water slides (a toilet bowl ride and a freefall slide). No outside food is allowed, but food is sold on site. There are also private cabanas with wait service, volleyball courts, group picnic areas and banquet area.

The park is generally open from May to October. Check the website for hours.

River Oaks Golf Course

700 Clubhouse Drive

(805) 226 - 2096

www.riveroaksgolfcourse.com

$-$$

From Highway 101 take Highway 46 east, turn left onto North River Road, right onto River Oaks Drive and then left onto Clubhouse Drive.

This unique 6-hole, par-19 player development golf course offers three sets of tees offering different angles of approach rather than simply extending distance to the greens. The course encourages family use with low rates and flexible play. The property also includes water features, a clubhouse and hitting net. First Tee and other golf lessons are hosted here.

Robbins Field

826 7th Street

(805) 237-3991

www.prcity.com/government/departments/recreation/facilities

FREE!

From southbound Highway 101 take the Pine Street exit and proceed north to the park. From northbound Highway 101 take the Spring Street exit and continue north, then turn right onto 6th Street.

This is a 2.4-acre ballpark that includes a lighted softball field with bleachers, announcer's booth and restrooms. It is regularly used for adult league, Little League and Junior Giant practices and games.

Royal Oak Meadows Park

1100 Parkview Lane

(805) 237-3991

www.prcity.com/government/departments/recreation/facilities

FREE!

From Highway 101 northbound take Spring Street, turn right onto Niblick Road. From southbound Highway 101 take Paso Robles Street exit and proceed straight, turn right onto Creston Road, then left onto Niblick Road. Continue east on Niblick Road as it jogs and becomes Linne Road. Turn right onto Airport Road and left onto Parkview Lane.

This 2.4-acre park includes a playground, grass ball field with backstop and two small group barbecue areas. There are no restrooms here.

Sherwood Park

1860 Creston Road

(805) 237-3991

www.prcity.com/government/departments/publicworks/maintenance/little-league.asp

FREE!

From Highway 101 northbound take Spring Street, turn right onto Niblick Road, then right onto Creston Road. From southbound Highway 101 take Paso Robles Street exit and proceed straight, turn right onto Creston Road.

The 12.6 acre park is a focal point for the city's youth sports program. It includes a Little League field, softball field with bleachers, soccer fields, basketball court, sand volleyball court, four tennis courts and horseshoe pits. There are also group barbecue areas and restrooms.

Turtle Creek Park
700 Brookhill Drive
(805) 237-3991
www.prcity.com/government/departments/recreation/facilities
FREE!
From Highway 101 northbound take Spring Street, turn right onto Niblick Road. From southbound Highway 101 take Paso Robles Street exit and proceed straight, turn right onto Creston Road, then left onto Niblick Road. Continue east on Niblick Road as it jogs and becomes Linne Road. Turn right onto Airport Road, then right onto Brookhill Drive.

This 4.6-acre park includes a shuffle board, horseshoe pits, walking path, and four small barbecue areas but no restrooms.

OTHER ADVENTURES
George Stephan Oak Park Community Center
3050 Park Street
(805) 237-0845
From Highway 101 take Highway 46 west, turn right onto Spring Street, right onto 30th Street, then left onto Park Street.

This child-centered community center offers afterschool childcare, study nights, a computer lab, recreational facilities and a variety of classes and special events throughout the year. Outdoor facilities include basketball courts and plenty of lawn space for a quick game of catch or an afternoon of Frisbee.

Kennedy Club Fitness Center Pool
500 S. River Road
(805) 239-8488
www.kennedyclubs.com/pasorobles
$$
From northbound Highway 101, take Spring Street, turn right onto Niblick Road, then right onto River Road. From southbound Highway 101, take Pine Street exit, turn left onto 4th Street, left onto Spring Street, left onto Niblick Road, then right onto River Road.

Although this fitness club promotes membership, it also provides public access to its aquatic facilities for a fee. The club offers lap swim as well as a youth swim team, water polo, Masters swimming and private and semi-private lessons.

Paso Bowl
2748 Spring St.
(805) 238-5020

$

From Highway 101 take the 24th Street exit and turn west onto 24th Street, then turn right onto Spring Street.

While other bowling alleys continue to fall off the map, this old favorite holds strong with new synthetic lanes, a pizza parlor and lounge. Each of the 16 lanes can be quickly adapted to accommodate those in need of bumper aids. Shoe rental and bowling balls are also provided.

Paso Robles Children's Museum
623 13th Street

(805) 238-7432

www.pasokids.org

$

From northbound Highway 101 take Paso Robles Street north, then turn left onto 13th Street. From southbound Highway 101 take the 16th Street exit, turn left on Spring Street, then right onto 13th Street.

This three-story museum in the city's historic firehouse focuses on early childhood development. Don a uniform and climb on the fire truck, creep through the trunk of an old oak tree, cook pizza in the kitchen or dress up and take to the stage. Newton's Playhouse is a clear favorite among active children interested in puzzling out the pneumatic ball launching system.

The museum also hosts hands-on events including camps, birthday parties and field trips. The facility can also be rented for special events. The museum is open Wednesday through Sunday. Check website for current hours and special events.

Senior Citizens' Center
270 Scott Street

(805) 237-3880

tinyurl.com/6gzaq3n

From northbound Highway 101 take Spring Street, turn right onto Niblick Road, right onto Creston Road and left onto Scott Street.

The city's 5,000-square-foot center for those "50 and better" is a hub of senior activity weekdays from 8 a.m. to 5 p.m. Swing in for hot coffee, available all day and every day, a loan from the library, some computer time among friends or to get involved in any number of classes, workshops, special events and outings.

Tobin James Tasting Room
8950 Union Road (off Highway 46)

(805) 239-2204

www.tobinjames.com

FREE!

From Highway 101 take Highway 46 east about 8 miles. Turn right onto Union Road.

Wine tasting is not traditionally a family affair, but Tobin James makes it possible at his rural tasting room. With a designated driver at the ready, adults can sip creative labels while kids enjoy the Old West theme of the tasting room (complete with 1860s-era mahogany bar from Blue Eye, Missouri), free arcade games and a bit of running room outside. The tasting room offers James Gang Juice, a non-alcoholic carbonated juice beverage. There's also a bed & breakfast in the original stagecoach stop next door.

Chapter 19

Outlying Areas & Day Trips

The outlying areas of San Luis Obispo County and extending into Santa Barbara and Monterey counties include miles upon miles of spectacular scenery and family entertainment opportunities.

LETTERS

Creston Library
6290 Adams Street
Creston
(805) 237-3010
slolibrary.org/branch.htm
FREE!
From Highway 1 in Atascadero take Highway 41/Creston Eureka Road east. Turn right onto Highway 229/Webster Road, left onto Swayze Street, and then right onto Adams Street.

This San Luis Obispo County Library branch located across the street from Creston School is very small, but provides access to the the countywide collection. This library also provides a summer reading program. The branch is open Tuesday through Thursday. Call for current hours and special events schedule.

Shandon Library
240 East Centre St.
Shandon
(805) 237-3009
slolibrary.org/branch.htm
FREE!
From Highway 101 take Highway 46 east, turn right onto McMillan Canyon Road/Highway 41 and proceed into Shandon.

This branch of the San Luis Obispo County Library is open Thursday through Saturday for collection loan and offers special family-friendly events during the summer when a reading program is also in place. Call for current events schedule.

The long hike from Main Street to Devil's Slide in Guadalupe-Nipomo Dunes Complex
rewards intrepid sand walkers with peace, spectacular native plant shows
and panoramic ocean views ideal for whale watching.

HISTORY

Camp Roberts Military Museum

Building 114, Camp Roberts

12 miles north of Paso Robles off Highway 101

(805) 238-8288

Camprobertshistoricalmuseum.com

FREE!

Camp Roberts has served as a training center for the Army Reserve, National Guard and other military units since World War II. The museum boasts more than 3,000 items displayed in three buildings including the main museum, building 114 (Red Cross Headquarters) and Building 6585 (a World War II U.S. Post Office). Unusual features include regularly rotated exhibits that may include the Women's Army Corps, the WW II rail station, celebrities, and the hospital. The museum also includes a large collection of vintage vehicles as well as two video viewing rooms in which to further immerse visitors in Camp Roberts history. The site offers a reference library and gift shop as well.

The ADA-compliant museum is open Thursday and Saturday from 9 a.m. to 4 p.m. Tours are available by reservation.

☞ Mission San Antonio de Padua

17 Mission Road

South of King City

(831) 385-4478

www.mchsmuseum.com/missionsant.html

FREE!

From Highway 101 take Jolon Road/Fort Hunter Liggett exit and head west

to Mission Road. Access is through the military reserve which requires vehicle registration, insurance and driver's license.

This mission in southern Monterey County is unique among the 21 historic missions in that no city ever developed around it. The result is an opportunity to view the mission surrounded by wild California, much as it would have appeared more than 200 years ago. Look closely and you may still be able to spot portions of the aqueduct that brought water from the San Antonio River to the mission's grist mill, the first in California. Vandals have, unfortunately, damaged the original millstone and other historic elements, but the mission's setting remains one of the most authentic in the state.

The mission is open daily from 10 a.m. to 4 p.m. October through May, 8:30 a.m. to 6 p.m. June through September, and closed some holidays. Mass is held Sundays at 10 a.m. Docent-led group tours are available by reservation.

Mission San Antonio de Padua, a National Historic Landmark and California Historic Place, is located on Fort Hunter Liggett Military Reservation, an active military training base. Base police aren't messing around when they enforce road closures, speed limits and other potential delays. Call ahead for current schedules, conditions and foreseeable delays.

Mission San Miguel Arcangel

Mission Street
San Miguel
(805) 467-3256
www.missionsanmiguel.org
FREE!

From northbound Highway 101 take the Mission Street exit and proceed straight. From southbound Highway 101 take the 10th Street exit, turn left onto 10th Street, then right onto Mission Street.

The 16th of the California missions was erected in 1797 to close the gap between Mission San Luis Obispo de Tolosa and Mission San Antonio. In 1806, the original structure burned to the ground. By 1821, the mission was back to full service, but in 1834 the missions were disbanded and the property granted to the Reed family. In 1859 the Catholic Church reclaimed the mission and in 1928 it was returned to the Franciscans who still maintain it as a novitiate training ground. The mission was heavily damaged in the 2003 San Simeon Earthquake, but its designation as a National Historic Landmark led to its preservation.

The mission, grounds and gift shop are open for self-guided tours daily from 10 a.m. to 4:30 p.m. Phone in advance to arrange group tours. And always be mindful that this is a place of religious worship; be respectful of services and church-related activities that may be in service during your visit.

Rios-Caledonia Adobe

700 S. Mission St.

San Miguel

(805) 467-3357

rios-caledonia.org

FREE!

From northbound Highway 101 take the Mission Street exit and proceed straight. From southbound Highway 101 take the 10th Street exit, turn left onto 10th Street, then right onto Mission Street.

The two-story adobe built in 1846 for Petronilo Rios is open Friday through Sunday from 11 a.m. to 4 p.m., though the grounds are open year-round during daylight hours. The site includes restrooms, landscaped grounds with picnic benches, plentiful parking and a gift shop.

The structure originally served as the Rios family home. After a change in ownership, the property was opened to the public as Caledonia Inn. It later served a variety of functions including home to various families, a mattress factory, a post office and a school.

NATURE

Big Sandy Wildlife Area

Indian Valley Road

San Miguel

(831) 649-2870

FREE!

From Highway 101 take the San Miguel/10th Street exit, turn east onto 10th street, left onto Mission Street, right onto River Road, then left onto Cross Canyons/Indian Valley Road, veering left as Indian Valley Road splits off.

This 850-acre wildlife area managed by the Department of Fish and

Game is a designated hunting area. Archery equipment and shotguns are allowed here with hunting license, but no rifles or pistols are allowed. The area is also accessible to non-hunters. No camping is allowed, and since its primary purpose is to provide habitat for area wildlife, there are no maintained trails. Beware squirrel holes, rattle snakes, wild pigs and poison oak.

Big Sur
Highway 1 between San Simeon and Carmel
(831) 667-2100
www.bigsurcalifornia.org

Halfway between Santa Maria and San Francisco on world-famous Highway 1 is the rugged shoreline that served as inspiration for the likes of Jack Kerouac, Ansel Adams and just as likely your neighbor.

Ask friends, family, even random strangers to describe Big Sur and no two are likely to paint the same picture. One will reflect on family adventures building driftwood castles on the long stretch of sand at Andrew Molera State Park. Another will focus on the precipitous cliffs that separate Pacific Ocean from towering Santa Lucia mountain range. Some will recall heavy fog, dense shade, fresh incense of the forest. Others may reflect on crashing waves, waterfalls and windswept beaches.

In fact, all these visitors are right on target when describing the 70-mile-long coastal region. This storied stretch of Highway 1 offers spectacular views of California's most rugged coastal area, a challenging road, the state's southernmost redwood forest, plentiful camping and hiking for all abilities.

The most daunting aspect of Big Sur is the drive.

Given a straight, well-maintained, wide road, the drive up the coast would take only a few short hours. In reality, the trip up winding Highway 1 slows, often to jogging pace, just north of San Simeon. Hairpin turns and treacherous cliffs slow even the most aggressive drivers. Lumbering motorhomes and gutsy bicyclists slow the rest of us.

Thanks in no small part to this challenging access, the area has gone largely unchanged since Juan Cabrillo first noted it in 1542. While trails metamorphosized into roads crisscrossing the state for the following three and a half centuries, access to Big Sur was limited to trails. It wasn't until 1937 that a treacherous wagon trail from Carmel to Big Sur was improved and extended to become today's well-traveled route to San Simeon.

Once in Big Sur, expect no strip malls, no big box stores, not even a large grocery store.

There is, however, plenty of room for tents, backpacks, hiking boots, children and those seeking to commune with nature. There are thick forests of fragrant redwoods and Monterey pine, miles upon miles of mountainous hiking trails, blufftop trails and beachcombing opportunity galore.

Parks include: **Andrew Molera State Park**, featuring an easy 1-mile hike to the driftwood-laden beach; **Pfeiffer Big Sur State Park** with riverside and redwood camping, hiking trails directly out of the campground into redwood forests and to the Pfeiffer Falls; **Julia Pfeiffer Burns State Park** with its famous view of McWay Falls; **Plaskett Creek Campground** just across Highway 1 from Sand Dollar Beach.

Among the most popular hikes in the area is **Salmon Creek Trail** about 5 miles north of the county line on the outside edge of a horseshoe curve. In spring, the waterfall toward the lower end of this rugged, single-track trail draws a lot of attention, but carry on up the steep route an you'll find abundant wildflowers (spring) and wildlife (year round). At two miles, a trail to the left drops steeply to Spruce Creek Camp. Continue along the main trail to oak-shaded Estrella Camp, then over the ridge to the meadow at Dutra Flats.

Winter weather can create landslides that close Highway 1 fairly regularly. Beware of poison oak which grows abundantly along the coastal region and keep an eye out for traffic. Pull over at any of a number of scenic turnouts to let faster vehicles pass while you safely take in the view. And remember: slow-going vehicles that cause five vehicles to bunch behind are required by California's Vehicle Code to pull off the roadway at the first safe opportunity to relieve congestion.

C.W. Clarke Park

101 West Centre Street
Shandon
(805) 781-5930
www.slocountyparks.com
FREE!

From Highway 101 take Highway 46 east, turn right onto McMillan Canyon Road/Highway 41 and proceed into Shandon.

This 11-acre park offers plenty of lawn as well as volleyball courts, horseshoe pits, basketball courts, tennis courts, a football and baseball field, and two group barbecue areas that are available by reservation. Together, the group areas can accommodate 130 guests.

This park also houses the County Parks Department's largest public pool which is open summer days.

Guadalupe-Nipomo Dunes Preserve

West Main Street
Guadalupe in Santa Barbara County
(805) 343-9151
Tinyurl.com/6cchzqn
www.dunescenter.org
FREE!

From Highway 101 in Santa Maria take Main Street/Highway 166 West through town, and fields before arriving at its end at the beach.

This 18-mile stretch of coastline, dunes and estuaries offers seemingly endless walks, wildlife viewing opportunities and plenty of sand for castles. Whales are often spotted from this stretch of coastline that is also home to endangered California least tern and California red-legged frog, and the threatened Western snowy plover. The area is also home to the Guadalupe-Nipomo Dunes National Wildlife Refuge.

Though the waves may be inviting, this is not an ideal place to enter the Pacific. Riptides abound here, the waves can be enormous and the sandy edge quickly drops to a deep shelf. Children should be attended closely. Wading is discouraged since sweeper waves occur regularly here.

The non-profit Guadalupe Dunes Center in nearby Guadalupe (1055 Guadalupe St., 805-343-2455) offers docent-led walks and other educational programs throughout the year.

The Nature Conservancy controls the southernmost access to the complex and encourages donations at the entrance kiosk, but there is no mandatory fee.

Lake Nacimiento
10625 Nacimiento Lake Drive
Paso Robles
(805) 238-3256
www.co.monterey.ca.us/parks/nacimiento.html
$$
From Highway 101 take the 24th Street exit and proceed west through town. Follow Nacimiento Lake Drive to the right as it splits off from 24th Street.

Generations of Central Coast families have spent countless weekends, holidays and lazy summer afternoons along the shore of this man-made lake. With 167 miles of shoreline and 5,370 surface acres of water there's usually enough room for waterskiing and fishing, camping and hiking. The marina offers boat and jet ski rentals and there is a slalom course on the lake. There are more than 350 campsites of varying levels of services, from primitive to full hook-ups, located throughout the park. Nearby Nacimiento Resort offers a restaurant, groceries, fuel, bait, tackle and other supplies.

Parkfield
Cholame Valley Road
(805) 463-2421
www.parkfield.com/parkfield
FREE!
From Highway 101 turn east onto Highway 46 and continue out of town, past Shandon and through Cholame. Turn left onto Cholame Valley Road just a couple hundred feet before the Highway 41/Highway 46 split.

This tiny rural community on the San Andreas Fault has been made famous by its relatively regular significant earthquakes. As a result, it was selected by the U.S. Geological Survey for a comprehensive, long-term earthquake research project aptly named The Parkfield Experiment.

The area also offers spectacular shows of wildflowers in the spring, an annual bluegrass festival (www.parkfieldbluegrass.com) held every Mother's Day weekend and a rodeo each spring.

Pinnacles National Monument

East of Soledad in Monterey County

(831) 389-4485

www.nps.gov/pinn

$

East entrance: From Highway 101 at King City take Bitterwater Road north to Highway 25. Turn left and continue, following signs to the entrance.

West entrance: From Highway 101 at Soledad, take the Front Street/El Camino Real exit, turn east onto Highway 146 and follow the signs to the park.

The dark recesses of Balconies Caves offer an ants-eye view of the world. Gigantic boulders are wedged precariously in the cracked cliffs overhead like the gravel and sand that form the delicately balanced anthill. For some, the caves are the high point of Pinnacles National Monument. Other favorites include technical rock climbing opportunities, the park's 30 miles of trails, and more than 160 species of birds.

Formation of the namesake peaks began millions of years ago inside the heart of a volcano. Erosion, plate tectonics and faulting have washed the volcano's shell away, some of it as far south as the Los Angeles basin. The remaining spires are best viewed from the park's west entrance or along the steep and strenuous High Peaks Trail. There are no roads connecting the two park entrances, so visitors interested in both angles must either drive the long way around or plan to spend some time on the foot trails that link the two entrances.

This 24,200-acre park set aside in 1908 as a natural preserve and recreation area offers plentiful opportunity for hands-on lessons in geology, botany, wildlife and outdoor survival. The nearest campground is a half mile east of the eastern gate. The privately operated camp includes flush toilets, pay showers, a pool and well-stocked little store. Raccoons and wild boars sometimes plague campers. We learned the hard way that raccoons, just like cats, will climb atop cars to reach their booty. The sites were well spaced, though sound traveled clearly from one fire ring to the next. Morning wakeup calls included the tunes of magpies, bluejays, Stellar jays, quail, hawks, doves, owls, woodpeckers, towhees, hummingbirds, junkos and woodpeckers.

The store clerk said the park is usually busiest in spring months as wildflowers spread their petals and temperatures are most comfortable. During summer months, trailside temperatures can often reach 100 degrees.

Old Pinnacles Trail is a good place for families to start. Wildflowers along the route include sticky monkeyflower, indian paintbrush, wooly blue curls,

California poppy, miner's lettuce and fiddleneck. The trail starts easy enough, but gives way to a more moderate stretch just over two quiet miles from the trailhead at Chalone Creek Picnic Area. As we rounded a corner, we suddenly faced a wall of rock. A clearly marked trail led us into the talus cave where the going got pretty rough, but was much more entertaining. A flashlight is a must for anyone interested in passing completely through the half-mile natural tunnel. At points, hikers are completely enveloped in blackness. Finding the way without a light may not be impossible, but certainly would be dangerous.

We climbed up and over, sidled through, squeezed between and, at times, crawled under boulders varying in size from small treasure chests to large homes. And just as quickly as we had come upon the caves we were out of them. In the narrow canyon above, we found a fantastically cool spot to rest our packs, enjoy lunch and take a close look at the rocks and plants.

For those seeking direction, park rangers lead nature hikes every Saturday and Sunday through May. The hikes begin at 10 a.m. from the Bear Gulch Visitor Center on the east side of the park and at 2 p.m. from the Chaparral Ranger Station on the west. The park also offers interpretive talks, night hikes, and bat education programs.

No dogs are allowed on any trails, though they are allowed in parking and picnic areas. The park is open 7:30 a.m. to 8 p.m. daily. No overnight camping inside the park boundary. Bear Gulch Cave closed indefinitely. Watch out for poison oak, rattlesnakes and heat.

☞ Point Sal State Beach
Point Sal Road
Near Guadalupe in Santa Barbara County
(800) 777-0369
www.parks.ca.gov/?page_id=605
FREE!

From Highway 101 take Main Street exit in Santa Maria and head west. Turn left onto Ray Road, then right onto Brown Road. Continue west on Brown Road across Highway 1 then follow the road as it curves toward the locked gate at the bottom of Point Sal Road.

While the Bureau of Land Management does not provide public access to its 77-acre Point Sal promontory, State Parks does allow hikers to access Point Sal Beach south of the point. The 9-mile roundtrip isn't for the faint of heart; what climbs in must climb out.

The road that once provided public access to this beautiful stretch of white sand was wiped out by winter storms in the 1990s and the powers that were opted not to restore the road. While many portions of the road remain in decent repair, complete sections have been demolished. There only single-track trails remain.

The trek to the beach and back involves a long, unrelenting climb/descent. But the graded dirt road, sections of pavement and even the single-track that leads down toward the beach are clearly well traveled.

The joy in this journey doesn't require reaching the beach. Adventurers to the ridge are rewarded with 360-degree views often accompanied by the sounds of waves and sea lions from the beach below.

Keep in mind that there are no lifeguards at the beach an no facilities anywhere along the route.

San Antonio Lake
Nacimiento Lake Road
Paso Robles
(805) 472-2311
www.lakesanantonioresort.com
$$

From Highway 101 take the 24th Street exit and proceed west through town. Follow Nacimiento Lake Drive to the right as it splits off from 24th Street. Continue past Nacimiento Lake and past Interlake Road to San Antonio Lake.

Like Nacimiento Lake, its neighbor to the south, San Antonio Lake serves up plenty of fishing, waterskiing and general family fun. The man-made lake boasts 5,500 surface acres of water and 60 miles of shoreline. Boat rentals are offered at the marina, and shoreline camping is plentiful.

San Miguel Park
1221 K Street
(805) 781-5930
www.slocountyparks.com

From Highway 101 take the 10th Street exit, turn east onto 10th Street, then left onto K Street.

This park is located on the site of a school dating back to the 1800s. Today it includes a skinned ball field, playground and restrooms. It is also home to the community pool that is open summer months only.

Star Farms
7835 Estrella Road, San Miguel

(805) 467-3389

$$$

From Highway 101 Mission Street into town, turn right onto North River Road then left onto Estrella Road.

This working alfalfa farms opens its doors to group by reservation only. Rent the facilities for access to the palm-tree-lined lake, cabanas, beach, horseshoe pits, croquet court, trampoline, hammocks, barbecue pits (from kettle to giant pit), full-kitchen facilities, bonfire pit. No dogs allowed.

Wolf Natural Area

North River Road, San Miguel

(805) 781-5930

FREE!

From Highway 101 Mission Street into town then turn right onto North River Road.

This 58-acre, county-owned property in the Salinas River corridor is not maintained nor are there facilities, but there are many unofficial trails open to any non-motorized use. Bring your horse, your mountain bike, your hiking boots and the dog, but don't bring a motorcycle or other OHV.

Resources

Books
Some things are better left alone. For a complete rundown on the great outdoors, check out these books, most of which are available at local bookstores and other local retailers:

San Luis Obispo County Trail Guide, by Santa Lucia Chapter, Sierra Club
Day Hikes San Luis Obispo County California, by Robert Stone
Mountain biking the Central Coast, by Carol Berlund

Chambers of Commerce
These business associations promote their communities with an emphasis on membership. While these are great places to start your search for local information, keep in mind that most fail to mention non-member businesses, so their information isn't always all inclusive.

Arroyo Grande Chamber of Commerce
800 West Branch St.   (805) 489-1488
Arroyo Grande, CA 93420
arroyograndecc.com

Atascadero Chamber of Commerce
6550 El Camino Real   (805) 466-2044
Atascadero, CA 93422-4202
atascaderochamber.org

Cambria Chamber of Commerce
767 Main St.   (805) 927-3624
Cambria, CA 93428
cambriachamber.org

Cayucos Chamber of Commerce
158 N. Ocean Ave.   (805) 995-1200
Cayucos, CA 93430
cayucoschamber.com

Grover Beach Chamber of Commerce
180 Highway 1   (805) 489-9091
Grover Beach, CA 93433
groverbeachchamber.com

Los Osos/Baywood Park Chamber of Commerce
781 Los Osos Valley Road   (805) 528-4884
P.O. Box 6282
Los Osos, CA 93412
www.lobphchamber.com

Morro Bay Chamber of Commerce
845 Embarcadero, #D   (805) 772-4467
Morro Bay, CA 93442-2147
morrobay.org

Nipomo Chamber of Commerce
671 West Tefft St., Ste 8   (805) 929-1583
Nipomo, CA 93444-8988
www.nipomochamber.org

Paso Robles Chamber of Commerce
1225 Park Street   (805) 238-0506
Paso Robles, CA 93446
pasorobleschamber.com

Pismo Beach Chamber of Commerce
581 Dolliver St.   (805) 773-4382
Pismo Beach, CA 93449
pismochamber.com

San Luis Obispo Chamber of Commerce
1039 Chorro St.   (805) 781-2777
San Luis Obispo, CA 93401
slochamber.org

Templeton Chamber of Commerce
P.O. Box 701   (805) 434-1789
Templeton, CA 93465
www.templetonchamber.com

San Luis Obispo County Visitors & Conference Bureau
811 El Capitan Way, #200   (805) 541-8000
San Luis Obispo, CA 93401
SanLuisObispoCounty.com

Central Coast Agritourism Council
4665 Jack Creek Road
Templeton, CA 93465
www.agadventures.org

Recreation & Parks Departments

Atascadero Parks & Recreation Department	(805) 461-5000
Arroyo Grande Parks & Recreation Department	(805) 473-5474
Cambria Parks & Recreation Department	(805) 927-7776
Grover Beach Parks & Recreation Department	(805) 473-4580
Morro Bay Recreation & Parks Department	(805) 772-6278
Nipomo Area Recreation Association	(805) 929-5437
Paso Robles Recreation Division	(805) 237-3991
Pismo Beach Recreation Division	(805) 773-7063
San Luis Obispo Parks & Recreation Department	(805) 781-7283
Templeton Parks Department	(805) 434-4900
San Luis Obispo County Parks	(805) 781-5930

Farmers' Markets

On any given day you can find some sort of farmers' market going on in San Luis Obispo County. They are organized by a variety of associations, and all include produce from local (and sometimes not-so-local) farms.

Many of the markets also include crafts, games and live entertainment.

The following list of locations and times is subject to change. Check local newspaper listings or chambers of commerce for the latest information or check in with organizers.

Arroyo Grande
www.slocountyfarmers.org   (805) 544-9570
Saturday, Noon-2:30 p.m, in the Village behind City Hall
Wednesday, 8:30-11 a.m., 1464 E. Grand Avenue
Saturday, Noon-2:30 p.m. at City Hall Parking Lot off E. Branch St.

Atascadero
www.northcountyfarmersmarkets.com   (805) 466-2044
Wednesday, 3-6 p.m., Sunken Gardens on El Camino Real

Avila Beach
countryfarmandcraftmarket.com/market.html (805) 602-8266
April through October, Friday, 4-8 p.m., Front Street Plaza

Cambria
www.cambriachamber.org   (805) 927-3624
Friday, 2:30-5 p.m., Veterans Hall parking lot, 1000 Main St.

Cayucos
countryfarmandcraftmarket.com/market.html (805) 235-9498
April through November, Friday, 10a.m.-12:30p.m., Cayucos
Veteran's Hall, 10 Cayucos Dr.

Grover Beach
countryfarmandcraftmarket.com/market.html (805) 602-8266
June through September, Sunday, 3-6 p.m., Ramona Garden Park

Los Osos/Baywood Park
www.northcountyfamersmarkets.com   (805) 239-6535
Monday, 2-4:30 p.m., Santa Maria Ave. between 2nd and 3rd Streets

Morro Bay
www.slocountyfarmers.org   (805) 544-9570
Thursday Fishermen's & Farmers' Market, 2:30-5 p.m., 2650 Main St.
Saturday, 4-7 p.m., 800 block Main St.

Nipomo
Nipomofarmersmarket.com   (805) 929-3081
Sunday ,11:30 a.m. to 2:30 p.m., 1645 Trilogy Parkway

Paso Robles
www.northcountyfarmersmarkets.com   (805) 237-9254
Tuesday, 3-6 p.m., City Park, 11th and Spring St.
Friday, 3-6 p.m. (winter), 4-7 p.m. (summer), 2445 Golden Hill Road.
Saturday, 9 a.m.-1p.m., City Park, 11th and Spring Streets

Pismo Beach
countryfarmandcraftmarket.com/market.html (805) 305-7017
Wednesday, 5-8 p.m., Main and Dolliver streets

San Luis Obispo
www.slocountyfarmers.org   (805) 544-9570
Thursday, 6- 9 p.m., Higuera Street from Osos St. to Nipomo St.
Saturday, 8-10:30 a.m., Madonna Shopping Center, Madonna Road

San Miguel

www.discoversanmiguel.com/market.html   (805) 286-1436

Thursday, April-September, 3-6 p.m., San Paso Truck Stop, Hwy. 101

Shell Beach

countryfarmandcraftmarket.com/market.html (805) 305-7017

Saturday, 9 a.m.-1 p.m., Dinosaur Caves Park

www.discoversanmiguel.com/market.html

Templeton

www.northcountyfamersmarkets.com   (805) 239-6535

Saturday, 9 a.m.-12:30 p.m., 6th and Crocker streets

Arts Associations

Many of these associations welcome junior members and/or provide training, workshops and camps for artists of all ages and ability. Contact each directly for details.

Allied Arts Association Schoolhouse Gallery

P.O. Box 184, Cambria, CA 93428   (805) 927-8190

artistsofcambria.com

ARTS Obispo

P.O. Box 1710, San Luis Obispo, CA 93406   (805) 544-9251

Artsobispo.org

Atascadero Art Association

P.O. Box 28, Atascadero, CA 93423   (805) 462-0632

.atascaderoartassn.fix.net

Cal Poly Arts

1 Grand Ave., San Luis Obispo, CA 93407   (805) 756-7110

www.calpolyarts.org

Cayucos Art Association

10 Cayucos Dr., Cayucos, CA 93430   (805) 995-2049

cayucosart.org

Paso Robles Art Association

1315 Vine St., Paso Robles, CA 93446   (805) 238-5473

Pasoroblesart.org

San Luis Obispo Museum of Art

1010 Broad St., San Luis Obispo, CA 93401   (805) 543-8562

www.sloma.org

Music Associations

Many of these associations welcome junior members or offer skill-building camps and workshops. Contact them directly for offerings and schedules.

Arroyo Grande Community Chorus

Arroyo Grande   (805) 489-1814

Central Coast Celebration, Sweet Adelines International

Pismo Beach   (805) 709-1591

www.celebration-chorus.com

Central Coast Children's Choir
P.O. Box 15757, San Luis Obispo, CA 93406   (805) 541-5323
Centralcoastchildrenschoir.org

Festival Mozaic
P.O. Box 311, San Luis Obispo, CA 93406   (805) 781-3008
www.festivalmozaic.com

Gold Coast (Barbershop) Chorus
San Luis Obispo   (805) 543-2265
www.evg.org/~slogold

Pacific Horizons Chorus, Sweet Adelines International
P.O. Box 30, San Luis Obispo, CA 93406   (805) 528-6106
www.celebration-chorus.com

San Luis Chamber Orchestra
1950 Aspen St., Los Osos, CA 93402   (805) 528-7795
www.sanluischamberorchestra.org

San Luis Obispo Blues Society
P.O. Box 14041, San Luis Obispo, CA 93406   (805) 541-7930
home.kcbx.net/~sloblues/

San Luis Obispo County Band
www.slocountyband.org   (805) 929-0552

San Luis Obispo County Jazz Federation
P.O. Box 1888, Morro Bay, CA 93443   (805) 546-3733
slojazz.org

San Luis Obispo County Youth Symphony
P.O. Box 430, San Luis Obispo, CA 93406   (805) 543-3533
sloyouthsymphony.org

San Luis Obispo Folk Music Society
2465 Tierra Drive, Los Osos, CA 93402   (805) 528-8963
slofolks.org

San Luis Obispo Opera
P.O. Box 14760, San Luis Obispo, CA 93406   (805) 541-5369
www.operaslo.org

San Luis Obispo Symphony
P.O. Box 658, San Luis Obispo, CA 93406   (805) 543-3533
slosymphony.com

San Luis Obispo Vocal Arts Ensemble
P.O. Box 4306, San Luis Obispo, CA 93406   (805) 541-6797
vocalarts.org

Theatrical/Dance Organizations

Many of these organizations welcome junior members or offer skill-building camps and workshops. Contact them directly for offerings and schedules.

Cal Poly Theatre and Dance
1 Grand Ave., San Luis Obispo, CA 93407   (805) 756-1465
cla.calpoly.edu/thtrdanc

Central Coast Shakespeare Festival
P.O. Box 175, San Luis Obispo, CA 93406   (805) 546-4224
Centralcoastshakespeare.org

Civic Ballet of San Luis Obispo
> 672 Higuera St., San Luis Obispo, CA 93401   (805) 544-4363
> civicballetofslo.org

Clark Center for the Performing Arts
> 487 Fair Oaks Ave., Arroyo Grande, CA 93420 (805) 489-9444
> clarkcenter.org

Corners of the Mouth Poetry Festival
> 393 D Buchon St., San Luis Obispo, CA 93401 (805) 547-1318
> www.languageofthesoul.org

Cuesta College Performing Arts
> Cuesta College, Hwy. 1, SLO, CA 93401   (805) 546-3100
> academic.cuesta.edu/performingarts

Foundation for the Performing Arts Center
> P.O. Box 1137, San Luis Obispo, CA 93406   (805) 541-5401
> fpacslo.org

The Great American Melodrama & Vaudeville Revue
> 1863 Pacific Blvd., Oceano, CA 93475   (805) 489-2499
> Americanmelodrama.com

Kelrik Productions
> 1490 Southwood Drive, SLO, CA 93401   (805) 543-7529
> kelrikproductions.com

Pewter Plough Playhouse
> P.O. Box 494., Cambria, CA 93428   (805) 927-3877
> pewterploughplayhouse.org

San Luis Obispo Little Theatre
> 888 Morro St., San Luis Obispo, CA 93406   (805) 786-2440
> www.slolittletheatre.org

Public Transit

The county is full of public transportation options, though some are more convenient than others. Many of the area's buses include bike racks. All require exact change, and any transfers needed should be requested upon boarding. See each city for local listings. The following are offered countywide.

Regional Transit Authority (RTA) / South County Transit (SCAT)
(805) 541-2228
www.slorta.org
www.cattransit.org
Countywide bus system includes most cities in the county, plus Cal Poly, Cuesta College, Hearst Castle and Santa Maria in neighboring Santa Barbara County. The service also runs the Avila Beach Trolley.

SLO Transit
This public bus service canvases the city and operates the Downtown Trolley.
(805) 541-BUS (541-2877)
www.slocity.org/publicworks/transit.asp

Paso Robles Express
(805) 239-8747
www.pasoexpress.com

This bus service serves the city from 7 a.m. to 7 p.m. Monday through Saturday except holidays.

Atascadero Transit/El Camino Shuttle

(805) 466-7433

Tinyurl.com/63msqtw

This service runs from 7 a.m. to 7 p.m. Mondays through Saturdays throughout the year except holidays. Serves Atascadero and runs shuttles to Templeton, Cuesta College and Paso Robles.

Cambria Otter Bus

(805) 541-2228

Tinyurl.com/6jgp71k

Free summertime transportation linking Cambria Village businesses and Highway 1 is also available Fridays through Sundays the rest of the year.

Morro Bay Trolley

(805) 772-2744

tinyurl.com/3vl5pfe

Offers three routes: Waterfront, Downtown and North Bay. Runs Fridays through Mondays from Memorial Day weekend to the first weekend in October.

Ride-On/Senior Shuttle

(805) 541-TRIP (541-8747)

ride-on.org

This non-profit organization promotes community transportation through ridesharing, busing and shuttle services. It provides airport shuttles, lunchtime express shuttle service and carpooling information as well as current information about all area public transportation options throughout SLO County.

It also provides low-cost senior transportation from 9 a.m. to 5 p.m. by reservation. South County service runs Tuesdays and Thursdays. North County and North Coast services are available Mondays and Wednesdays.

Clubs, Groups and Other Gatherings

Almond Country Quilters Guild

almondcountryquilters.org

Trinity Lutheran Church

940 Creston Road, Paso Robles

Meets 6:30 p.m. the first Monday of each month.

Paso Robles Amateur Radio Club

(805) 226-9990

www.pasoroblesarc.org

Paso Robles

Meets at 7 p.m. the first Monday of each month at Estrella Warbird Museum (p. 201).

Atascadero Horsemen's Club
Atascaderohorsemensclub.com
Meets at Players Restaurant
8845 El Camino Real, Atascadero
Meets at 7 p.m. on the second Tuesday of each month to plan and discuss rides, projects and other club events.

Atascadero Native Tree Association
(805) 466-8781
Meets at Ranger House, Atascadero Lake Park
Meets at 5 p.m. the second Monday of each month.

Backcountry Horsemen – Los Padres Unit
(805) 238-6393
www.bchc-lpunit.org
Family-focused horse enthusiasts meet monthly at rotating locations to plan rides, campouts and community service events.

Bear Valley Quilters
(805) 528-2183
Meets at South Bay Community Center
2180 Palisades Ave., Los Osos
Meets at 6:30 p.m. the fourth Monday of each month.

Boy Scouts of America
(805) 543-5766
beascout.scouting.org
Cub Scouts, Boy Scouts, Venturing and Volunteer programs countywide

Cambria Computer Club
(805) 927-8844
Meets at Joslyn Recreation Center
950 Main St., Cambria
Meets at 2 p.m. the first three Thursdays of the month. Novice meeting the first, Mac meeting the second, general meeting the third.

Central Coast Art Doll Club
(805) 481-4478
Art doll artists meet at 10 a.m. to 12:30 p.m. on the third Monday of each month at private homes for projects, exhibits and classes. Group is interested in three-dimensional, dressed, figurative dolls from historical to fantasy originals. Bring a project to share.

Central Coast Classy Birds Car Club
(805) 773-3626
This club is for owners of 1955-57 Thunderbirds. Call for meeting info.

Central Coast Follies
(80t) 474-1525
Singers and dancers of all ages gather Wednesdays from 11:15 a.m. to 1:15 a.m. for performances at Moose Hall, 180 Main St., Pismo Beach.

Central Coast Mothers of Multiples
(www.centralcoasttwins.com
Meetings and playdates designed specifically for moms of multiples.

Central Coast Natural History Association
(805) 772-2694
Through the efforts of its members, the association supports educational and conservation works throughout state parks located on the Central Coast.

Central Coast Quilters
(805) 489-9786
Meets at 6:30 p.m. the fourth Tuesday of each month at Arroyo Grande Community Center, 211 Vernon Ave., Arroyo Grande

Central Coast Treasure Hunters Association
www.cctha.org
This club of metal-detection enthusiasts, featured in Life Magazine, meets at 7 p.m. the fourth Wednesday of each month at the County Board of Education Office, 3350 Education Drive off Highway 1 north of Cuesta College.

Central Coast Weavers Guild
www.centralcoastweavers.org
Meets the second Thursday of each month from 10-12:30 at Congregation Beth David, 10180 Los Osos Valley Rd., SLO. Refreshments provided. Bring something for "Show & Tell," and something for the raffle. Also meets the last Saturday of the month, 10:00 - 2:00, in member's homes - potluck lunch and show and tell.

Central Coast Woodcarvers
(805) 927-5240
Meets from 10 a.m. to 2 p.m. Wednesdays at the Cayucos Veterans Memorial Building, 201 Ocean Front Ave., Cayucos.

Central Coast Woodturners
(805) 929-1423
Members meet at 9 a.m. on the third Saturday of each month at the Oddfellows Hall, Dana Street, SLO to talk about current projects, show their work, see guest presenters and introduce a new challenge project each month. Amateurs to pros alike are invited.

Pismo Derelicts Car Club
(805) 473-5801
Pismoderelicts.com
Car enthusiasts of all sorts, particularly sports cars, antiques, collector cars

and hot rods, meet at 8 a.m. Saturdays in the shopping center parking lot at Oak Park Road and James Way.

Embroiderers' Guild of America, Bishop's Peak Chapter
(805) 473-9268

www.egausa.org

Meets from 10 a.m. to 1 p.m. the third Saturday of each month at Grover Beach Community Center, 1230 Trouville Ave., Grover Beach

Estero Radio Club
(805) 528-8900

www.sloradio.net

Amateur radio operators, many of whom are active in disaster and emergency communications systems, meet Mondays at 7:30 a.m., Hungry Fisherman, 399 Beach Street, Morro Bay; general meetings 7 p.m., fourth Wednesdays, SLO Sheriff's Auditorium, Kansas Ave. Topics of interest include Amateur Radio Emergency Service (ARES), administered by the American Radio Relay League, Radio Amateur Civil Emergency Service(RACES) and San Luis Obispo Emergency Communications Council. The club also provides ham radio training and license testing.

ECOSLO
(805) 544-1777

Ecoslo.org

Non-profit organization provides environmental advocacy, education, conservation and stewardship programs as well as monthly hikes.

For Youth's Interest (FYI)
(805) 461-5000

City-organized youth group for Atascadero area teens interested in building positive friendships and leadership skills.

Friends of the Adobes
(805) 467-3357

Regular meetings and projects organized to further the best interests of the area's historic adobe structures.

San Luis Obispo Gem & Mineral Club
(805) 710-5053

Meets at 7 p.m. the first Tuesday of each month at SLO Senior Citizens Center, 1455 Santa Rosa St., San Luis Obispo.

German-American Club of the Central Coast
(805) 462-0717

Meets at 7 p.m. the second Wednesday of each month at Players Restaurant, 8845 El Camino Real, Atascadero.

Girl Scouts of California's Central Coast
(800)822-2427
www.girlscoutsccc.org
Provides Brownies, Juniors and Cadets programs throughout the county.

Homeschoolers of the Central Coast
jenhen16@yahoo.com
groups.yahoo.com/group/Homeschoolers_of_the_Central_Coast
Play groups, co-ops and field trips for and by homeschool families
throughout the county.

Italian-Speaking Group
(805) 922-6966 x3422
Meets from 2 p.m. to 4 p.m. the second and fourth Saturdays of each month
at Linnaea's Café, 1110 Garden St., San Luis Obispo.

Knitters' Guild
Meets from 10 a.m. to noon the second and fourth Saturdays of each month
at St. Stephen's Espiscopal Church, 1344 Nipomo St., SLO.

La Leche League of San Luis Obispo County
(805) 489-9128
sites.google.com/site/lllofslo
This breastfeeding support organization provides, through monthly
meetings and other events, mother-to-mother support, encouragement,
information and education to promote better understand of breastfeeding as
an important element in the healthy development of baby and mother. Meets
at 10 a.m. the second Tuesday of each month at Santa Lucia Birthing Center
4251 S. Higuera, suite 300, SLO.

Mid-State Cruizers Classic Car Club
(805) 466-3853
www.midstatecruizers.org
Meets at 7 p.m. the third Thursday of each month at Player's Restaurant,
8845 El Camino Real, Atascadero, and 6 p.m. second Saturdays from April
to October in the shopping center parking lot at 3980 El Camino Real,
Atascadero.

Moms Offering Moms Support (MOMS) Clubs
These non-profit support groups for mothers meet regularly for activities,
field trips, moms' nights out. Some include babysitting cooperatives. Call for
current schedule of activities and locations. **MOMS Club of Atascadero,**
(805) 438-3531, www.momsclubofatascadero.com.. **MOMS Club of SLO,**
(805) 783-2103, www.slomomsclub.com.

Muddy Bog Juggling Club
(805) 772-2759
Meets from 6:30 p.m. to 8:30 p.m. Tuesdays in the cafeteria at Cuesta

College and from 5 p.m. to 7 p.m. Thursdays at Cal Poly's student government room.

National Association of Watch and Clock Collectors
(805) 528-3100
Meets 12:30 p.m. second Sunday, Senior Center, 1580 Railroad St., Oceano.

Newborn Feeding Class
(805) 543-6988
Mothers and fathers alike are welcome to these free weekly classes to discuss feeding, crying and sleep (or lack thereof).

North County Aquatics
P.O. Box 1933
Paso Robles, CA 93447
(805) 239-3013
www.northcountyaquatics.org
A USA Swimming-affiliated competitive swim team serving residents of northern San Luis Obispo County. Swimmers of all abilities ages 5 to 18 are eligible for the program.

Olde Towne Quilters of Nipomo
(805) 929-3704
Two meetings held the fourth Thursday of each month. The 10 a.m. meeting, held at St. Joseph's Church, 298 S. Thompson Ave., includes trunk shows, guest speakers and other presentations. The guild meets again at 6:30 p.m. for a friendship gathering.

Pale Kai Outriggers
(805) 773-5597
www.palekai.org
This outrigger canoe racing club promotes team work with regular training sessions and competitions. Open to paddlers of all levels ages 16 and older.

Parent Participation Preschool
(805) 773-5597
These interactive preschool opportunities offered throughout San Luis Obispo County educate both children and adults. Parents are required to take active roles in their preschoolers' education, and parents receive their own training sessions from a rotating slate of guest speakers. Oceano (805) 474-3900. San Luis Obispo, Morro Bay and Los Osos (805) 549-1253. Atascadero (805) 544-5033.

Pismo Beach Walking Club
(805) 481-7887
pismobeachwalkers@att.net
Meets south of Pismo Pier at 7:55 a.m. Mondays, Wednesdays and Fridays. Call to confirm.

Poison Oak Cachers

Poisonoakcachers.com

Local geocachers join forces in this informal club that promotes family-friendly outings, exploration of the central coast and the high-tech treasure hunting called geocaching.

Puma Aquatics

(805) 709-7946

www.pumaswim.org

This USA Swimming-affiliated competitive swim team practices in Atascadero, Paso Robles, San Luis Obispo and Arroyo Grande. Swimmers of all abilities ages 5 to 18 are eligible for the program.

Ride Nipomo

Ridenipomo.org

(805) 343-9494

Meets regularly for horse-related events and to promote safe riding and advocate for public trail access.

San Luis Obispo County 4-H

www.slocounty4h.org

(805) 781-5943

4-H is a co-educational youth development program overseen by the University of California Cooperative Extension. The learn-by-doing program is designed for youth in grades 4 and up, though primary members as young as 5 years old may be allowed. Projects range from citizenship and leadership to science and technology. Clubs are available throughout the county.

San Luis Obispo Rugby Football Club

www.slorugby.org

(805) 786-6860

Fore more than a quarter century, this rugby club has provided competitive play for the ruggers in the community. Programs for men, women and youth.

San Luis Obispo Swim Club (aka San Luis Obispo Seahawks)

P.O. Box 142

San Luis Obispo, CA 93406

(805) 543-9515

www.sloseahawks.org

A USA Swimming-affiliated competitive swim team, all abilities ages 5 to 18.

SLO Bicycle Club

(805) 543-5973

slobc.org

Avid cyclists, primarily road riders, meet at 7 p.m. the first Thursday of each month at the SLO Library, Palm Street.

SLO Bytes PC Users Group
www.slobytes.org
Meets from 1 p.m. to 4:30 p.m. the first Sunday of each month at Odd Fellows Hall, 520 Dana St., San Luis Obispo.

SLO Chess Club
(805) 544-0717
All ages and levels are invited for the Thursday meetings from 6:30 p.m. to 10 p.m. All equipment is provided. Call for current location.

SLO County Four-Wheel Drive Club
www.slo4wheelers.org
Meets at 7 p.m. on the first Wednesday of each month at Player's Restaurant, 8845 El Camino Real, Atascadero.

SLO County Genealogical Society
(805) 785-0383
Meets at 12:30 p.m. the first Saturdays except July, August and December at Odd Fellows Hall, 520 Dana St., San Luis Obispo.

SLO Camera Club
(805) 786-0710
Meets at 7:30 p.m the fourth Tuesday, 6588 Ontario Road, San Luis Obispo.

SLO Muzzleloaders
(805) 528-6426
Meets at 9 a.m. second Sundays at SLO Sportsmen's Association, 3272 Gilardi Road.

SLO Philatelic Society
(805) 547-9022
Stamp collectors meet at 1 p.m. the first Tuesday and 7 p.m. the third Thursday of each month at Church of Christ fellowship hall, 3172 Johnson Ave., San Luis Obispo.

SLO Quilters
www.sloquilters.org
Meets at 7 p.m. second Mondays at Congregational United Church of Christ, 11245 Los Osos Valley Road, San Luis Obispo. The club offers a book loan library, seminars and workshops, Block-a-Month activities, community service quilting projects, quilt shows and challenges.

SLO Rowing Club
(805) 466-9507
Meets at 8 a.m. Saturdays and Sundays, 7 a.m. Thursdays at Santa Margarita Lake. Club boats are provided for members.

SLO Vettes Car Club
(805) 434-2724

slovettes.org

Corvette owners meet at 6:30 p.m. second Fridays at Players, 8845 El Camino Real, Atascadero.

Santa Lucia Flyfishers
www.santaluciaflyfishers.com

Avid flyfishers gather to hear speakers, meet other fishers and make plans for fishing outings. Meetings held the second Thursday of each month at 6 p.m. at Margie's Diner, 1575 Calle Joaquin, San Luis Obispo.

Santa Lucia Rockhounds
(805) 467-2966

www.slrockhounds.org

The club encourages learning and good citizenship through the study of mineralogy, lapidary, metalworking, jewelry design and fabrication, geology, field trips for collecting and related history. Meets at 7 p.m., third Mondays, Paso Robles Pioneer Museum (p. 202), 2010 Riverside Ave., Paso Robles.

Stillehavet Lodge – Sons of Norway
(805) 748-5674

Learn Scandinavian tradition, dance and more with this group of jokesters at 1 p.m. second Saturdays most of the year, Odd Fellows Hall, 520 Dana St., San Luis Obispo. Call for current schedule.

Surfrider Foundation, San Luis Bay Chapter
(949) 492-8170

Perhaps known most for its storm-drain stenciling program, this organization promotes clean beaches, surf safety and public beach access.

Toastmasters International, Cambria
(805) 203-5072

Learn to speak publicly by practicing with the club at semi-monthly meetings.

TOO SLO Turtle Club
(805) 481-5222

tooslo.org

The local chapter of the California Turtle and Tortoise Club meets at 7 p.m. on second Wednesdays at the PG&E Community Building, 6588 Ontario Road, Avila Valley.

Sources

In addition to the websites sited throughout this book, the following sources were also used:

California State Parks, *Harmony Coast (Sea West) Project Inventory of Features/Resource Summary*

Thomas Guide: Santa Barbara & San Luis Obispo Counties. Rand-McNally. 2008.

California State Parks, *San Simeon Point Recommended Access Plan,* Oct. 7, 2003 (Updated July 8, 2004)

Greenwood & Associates, *Restoration Plan for the Cambria Chinese Temple,* July 2005

Mission Tour - http://missiontour.org/sanluisobispo/santamargarita.htm

San Luis Obispo: a History in Architecture, Janet Penn Franks, 2004.

San Luis Obispo County Dept. of Planning and Building, *Cambria Commercial Design Plan,* May 9, 2002 (Amended Nov. 2007)

San Luis Obispo County Parks & Recreation Element-Planning Commission Review Draft, March 2006

Santa Margarita Historical Society, santamargaritahistoricalsociety.org

State of California, *Hearst Ranch Draft Transaction Documents,* Feb. 18, 2005

U.S. Census Bureau (quickfacts.census.gov)

Index

Notes

Notes

Notes